SHOWBUSINESS with BLOOD

For Cynthia Lowe, who has always punched above her weight.

EAMON CARR

SHOWBUSINESS with BLOOD

A GOLDEN AGE OF IRISH BOXING

with every good wish!
Eamon Carr

THE LILLIPUT PRESS
DUBLIN

First published 2023 by
THE LILLIPUT PRESS

62–63 Sitric Road, Arbour Hill
Dublin 7, Ireland
www.lilliputpress.ie

ISBN 9781843518730

10 9 8 7 6 5 4 3 2 1

The Lilliput Press gratefully acknowledges the financial support of the Arts Council/
An Chomhairle Ealaíon.

Set in 11pt on 15pt with Adobe Caslon Pro by Compuscript
Printed in the Czech Republic by Finidr

Contents

Illustrations between pages 82 and 83.

Prologue

IN 1885 A LARGE bronze statue was unearthed during excavations on
the Quirinal Hill in Rome. An imposing, lifelike figure of a seated boxer, the
discovery was dated to the second to first century BC and believed to have
been from Greece. Those on the site of the dig were astounded. 'I have never
felt such an extraordinary impression as the one created by the sight of this
magnificent specimen of a semi-barbaric athlete, coming slowly out of the
ground, as if awakening from a long repose after his gallant fights,' wrote
Rodolfo Lanciani in 1888.

On close inspection, the muscular bearded figure is scarred. Some
wounds appear new. Others, such as the broken nose, are older. Seated
with his elbows resting on his thighs, the wraps on his hands are in full
view. In real life, they would have been leather, probably with metal and
wool between the thongs. Then, as now, these coverings were designed
to protect the fists from damage. Deft application of red copper was
used to signify the blood stains and darker alloys of bronze to create the
bruised swellings.

Boxing was included in the ancient Olympic Games, 688 BC, and the combatants were professionals, not amateurs. The boxer we see in the museum in Palazzo Massimo alle Terme presents an accurate interpretation of how it was, and brings within touching distance Virgil's epic account in the *Aeneid* of the bout at the funeral games of Anchises. From over two thousand years before the world could read ringside scribes Gerry Callan or Budd Schulberg, the report is of the Prizefighter series in the raw.

An ox with gilded horns awaited the winner. Just one contender stepped forward. 'An immense man' named Dares, he had a fearsome reputation. He had crushed Butes ('that gigantic hulk') and was the only man to have taken on Paris, the strongest boxer in Troy. Dares was super confident. He dazzled the crowd with a bit of shadow-boxing. 'Hand over the prize,' he demanded. 'There's no one to face me.' He may possibly have said, 'I am the greatest.' But Virgil didn't record it. In the crowd a previous champion, Entellus, looked on. His friend goaded him, 'You've lost it, mate. Where's it gone?' Entellus complained of growing old and slowing down. But he took the bait. 'My pride remains strong,' he said, throwing down the gauntlets. These were solid, heavy gloves, rows of ox-hide stitched to hold lead and iron. We're told they were still 'crusted with blood and spattered brains'. No wonder Dares looked a bit worried. But Entellus agreed to both boxers being given new gloves of equal weight. Their hands taped, the boxers squared up in the centre of an outdoor ring.

There was a hint of the Clay–Liston bouts about this ancient duel. Dares, quick on his feet, danced around the older fighter, jabbing, probing, trying to find an opening. Both men landed impact punches but neither relented. And on they went. Entellus, conserving energy, used his upper-body movement to avoid his busy opponent's combinations. His plan was to finish the bout with one big punch. Lumbering and breathing heavily, he unleashed a monster right hook, which Dares ducked. The momentum carried Entellus forward and he toppled over. He hit the ground. The crowd went wild. Winded, Entellus struggled to his feet. Pride dented, he took the fight to Dares, letting rip with a series of combinations and crunching power shots. The younger fighter retreated but there was no escape. Entellus kept up his onslaught. Dares was out on his feet as the older man's fists hammered a rapid-fire tattoo on his head and body.

Eventually, the official stepped in and saved him from further damage, because Entellus was in no mood to stop. The old man was declared the winner. His vanquished opponent, semi-conscious and reeling, was helped from the scene spitting blood and bits of broken teeth. Entellus then turned his attention to his prize, a live bull. Pulling back his fist, he delivered a death blow between the animal's horns, crunching its skull and bursting its brains. Then he threw down his gloves and officially retired. In ancient Greece, as now, boxing was a serious business.

I

The core principle of a boxing bout remains the same as when the Greeks first formalized the sport. It's about hitting and trying not to get hit. Or, as journalist Hugh McIlvanney once put it, 'Boxing is a sport in which two men try and batter each other senseless. No matter how you dress it up, the basic objective in boxing is to render the opponent unconscious.'

Boxers are by definition brave. Whatever mix of emotions they may be feeling, they display enormous courage every time they step forward to fight. Even when surrounded by thousands of enthusiastic spectators, the ring is the loneliest place in the world. As Joe Louis said, 'Once that bell rings you're on your own. It's just you and the other guy.'

I was introduced to the sport years before television became commonplace in Ireland. As a small boy, I accompanied my father to the local amateur boxing gym, where he was on the coaching team. He also took me along to various tournaments. It was exciting. Around this time I also spent months in a sanatorium with chronic bronchiectasis, the dilation and destruction of the airways. Visiting uncles would regale me with accounts of the latest big fight they'd heard on the radio or seen on newsreels in the cinema. It wasn't until years later that I discovered my illness had, for a time, been life-threatening. Looking back, it's obvious that, in attempting to raise my spirits, my uncles resorted to the kind of psychology trainers like Eddie Futch used to motivate fighters. Gathered around my bed, ducking, weaving and throwing punches, they'd engage me with vivid, epic stories of real flesh-and-blood superheroes who fought against the odds. And won. Their kidology worked. I eagerly awaited the following week's instalment. Rocky Marciano sounded the most exotic. He'd defeated everyone's favourite, Joe Louis. I knew that Louis was a colossus who'd held the world on his broad shoulders. But no one could beat Marciano. Knocking people out was his speciality.

I knew I was ill. There were innumerable painful injections daily and various scary tests. The days lying in bed on a veranda in the open air, watching the clouds and listening to birds in nearby trees, were the best. When some patients disappeared suddenly, we assumed they'd been allowed go home. Nurses smiled wanly and seemed sad. I was too young to know that this was primarily a TB hospital. I hadn't heard of tuberculosis and didn't realize I was surrounded by children at death's door.

Neighbours sent relics of the saints: Don Bosco, Blessed Martin, Dominic Savio. I sensed these guys were on my side but, always triumphant, St Marciano was the one I thought about most. Because of him, I had something to aim for. I desperately wanted to get home to my friends and revisit the gym – the crackling excitement of the young boxers in training, skipping ropes beating mesmeric rhythms on the wooden floor, the staccato snap of the speed bags, the thud of gloved fists sinking into the heavy bags and the acrid air heavy with the pungent aroma of wintergreen and liniment.

Though bedridden, I was already there, training with the big boys. In my innocence I convinced myself that I might even become a champion one day. If not of the world, then maybe of my school. Or even my street. But most of all I just wanted to be allowed out of my iron bed. Much deeper down was a profound wish that somehow or other I'd get to star in the ring at the National Boxing Stadium in Dublin. Childish dreams. As Lucinda Williams sings, 'If wishes were horses, I'd have a ranch.'

And so, on those dark terrifying nights, as I lay sweating, struggling for breath, retching and spewing mucus into an enamelled basin and hearing my fragile chest wheezing like a battered old accordion, I wasn't alone. I was part of the great boxing universe. A tiny pinprick of light circling the heavens, orbiting an endless celestial ring in the company of glowing and fiery stellar giants. In my imagination, I was a southpaw, jabbing, hooking, keeping my guard up, boxing shadows. Yes. I was going to come out fighting. That's what we boxers, big and small, did. One more round. One more chance. Please.

II

With six boxers representing Ireland in the Melbourne Olympics in 1956, we followed the team's progress with interest. Four of them won medals. While Fred Tiedt, John Caldwell and Freddie Gilroy became legends, Tony Byrne was the most celebrated in our house. Known as 'Socks', he had carried the Irish flag at the opening ceremony. On our way to the seaside we would detour to drive past his house in Drogheda. Such is the fate of local heroes.

The following year, disaster struck. My mother died young. Grief-stricken and confused, I became somewhat wayward and, though still in short pants, fell in with a bunch of older delinquents. With the wildness of rock 'n' roll and the reckless abandon of the Teddy Boy ethos now taking precedence, concerned relations staged an intervention and I was packed off to boarding school, a uniquely alien environment. In St Finian's College, the diocesan school for Meath, contact with the outside world was forbidden. Newspapers, radio and TV were banned but, like a POW planning an escape, I listened through static on a borrowed crystal set in the middle of the night to 7:1 underdog Cassius Clay's challenge in Miami for the world heavyweight title held by Sonny Liston. The man who was about to become Muhammad Ali was overjoyed when Liston failed to come out for the seventh round; so hyped up, the commentators couldn't pin him down. Suddenly he exclaimed, 'Sam Cooke! Hey, let that man up here. This is Sam Cooke!' Sam, who'd been a staple on the jukebox that became my devotional shrine during those nascent feral years, was a friend of the new world champion! And in the gym a week earlier, the young contender had his photo taken with a young band visiting from England, The Beatles. Right then, I couldn't have been happier. My two boyhood passions, boxing and rock 'n' roll, had merged.

Gradually, in my study-hall reveries, boxing was replaced by beat groups. Trainers and boxers' CVs made way for lists of obscure record producers and forgotten 45 rpm vinyl discs. I became convinced that this was a world I could live in. Back on Civvy Street, music dominated my life. After a few years scuffling around, Horslips, an unlikely band assembled by me and friends, released a record. At the time, I was sharing a house with legendary Scottish boxing correspondent Jim McNeill, who worked with the *Irish Press*. Jim's wife, Jackie, was a talented seamstress and on more than one occasion Jim would arrive home from work to find me half-undressed with Jackie fitting me for an outlandish glam rock costume. Jim would snort with derision but, in public, he'd be first to defend my reputation.

As the band began to find an audience in the early 1970s, with David Bowie and Marc Bolan dominating the charts, I made a discovery that was to change my life. While guitarist Johnny Fean was quietly running through some scales and finger exercises, a curious cadence caught my attention. What was that? I had Johnny retrace his steps. And there it was, taunting like a ghostly tribal war cry. An ancient sequence of notes, interpreted by my new flatmate with the authority of a Chicago bluesman, conjured up dramatic widescreen images. I felt the rush of history but I also glimpsed a future of sorts. This felt like a once-in-a-lifetime encounter. Stamping my foot on the floor, I urged him to hammer out the riff again so as not to lose it. 'If I write some lyrics, will you flesh out a melody?' I asked. Of course he would.

At the time, I was working on reshaping the old Irish tale, 'The Cattle Raid of Cooley' ('An Táin'), as a rock 'n' roll concept album and now I had my centrepiece. The mythical hero Cú Chulainn was the central character in the story. A fighting man, his named translated as the Hound of Culann. Featuring in the many books in my grandfather's library, he'd been my childhood companion. I knew him well. He was volatile and dangerous. A man with supernatural powers. A voodoo man, both charming and menacing. 'When you see me coming, you had better run, run, run …' From who exactly? From Cú Chulainn? No. From the Hound of Culann? No. He was more sinister than that. He was Dearg Doom. 'Dearg' being the Irish word for 'red', here was Ulster's bloodied Red Hand. 'I'm The Red Doom!' A warrior boast and a unique comic-book, rock 'n' roll character. His name would be spat out like a hermetic oath. Its very utterance was like unleashing a cabbalistic invocation.

Years later, I was gratified to see the figure of Cú Chulainn, based on Oliver Sheppard's famous statue in the GPO, feature as the logo for the Boxing Union of Ireland (BUI). Recalling the legend, the hero has tied himself to a stone pillar in order to fight his enemies to the last. An inspired choice by the BUI. I spent long hours researching the occult dimension of this totemic figure through the notebooks and papers of W.B. Yeats in the National Library of Ireland, and the significance of having him draw together various strands of my life seemed uncanny, if not oracular.

If Dearg Doom was a spell, it certainly worked. The song proved successful. It opened doors worldwide. Much later, the riff would form the core of the great Ireland football anthem 'Put 'Em Under Pressure'. In the 1970s, as Horslips began touring internationally, occasional headline title fights were the only ones that registered. For over a decade, the cycle of writing, rehearsing, recording and touring felt like being permanently in training camp concentrating on the next big fight. And, while it wasn't exactly what I'd envisaged as a child, no one in the audience could have guessed the profound personal significance of finding myself headlining on stage in the National Stadium. It was the country's premier rock-music venue back then, hosting The Who, Led Zeppelin, Fleetwood Mac ... and me.

III

In 1985, when Barry McGuigan became WBA world featherweight champion, the country experienced a joyous communal sense of hope and celebration. In those troubled times, Barry's achievements were beyond the range of Irish expectation. It was as if, as McGuigan's biographer Jim Sheridan put it, 'A boyhood hero stepped from the comics of our childhood, fearless, strong and full of insane life.' We weren't to know it at the time, but the future was exceptionally bright. Many more glorious boxing nights lay ahead.

Around this time, I'd begun writing about my interests for newspapers and magazines. As fate would have it, a new career as a journalist coincided with a steady boxing renaissance in Ireland. Michael Carruth won a gold medal at the Barcelona Olympics in 1992. Steve Collins became WBO world super-middleweight champion in 1995. As many more Irish fighters began winning world titles, the skinny, pale youngster from the sanatorium was with them, every step of the way. Through a curious alchemy of fate and fortune, the wish he'd nurtured as he'd received extreme unction – an anointing with oils of the sick and dying – saw him afforded opportunities denied his father. He became a regular at ringside on the big nights. Got to be in the gym, at the weigh-in and even in the changing room. He observed the fighters' extreme training regimes, glimpsed their private torment and probed their self-belief. He shared their joy and celebration and felt their loss, their dejection, their despair.

This being boxing, the dramatic painful interface between glory and failure, fulfilment and frustration, he watched, time and again, the lives of brave men, and women too, turn, to reference Virginia Woolf, on 'moments of humiliation and triumph'.

The frail, 'delicate' kid lived to witness, first-hand, a golden age for Irish athletes in the toughest, most ruthless, most demanding sport of all.

Profound gratitude is due to all those boxers, trainers, managers, promoters and officials who made him welcome and impressed with their commitment, their knowledge and their zeal.

What follows are stories of aspiration, violence and catastrophe. Yet amid the chaos and destruction are inspirational studies in courage, resilience and personal redemption: boxing's enduring saving grace.

1
WARRIOR

'All boxers live with the presence of death.'
Steve Collins

I

'I'M NOT GOING TO be able to hurt him enough.'

Regret trumps animosity as Chris Eubank delivers his lamentation with clinical precision. No histrionics. No braggadocio. A calm, conversational tone makes the world champion's promise of egregious violence all the more chilling.

Eubank has had time to ruminate on a simmering feud, which reached boiling point in Dublin earlier in the week. In the lobby of a luxurious hotel in Brighton, he's relaxed. But there's no disguising his indignation. Since time immemorial, a sense of retribution has provided powerful motivation. Today, the message is shared with missionary zeal. The object of this vengeful wrath is Steve Collins, the WBO world middleweight champion, who is set to contest Eubank's WBO world super-middleweight title in a few weeks' time. The clash will be televised in Ireland, and Eubank, unbeaten in forty-three pro fights, is intent on punishing the disrespectful Dubliner with as much pain as is legally permissible.

'It's kill or be killed,' says Eubank, on a bright mid-February morning. 'You're going to have to kill me to win.'

Alarmingly, these studied remarks carry a reminder of Eubank's most notorious bout. On a Saturday night in White Hart Lane in September 1991, he picked himself up off the canvas where he'd been dumped by the people's favourite, Michael Watson, just seconds from the end of the eleventh round. Cut and bleeding for the first time in his career, Eubank looked finished. But, with one almost superhuman effort, he connected with a right uppercut, which pulverized the blood vessels in Watson's brain. Watson's chances were saved by the bell. As he gamely went out for the last round, it was obvious to referee Roy Francis that Watson was seriously injured. The fight was terminated, much to the chagrin of many spectators, who responded by rioting. Disoriented, Watson slipped into unconsciousness in his corner and appeared lifeless as they manoeuvred him from the ring onto a stretcher. He was lucky to survive. Despite a series of complex neurosurgeries, he remained in a coma for six weeks, spent a year in intensive care and, paralyzed in a wheelchair for six years, had to re-learn how to speak, read and walk.

Before that fateful encounter, Michael Watson had publicly mocked Eubank's speech patterns. As I sip my coffee, Eubank holds eye contact and coolly lisps his grievances. 'You've beaten me,' he says. 'You've humiliated me. You've downed me. I'm true to the man within. I don't care about my life, my family, money. All I care about is beating you.'

There will be no mercy shown.

II

A few days earlier, arriving for the Dublin press conference, a familiar voice rings out. 'Howaya, Eamon.' I turn to see Steve Collins perched like a supermodel on the bonnet of a vintage Jaguar car: the hard man from Cabra is nattily attired in a smart tweed jacket with matching waistcoat and flat cap. The country-gent look is offset with an eye-catching bow tie. Nor has this unlikely doyen of high-style forgotten to accessorize for the photographers. One meaty hand grasps the lead of an imposing Irish wolfhound while the other fist brandishes a rugged blackthorn walking stick in the manner of an offensive weapon. 'There y'are, champ,' says I.

Arriving in the penthouse suite ahead of Collins, I study the players waiting at the top table. The promoters' upbeat demeanour fails to distract from the aura of irritation radiating from the man being kept waiting, the man Collins will fight for the world super-middleweight title, Chris Eubank.

Scheduled to interview Collins in London later in the week, I'm interested in observing the dynamic between the fighters. Eubank is both a sports superstar and a major celebrity whose artfully cultivated image of aristocratic elegance is as challenging and entertaining as the plummy to-the-manor-born persona he's adopted. He often wears a monocle and jodhpurs, carries a silver-tipped cane and enunciates a faux upper-class accent. While he might seem like an effete toff from the pages of a P.G. Wodehouse novel, there is no disputing that Eubank can fight. By the time he'd agreed to Collins as a contestant, the reigning champion had staged fourteen successful defences of the world title he'd won four years earlier.

By keeping the champion waiting and attempting to upstage him in the fashion stakes, Collins is clearly deploying a barbed display of disrespect. It's a high-stakes gambit.

While Collins had been based in the US, the middleweight division in England exploded with a series of rivalries that created huge box-office bonanzas. A lucrative but dangerous zone, the middleweight division was populated by several contestants who combined technical skill, raw courage and savage barbarity. Public interest in the middleweight division had been cranking up when, in 1989, Michael Watson defeated Commonwealth middleweight champion Nigel Benn, a former soldier with the Royal Fusiliers. Despite the setback, Benn went on to claim the WBO world middleweight title in April 1990 in Atlantic City. Seven months later, he lost his title when Eubank forced a stoppage after nine vicious rounds in Birmingham. The triangle of animosity that developed between Watson, Benn and Eubank dominated boxing in Britain.

In June 1991 Eubank beat Watson by a hotly disputed majority decision. Three months later, the pair fought again, with catastrophic results for Watson's health. The following year Benn, the self-styled 'Dark Destroyer', went to Italy and stopped his opponent to claim the WBC world super-middleweight title. Following three successful defences, Benn met Eubank again. Television rights sold to sixty countries, as each man put their

3

respective world titles on the line. The result was a draw. In Britain alone, 16.5 million people viewed the fight on ITV.

Eubank's flamboyant image, stylized ring choreography and often inflammatory pronouncements attracted a growing audience. Boxing fans shared a degree of disquiet when Sky Sports agreed a £10-million deal with Eubank to fight eight bouts in a year. A top-level prize fight every seven weeks seemed an impossible task. 'I'm here to prove I'm not the normal man,' declared Eubank. Appropriating Tina Turner, he began marketing himself as 'Simply the Best'. 'Farcical,' snorted rival promoter Frank Maloney. 'Simply the best conman is more like it.'

When Eubank's first opponent of 1995 failed a brain scan, Eubank's manager cast around for a replacement. Steve Collins had never fought at super-middleweight, and hadn't boxed since he'd won the WBO middleweight belt in May '94, but after intensive negotiations, the Dubliner landed a £150,000 purse, an unprecedented fee for a challenger. His biggest payday ever came with the possibility of further big-money fights.

The stage was set for one of the most astonishing sagas ever in Irish sporting history.

III

The escalating rivalry between Chris Eubank and Steve Collins marked the beginning of a golden age for Irish professional boxing.

Collins had been Irish middleweight amateur champion before making his professional debut in October 1986 in Massachusetts. He returned with a record of twenty-one wins and three losses. The statistics didn't tell the full story. Collins took champion Mike McCallum the distance in a world-title fight. His two other narrow defeats had also been in championship fights. Still without a meaningful belt, Collins landed a shot at the WBO world middleweight title held by Chris Pyatt. Presenting as the 'Celtic Warrior' for the first time, Collins fought Pyatt in Sheffield in May '94. Channelling years of disappointment into a furious fifth round, he forced a stoppage. The Dubliner was now a world champion.

The Eubank–Collins fight was set for the lavishly titled Green Glens Arena, a draughty equestrian venue that, two years earlier, had been pressed into service as the venue for the Eurovision Song Contest finals. On the national festive weekend in March 1995, the market town of Millstreet, County Cork, would become the most unlikely setting for a high-profile fight between an Irishman and an Englishman since Dan Donnelly hosted George Cooper in Belcher's Hollow on the Curragh in County Kildare in 1815. Donnelly settled the fight in the thirty-fourth round. Following the Dublin fighter's death five years later, his body was stolen by grave robbers. At the time of the Eubank–Collins fight, Donnelly's severed right arm, as weathered as ancient bog oak, was on permanent display in a custom-made exhibition cabinet in a pub in Kilcullen in County Kildare.

Supercilious and condescending, Eubank drove opponents to distraction. In Dublin, Collins set about turning the tables. No sooner had Barry Hearn made the introductions than Collins fired his first volley. Purposely referring to the visitor as 'Eubanks', he proceeded to read a statement in Irish, welcoming the champion and declaring, '*Go mbeidh an bua agam ar Christó MacEubank.*' 'I will have victory over Christó MacEubank.' The crowd hooted with laughter. Clearly stung, Eubank announced imperiously, 'Steve gets beat.'

Both fighters ran through the obligatory litany of threats and promises until, hearing Collins assert that he deserved to win, Eubank retorted, 'That has nothing to do with it. Why are people in Africa suffering or dying of famine? Do they deserve that?'

Collins responded, 'You're an African, an Anglo-African, of African descent, right? Why do you deny your African heritage and try to impersonate and behave like an Englishman when you're not? You should be proud of your roots and your people.' Collins' supporters cheered.

Eubank fumed. Repeating his claim that Collins would be beaten, he turned abruptly and strode out of the room in a huff. His seething anger was lost on Dublin Lord Mayor John Gormley, who shared the lift with him. Misjudging the mood, the Green Party stalwart enquired brightly if the visiting boxer might be taking a sightseeing trip around the city. The furious Eubank snapped, 'Fuck this city.' The quote was widely reported and a media firestorm ensued.

Colleagues at FM104, where I presented a rock show, pressed me to discuss the matter on that evening's phone-in programme. When I joined the conversation, the show's host was complaining that, 'dressed up as a leprechaun', Steve was 'stage Irish'. The presenter then began to discuss the possibility of racism in Steve's barbs.

A phone-in show is no place for nuance. Explaining that boxing press conferences are usually games of banter and one-upmanship, I said I felt Steve had simply been ill-informed in claiming that Eubank was impersonating an Englishman when, in fact, he'd been born in Peckham.

Five minutes later, a second call told me, 'Steve Collins wants to talk to you.' Live on air, I was amazed to hear the distinctive Dublin accent of the WBO champion going hammer and tongs with the presenter. Dragged back into a conversation that was on the verge of overheating, I pointed out for the benefit of the presenter and his listeners that Collins and Eubank were both managed by Barry Hearn. Quizzed by the host, Collins explained:

> Although it's a tough business, it's a business of entertaining. The entertainment starts with the head-to-head press conference. I don't think Eubank meant what he said about Dublin city or the Lord Mayor. Neither did I mean anything racial. Although it might be a touchy subject, I knew it would hit a nerve. It's not just a physical fight. There's a lot of psychology involved as well.

While outwardly confident he could beat Eubank, privately Collins was beset by worries. He was distracted by a high-stakes legal dispute with the Petronelli brothers in Boston. He hadn't fought for nine months and was suffering from the after-effects of a viral illness. Physically and mentally, Collins wasn't at his best. But, unknown to most, he had taken a bold initiative, which he hoped would give him an advantage. In the gamble of a lifetime, Collins had hooked up with health-shop business guru and hypnotherapist Tony Quinn.

IV

As the row rumbled on in the Irish media, Eubank agreed to an exclusive interview in Brighton. I had coffee while he sipped water. Surprisingly polite, he would have chatted for ages but for the fact that I urgently needed to phone through a news report for the later editions of the *Evening Herald*.

Under the headline 'I'M OUT FOR BLOOD!' the following piece is as it appeared on page 3:

> *Loud-mouth boxer Chris Eubank today warned Steve Collins that he is out for blood at their Millstreet clash next month.*

The controversial world champion angrily declared that he is not going to forgive and forget.

'I will not be able to hurt him enough,' he said. 'The man has caused me hurt.'

Speaking in Brighton, the fighter declared, 'I'm not interested in anything except beating Steve Collins. I'm only interested in out-thinking, out-boxing and hitting harder.'

'I haven't been this way since the Nigel Benn fight. It's not him, it's his ignorance I want to beat.'

Eubank called Steve Collins' remarks about his origins at their Dublin press conference earlier this week the 'insult of insults'.

And asked if he regretted swearing at Lord Mayor John Gormley, Eubank said, 'I've been insulted and you're asking me if I'm interested in your town? I'm not. I'm interested in Steve Collins. I'm supposed to walk around your town with a big smile on my face when I've been insulted? No. I will hurt.'

'When one wants to defend oneself and one can't, then one becomes hostile,' he explained.

Eubank today was outwardly calm and serene. As unruffled as the flat grey sea across the road from the hotel where we sat. But inside he was still an angry man.

'I do not see colour. I refuse to. It's made too many people bitter, twisted and warped and they become victims. I'm way past that. What hurt was that he must have thought about what he said. Is it my fault that my skin is black, but I'm English?'

'The forefathers of the English colonised my people. They enslaved my people and brought my forefathers to Jamaica. My parents emigrated from Jamaica to England. Here I am. I'm a citizen of this country.'

'I haven't a problem with who I am,' he added. 'What got me riled was that I was not going to be given the opportunity to explain myself. The man was behaving like a child. If his strategy was to get under my skin, he's done that.'

The boxer people loved to hate, Eubank reminded me of an old-style rude boy: the style-conscious anti-hero whose rebel philosophy was intertwined with the Jamaican ska and rocksteady music that swept popular culture in the 1960s and 70s. For me, Eubank echoed the mythical streetwise gangster

Johnny Too Bad, a maverick who challenged the system. Eubank warmed to my thesis. 'That fact that I adapt and overcome, that makes me even more the proper rude boy,' he enthused.

A bombastic and unrelenting moral stance added more than a touch of the comic-book character Judge Dredd to his character. 'The right way is the hardest way,' he declared. Saying goodbye in Brighton, Eubank climbed up into the cab of the gleaming Peterbilt truck he'd imported from America and roared off to his mansion in Hove.

V

The following morning, as arranged, I arrived at the offices of Matchroom Boxing, the fight promoters, to discuss the upcoming fight with Steve Collins and also hear his side of the story. There was a hitch. Steve had nixed the interview. Preparing to fly to a training camp in Las Vegas, he didn't need the distraction. Obligingly, he left me a written statement regarding the press-conference banter:

To Whom It May Concern

This letter is in reply to the accusation Chris Eubank made about me. Chris Eubank claimed that my remark about him forgetting his roots was a racial remark.

It was not in my opinion a racial slur. It was me expressing my opinion from observations.

Chris Eubank is definitely an Englishman, but he is an Englishman of African origins. Chris Eubank refers to the plight of starving millions in Africa due to war, crop failures and so on. Chris Eubank is only paying lip service and that is what annoyed me.

Chris Eubank is in a great position to help these people in many ways. It would not cost him any of the money that he loves and treasures so much.

All he would have to do is lend his time and participate in activities for Third World charities.

Since the late '80s I have been involved in GOAL. It is an organisation made up from sports stars throughout the world. I have been involved in fundraising for this charity. If you look back at photographs of the fight I had with Mike McCallum in February 1990, you will see me wearing

*the GOAL emblem on my boots. I still wear the GOAL emblem to date.
I do not intend to insult people, races or countries. If I did, it would be
unintentional and I would apologise immediately.*

Yours in sport,

Steve Collins

World Champ

VI

On fight night, the Millstreet equestrian venue was packed to the rafters.
Local bars were bursting at the seams with thirsty punters. Stewarding was
easy-going. The squash-faced Liverpudlian gent who joined me at ringside
didn't have a ticket. Nobody seemed to mind. In a corridor beneath the
stands a bookie was touting his odds. Fashionably dressed young men with
chiselled chins and laser-beam eyes tried to convince themselves they were
in Caesars Palace.

At ringside, I sat behind London legend Henry Cooper, the former
British and European heavyweight champion who once decked a young
Muhammad Ali before losing the fight on a technical knockout. 'Our 'Enry'
had seen it all but in the Green Glens Arena even he seemed bemused by
the pageantry of the ring walks. As blazing fireworks on the back wall of
the venue spelt out the name 'Eubank', the champion was raised aloft on his
Harley-Davidson like a mutant Minotaur, muscles and motorbike gleaming.
Despite the glitz and razzmatazz, this wasn't a Meatloaf concert. This was
the overture to an evening of orchestrated punishment.

Throughout the hullabaloo, Collins reclined in his corner. As
challenger, he had entered the ring first, a hooded figure of mystery,
seemingly lost in some trancelike state. The soundtrack from the *Rocky*
movie on the Celtic Warrior's headphones shut out Eubank's ritualistic
chest-beating display. The psychological warfare, waged by both men
since the controversial press conference in Dublin, had continued at
the weigh-in where Eubank complained that Collins was employing a
hypnotist to ensure he wouldn't feel pain. The war of nerves continued
throughout the twelve-round contest, with the unprecedented appearance
of bearded yoga teacher Quinn in Collins' corner apparently massaging

the Cabra man's chakras and whispering hypnotic hocus-pocus. On the back of his shirt, clearly legible from Eubank's corner, was Quinn's logo, 'The New Mind Technology'.

As the fight progressed, Collins seemed the more determined to win. He fought like a man possessed. Ruse or not, the hypnotism ploy was working and Collins advanced in strength until he walked into a crushing right hook in the tenth round. Eyes glazed, he began to flap in ungainly fashion as his legs buckled. Collins was down. Below him at ringside, his wife, Gemma, buried her head in her hands in horror. His friends looked shaken. But slumped on the lower ropes, the grotesque rictus of a smile that appeared on Collins's face further confounded Eubank.

Before the fight I had heard an account of Collins' resolve from Matchroom stablemate Garry 'The Hammer' Delaney who'd trained alongside the Dubliner in Las Vegas. 'As far as Steve's concerned, he's already won this fight,' revealed Garry. 'He locked himself away in his room, cooked his own food and concentrated on nothing else but this bout. No one can get near him. I've never seen him like this. It's uncanny.'

The fight went the distance and the hypnotism conspiracy was floated as an explanation for Eubank's failure to deploy his customary destructive capabilities. Finally, tension gave way to pandemonium as the judges' decision was announced. 'The winner and the new ...' The venue erupted in riotous celebration. Jubilation quickly turned to triumphalism as the capacity crowd taunted the defeated former champion and sang in one voice, 'On your bike, on your bike, on your bike' to the tune of 'Here We Go'. Even in victory there was to be no peace initiative. Steve Collins was now a double world champion. 'I'm not just the best Irish boxer ever,' he told the Sky interviewer after the fight. 'I'm the best pound-for-pound fighter in the world.'

Proper legends aren't commonplace. In binding folk belief and shared experience, they defy memory, logic and the phoney grandeur of death itself through confirming a community's wishful self-image. Collins created a legend in Millstreet. A legend as vibrant as that of Dan Donnelly in the Curragh in 1815. Against British boxing's hottest property, and in defiance of the bookmakers' odds, he fulfilled a long-standing dream and came to realize his twin ambitions of earning a million and riding down Dublin's O'Connell Street on an open-topped bus.

2
POCKET
ROCKET

'There's no way this guy is going to beat me. He'll have to kill me.'
Wayne McCullough

AN EERIE HUSH FELL over the Manchester crowd in 2006. They had just borne witness to the most brutal, uncompromising and destructive fight in recent history. At stake was the British light-middleweight title and the coveted Lonsdale Belt. As Matthew Macklin lay prone on the canvas, many feared they'd witnessed an execution. Before the medics slid the stretcher under the bottom rope, the victorious Jamie Moore dropped to his knees and whispered words of encouragement in Macklin's ear.

The media is obsessed with celebrity diet fads. But what's known in the fight game as *making weight* is less than compelling. Often the toughest, most challenging part of the sport – what's sometimes called 'the fight before the fight' – shedding pounds gives boxers an advantage by enabling them to qualify to fight in the lowest possible weight category. They then put the pounds back on after the weigh-in, hoping to be bigger and heavier than their opponent. Making weight correctly is a science and, if it isn't done properly, it can sometimes put a boxer in harm's way.

At the weigh-in Macklin had been five pounds overweight. Drastic action was called for. An hour on the treadmill, wrapped in a plastic sweatsuit, his body smeared with cream to make him perspire, was followed by a stint in a bath of nearly boiling water. The gruelling procedure worked. Macklin lost the necessary weight. Some say he looked a shadow of his former self.

The bout was scheduled for twelve rounds. Macklin usually finished work early by way of knockout. Anxious to build on his growing reputation, he began at a high tempo. Moore responded. Neither man relented. 'We both went to the darkest place,' recalled Jamie a few years later. Each man was taken aback by the other's formidable punching power, but neither opted to take a backwards step. After nine ferocious rounds, Macklin was running on empty and boxing on instinct. Under a crushing right-left combination from Moore in the tenth, he went down and remained unconscious for a worryingly long time. As he was carried from the ring, his friend Ricky Hatton surveyed the carnage with tears in his eyes.

'You don't know whether you've got it in you to be involved in a fight like that until it happens,' Moore told me. 'Some people would give in halfway through. Neither of us was willing to do that.'

Although he prefers not to revisit the trauma, Macklin later told me that even if he'd been standing at the final bell, he believes he would have collapsed unconscious in the dressing room afterwards from sheer exhaustion and dehydration. He'd lost a stone in weight and had given everything but his life in his pursuit of the title. He never fought at light-middleweight again.

I

It still pains coach Nicolas Cruz Hernandez that Wayne McCullough had to settle for a silver medal from the 1992 Olympic Games in Barcelona. 'There would have been two gold medals in Barcelona but for Wayne's injury,' he insists. 'He almost caught the guy in the third round.'

McCullough had earned his Olympic final place with convincing wins in the opening rounds of the competition. In the semi-final, he defeated Gwang-Sik Li by 21-16. But the sturdy North Korean had left his mark. McCullough's left cheek was swollen and painful. 'If there'd been proper medical testing they wouldn't have let him fight,' says Cruz. 'Don't you dare stop the fight,' McCullough warned his coach.

In the final, Cuban Joel Casamayor, a southpaw, peppered McCullough with jabs and power shots. 'I felt like I was being electrocuted with a live wire,' said McCullough. His shattered cheekbone caused blood to seep from the left eye socket. Despite a phenomenally brave final round, which he won, McCullough lost the bout. 'The damage to my face was a huge price to pay,' he said later, 'as I didn't fight again for a year.'

Six months later, McCullough turned professional and signed a lucrative contract with American promoter Mat Tinley.

Promised a minimum of seven fights a year in the first two years, with guaranteed television exposure, McCullough relocated to Las Vegas. He trained in the Top Rank gym under the guidance of Eddie Futch. Tinley was building a formidable team. 'It's not a risk-free sport,' he explained. 'Neither is motor-racing. There's always a gamble involved. We've got the best trainers in the world. We've got the most experienced guy in boxing. Eddie Futch.' Now in his early eighties, Futch knew more about the craft of boxing than most coaches could ever dream of learning. McCullough knew Futch had coached Mike McCallum and Joe Frazier among countless others. Hell, he'd been in Smokin' Joe's corner in Manila. He'd even trained and sparred alongside Joe Louis.

Together, Tinley and McCullough seized the day. McCullough knew the demands on a pro fighter are more onerous than those made on an amateur boxer. When he beat Victor Rabanales for the NABF belt in 1994, the twelve rounds had been his personal Rubicon. 'He hit me from directions I'd never been hit before,' McCullough told me. 'He's the only guy to ever have me out on my feet. We just beat the crap out of each other. There and then I knew, "I want it or I don't want it." … I knew then that nothing was going to stop me becoming a champion.'

Two years and five months after his first pro fight, McCullough was in Japan for the toughest test of his career. Under Tinley's guidance, he'd moved up the rankings and got to fight for the WBC world bantamweight belt against champion Yasuei Yakushiji in 1995. Having already successfully defended his title four times, Yakushiji was determined to keep the belt in Japan.

Eddie Futch had a plan. In the dressing room before the fight, he instructed McCullough to use his jab and to repeat it. The strategy worked. Yakushiji was tough but McCullough's jab upset his rhythm and caused problems. After twelve gruelling rounds, the judges declared McCullough champion by split decision.

In his seventeenth professional fight, McCullough had become world champion.

Travelling to the fight, McCullough asked why Tinley was so quiet. Tinley replied that he was just hoping McCullough would win. McCullough laughed and grabbed his arm, saying, 'Don't you worry. That's the least of my worries.' Tinley described the moment as 'chilling', telling me:

> He's like a fighter pilot. When you get up to that level as a boxer, if you make a mistake, it costs you. It's a high-pressure game. The next day was even more concerning. We were on our way into the hospital because the guy had headbutted him and he had a few stitches and his hand was hurting. McCullough told me, 'I knew my whole life was on the line last night. I knew I had to win or I'd be going back to square one.' He was twenty-four then and he said, 'When would I get another chance at the title? Maybe when I'm twenty-seven or twenty-eight? They won't want to fight me. And I can't make this weight much longer. I knew that if I win this fight I'd be on top of the world but if I don't I'd be scratching to get back.'

'He said he felt fatigued in the first two rounds from losing the weight just to get to 118 pounds' said the manager. 'The first round was close. He told himself, "There's no way I'm going to let anybody take this from me." Wayne is almost dangerously focused.'

Futch, who'd worked with nineteen world champions, rated McCullough in his top five. With a professional record of eighteen unbeaten, thirteen wins coming by way of knockout, McCullough's second title defence was planned for Dublin in March 1996.

II

Of Norman origin, the Luttrell family was widely hated in Ireland for centuries. For his role in helping to subjugate the native Gaelic population, Sir Geoffrey de Luterel was presented with a large tract of land on the outskirts of what is contemporary Dublin. For 600 years, the disenfranchised Irish regarded the Luttrell dynasty's homestead as a house of pain. Having played a role in suppressing the 1798 rebellion, Henry Laws Luttrell became such a reviled figure that his grandfather's grave was ransacked and the skull smashed. Luttrell wasn't stupid. He sold Luttrellstown Castle in 1800.

Luttrellstown Castle and Estate, now a splendid five-star country club and resort, became world famous as the wedding venue for Victoria Adams, aka 'Posh Spice', and Sir David Beckham. By the time I first visited the crenellated pile in 1994, to meet REM who'd based themselves in the castle while in Europe promoting their album *Monster*, my output as a journalist had expanded dramatically. I was covering a heady mix of cultural, political and sporting matters, reviewing theatre and music events, interviewing political leaders, reformed gangsters, convicted killers and showbiz celebrities and also reporting on major news stories. In Luttrellstown I was struck by how baronial splendour interfaced with contemporary country-club chic. Children's laughter echoed down the broad stairwells and along wood-panelled corridors as singer Michael Stipe and I discussed the cultural significance of *Beavis and Butt-Head*.

When I went back to the castle a couple of years later, the ambience was very different. This was where Wayne McCullough and his entourage pitched camp ahead of the world title defence against José Luis Bueno.

Emblematic of a new breed of boxing impresario, McCullough's charismatic manager Mat Tinley could have fitted comfortably into the REM entourage. 'You can't pick your relatives,' he joked. 'You can pick your friends and people you do business with. You do it on your terms.' A former TV executive with Prime International, Tinley had a similar grasp of the medicine-show hoopla that Tom Parker, the self-styled Colonel who managed Elvis Presley, once displayed. Cannily, Tinley had secured television coverage for all McCullough's fights. The Belfast man's unremitting aggression delivered the viewers. If, as Jim McNeill had informed me, boxing was showbusiness with blood, then the manager with music-industry smarts could be just the man to guide McCullough to superstardom.

'My main problem is I'm a bit of an elitist,' Tinley told me. 'I couldn't manage club fighters. I just want champions.'

It was obvious that, although razor-cheeked, McCullough was struggling to make weight days ahead of his Saturday night WBC world title defence against Bueno at the Point Depot. The central heating was on full blast even before we moved to sit by a roaring log fire. It was a mild March afternoon. I needed to take my jacket off. McCullough, on the other hand, wore a rubber sauna suit, designed to make him perspire, under his tracksuit. Towels were wrapped around his neck and tucked into his top. He appeared used to the ritual of shedding pounds. His focus was on Bueno who, anxious to depose the Irishman as reigning champion, had been winding things up. 'He can talk all he wants,' snorted McCullough. 'My fists will be talking faster than his. No one can help him.'

The Luttrellstown camp had been stung by the suggestion that Tinley had bolstered McCullough's record by picking easy competitors. 'What boxing is about is the fights you can remember,' Tinley declared:

> Fights like Ali–Frazier, Leonard–Hagler, even Benn–Eubank. Two guys who are perceived as evenly matched. A super-fight that can put fifty thousand people in a stadium, that's boxing's best moments. Eddie will tell you that Wayne's like the old guys of yesteryear. If he had his way, he'd fight every week. This will be the fifth world champion he's fought in nineteen fights. And he's beaten them all. A lot of boxers don't want to take a risk any more. When Jake LaMotta beat Sugar Ray Robinson they had a rematch nine weeks later. That's phenomenal. There are guys out there not boxing.

Tinley's marketing strategy was paying off. McCullough was world champion. A prime commodity. After a lifetime of investment in his trade, the 'Pocket Rocket' was expected to operate at the most lucrative end of his profession for the next few years. Being featured on the cover of *The Ring* magazine with Mike Tyson, Roy Jones Jr, Julio César Chávez and Marco Antonio Barrera was another high-end endorsement. Convinced that some big names were avoiding meeting McCullough, Tinley said, 'A loss to Wayne McCullough is no shame.'

Few people believed the fight with Bueno would last the scheduled twelve rounds. Knockouts were McCullough's speciality. But his Mexican opponent, who two years earlier held the WBC world super-flyweight title, had won twenty of his twenty-eight fights by stoppage. Their meeting would be explosive.

In hindsight, McCullough's avowed determination to hold on to his title belt has an aura of prophecy. 'It took me a long hard road to get to the top and nobody's going to take it away from me,' he insisted, his angular features glistening by the fire. 'I'd have to die in the ring before I let a guy take it away from me. He'll have to kill me.'

III

McCullough *v* Bueno defined the term 'slug fest'. In his book *Pocket Rocket* McCullough reveals how, the day before the weigh-in, he dropped four pounds. But at 8 st 8 lb (120 lb), he was still two pounds over the required weight.

On the day of the official weigh-in, he went to work again. Following physical exercise drills and twelve rounds of shadow-boxing in intense heat, he was still a pound and a half overweight. The pressure was on. More exercise. More heat. More sweating. 'I was so dehydrated that my lips were sticking together and I was exhausted,' he says. At the weigh-in, he tipped the scales at 8 st 5 1/2 lb. Few people knew of the torture he'd been forced to put himself through to make the weight. 'I can usually bring my weight down to about 8 st 7 lb without a problem,' he later admitted. 'But once I try to get below that I start losing my vision and I have no energy. That's exactly what happened. And the next day I still had to defend my world title.'

After a weigh-in, fighters strive to put weight back on before the fight. Every extra gram adds to the power of their punches. McCullough consumed litres of liquid and devoured a pile of chicken fillets. By fight night he'd piled on sixteen pounds. But he was bloated: 'I felt like garbage.'

Having grown up in in the poorest part of Mexico City, Bueno was on a mission. 'I promised my wife and children that I will return to Mexico with the championship belt,' he said. 'This is my big chance.'

McCullough looked classy in the early rounds, landing authoritative shots, but something strange began to happen. The Belfast man's normally chiselled features became indistinct. For a fighter renowned for his talent as a human-shock absorber, this was unprecedented. Seated about twelve rows from the ring, I watched as his face grew redder and inflated like a balloon. Both fighters dished out excruciating punishment. Full repertoires of crippling punches were unleashed. And still neither man gave way. McCullough's face became an amorphous mess, a raw hamburger. As the aggression continued unabated, we witnessed courage beyond measure. Or foolhardiness bordering on insanity.

When the final bell sounded at the end of the twelfth round, the predominant emotion in the venue was one of relief. Boxing fans aren't dumb. They could see McCullough was grotesquely disfigured. They knew the hazards. People felt they'd been privy to something close to a death duel. Two of the three judges gave the bout to McCullough. The referee told McCullough he'd held on to his title. Despite being at the centre of a noisy post-fight pageant, the reality didn't register. He couldn't remember the outcome when he woke the following day. He remembered nothing of what had happened from the third round onwards. Not even Bono coming to his dressing room and holding his hand in silent prayer. On the journey to the hospital, his anxious minders kept shouting to prevent him from slipping into unconsciousness. His blood pressure was dangerously high. His eardrum was burst. His body was in shock. Some of his coaching staff feared he was going to die. Following the ordeal, Wayne McCullough would never box at bantamweight again.

IV

At race meetings, aware of the dangers to both horse and jockey, trainers often say, 'I hope they come home safely.' That's not a phrase you hear in boxing circles. Fear is unspoken. It's often too easy to forget that tragedy can be just a punch away. The extremes McCullough and Bueno went to in their quest weighted heavily on me. The fight was a reminder of the harsh realities and brought back memories of hearing the shocking news decades earlier of how Benny 'Kid' Paret had been beaten to a pulp by Emile Griffith and was in a coma in hospital. There was uproar because the referee hadn't stopped what looked like a savage execution by Griffith who trapped the Cuban welterweight in the corner and punched him unmercifully. Paret, who had angered Griffith by publicly sneering at his bisexuality, died later in hospital. Griffith became tormented by his death.

Decades later, at the weigh-in at Madison Square Garden for Joe Calzaghe's fight with Roy Jones Jr, my notebook slipped off my lap. A hand tapped my shoulder and a gentle child-like voice chimed, 'Excuse me sir, you've dropped some important documents.' I turned to see a smiling, broad-shouldered Black man. I didn't immediately recognize Emile Griffith, who was accompanied by his attentive partner, Luis Rodrigo. We met again later that evening at a *Boxing Digest* soirée. I recall the evening clearly, not just for Griffith's zen-like serenity but also the ebullient presence of my sidekick George Kimball, esteemed boxing writer and friend of the Beats and the beaten-up.

Griffith was a calm, dignified man who appeared to have a slight cognitive impairment. In the wake of the Paret tragedy, he had been overcome with remorse. I remember a chilling quote of his from somewhere: 'It was the dreams that were getting to me. I'd doze off and wake up in a frightening sweat, scared of the dark, of shadows, afraid to stay awake and afraid to go to sleep.'

When boxers die on duty, their deaths steal a part of the soul of the man whose hands delivered the fatal blows.

Some years back, when sporting events promoter Scott Murray took Ray 'Boom Boom' Mancini to Dublin, I was invited to show them around. Following a visit to St Saviours boxing club, Mancini, who had sparred with Bob Dylan and was celebrated in a song by Warren Zevon, chatted with me and friends in a nearby hotel. The consequences of his brutal encounter with Korean hopeful Duk-Koo Kim in 1982 had been catastrophic. While Mancini held on to his world title, Kim died four days later from a brain haemorrhage. Two months later the dead man's distraught mother drank poison and died. Referee Richard Green, who stopped the fight in the fourteenth round, also committed suicide. The fight changed Mancini's life too. He became depressed and struggled to cope with the guilt. How did he survive?

'After the Kim fight, I had to get back in the ring right away,' he told us:

> 'Cos, if I didn't, I'd never move on. I rely on my faith. I say my prayers to get me through the hard times. For me that's the only way. People go so low they can't see a way out. My faith in Christ has kept me strong. I coulda banged the needle. Banged the bottle. No, no, man.

Once when I was with Barry McGuigan ('the Clones Cyclone'), we were approached by a group of English businessmen who wanted to shake his hand. Polite and cordial, Barry chatted with them and soon afterwards left for a meeting. When he'd gone, one of the men marvelled at the size of Barry's hands. 'His fists are enormous,' he exclaimed. They're sizeable weapons for sure. I remembered how, in the summer of 1982, Barry had travelled to London to fight Asymin Mustapha, a novice boxer from Nigeria known as 'Young Ali'. McGuigan had a record of ten wins and one loss.

The Clones Cyclone found the inexperienced Nigerian easy to hit. Despite the punishment, Young Ali kept coming. In the sixth round, McGuigan followed a series of headshots with a straight punch right between the eyes. Ali wobbled, fell back and lay prone on the canvas. *Irish Times* reporter Sean Kilfeather described hearing 'an eerie noise from Ali's throat'.

Still in a coma from a bleed on the brain, Ali was flown home to hospital in Nigeria. He never recovered and died in December. By that time, McGuigan had fought two more fights. But Ali's fate threw him into a spin. Tormented, he decided to quit. After months of soul-searching and prayer, he reassessed the situation. If he retired, Young Ali would become a forgotten statistic. If he fought on, he could carry the memory of the dead man with him. 'I wanted people to remember him,' he would say.

VI

Within a year of his fight with Bueno, Wayne McCullough became depressed. 'It sounds stupid and selfish but I spent weeks planning my suicide … I visualized myself tying my strong leather jump rope around the beam [in his Las Vegas living room], putting a noose on it and hanging myself.' He credits his wife Cheryl's intervention with saving his life.

When I met McCullough days before the Bueno bout, he was in love with his world. Bright-eyed, he was savouring the adventure that had brought him on an Olympic odyssey and onwards through an undefeated professional campaign. But the Bueno fight was a watershed. 'I still get shivers,' he told me years later, recalling the fight. 'I know I could have got him out of there. At the beginning of the third round I hit him a left hook and he sort of slid along the ropes. He was gone. From that moment it seemed like I got the life sucked out of me.' As he said to journalist Johnny Watterson, 'I had a punch. Then, all of a sudden, I didn't.'

Nine years passed before I met McCullough again. Superficially, he was the same guy but his eyes were now hollow. Here was a man who had stood above the abyss. The affection still shown by the Irish public did little to alleviate his smouldering frustration. Having always controlled his destiny in the ring, McCullough lacked a clear target for the rage caused by the innumerable logistical problems that beset him. Days and nights of hunger, and savage physicality, had taken the devout Christian from the Shankill Road to the edge of a cliff, the very borderline between this world and the next. Although McCullough didn't slip over, his familiar landscape was fundamentally altered by the psychic shockwaves generated in March 1996.

He had an acrimonious and protracted parting of the ways from Tinley and appointed his wife, Cheryl, as manager. His trainer, Eddie Futch, had retired. The complicated business side of boxing had sapped McCullough's enthusiasm for the sport he loved. Then came the cruellest blow. In October 2000, on the eve of his first home-town bout since 1995, he was diagnosed with having a cyst on his brain. This discovery prompted the British Boxing Board of Control (BBBofC) to cancel the fight and withdraw his licence to fight professionally. The boxer with a reputation for having a jaw as indestructible as an anvil was told he risked death if he was hit on the head. Shocked, McCullough sought further medical opinions. These contradicted the earlier findings. There was a cyst, yes, but it wasn't life-threatening. He could box on. Two years later, the BBBofC restored his licence. 'They stole my prime as a fighter,' he lamented.

McCullough had fifteen more fights and won eight. He fought at super-bantamweight, moved up to featherweight, came back down to super-bantamweight and back again to featherweight, to no avail. Tellingly, the seven losses were all in important title bouts. Something was missing. As they say in the trade, Wayne didn't bring his punch with him. It seemed that in his courage and determination, Wayne McCullough had unwittingly left something vital and central to his boxing persona in the ring when he battled Bueno in '96.

3
SERGEANT

'Sometimes I feel forgotten about.'
Michael Carruth

I

STANDING SIX FEET THREE inches, Cuba's Juan Hernández Sierra was eight inches taller than Michael Carruth when the pair met in the Olympic Games welterweight final in Barcelona in 1992. The Cuban had won gold at the previous year's World Championships. He'd also earned gold at the Central American and Caribbean Games in 1990 and gold at the 1991 Pan American Games. Hernández was in his prime. Nobody gave Carruth a chance.

Despite injuries to both his hands, Carruth made a silent vow in the dressing room. In something akin to an epiphany, he saw his lifelong connection to boxing. The years of effort. The cruel disappointments. His heady aspirations. His ultimate goal. Everything boiled down to the next nine minutes of boxing, his fourth tough fight in a week. Nothing would stop him beating the world champion and becoming Ireland's first boxer to win an Olympic gold medal.

His father, Austin, from Drimnagh Boxing Club, and Nicolas Cruz worked with Carruth on tactics to foil the rangy Cuban southpaw. Cruz had been a teacher at the Higher Institute of Physical Culture in Havana before being dispatched to Ireland on secondment to work with the Irish Amateur Boxing Association (IABA) in 1988. The Cubans wanted him back but Cruz liked Ireland so he stayed. His coaching style remained the same. 'I always preach, "Leave nothing to chance,"' he told me. 'You think you have it but then, one punch, and all your dreams are gone.'

Before the final in Barcelona, the pair worked on tactics for ninety minutes. 'We never went to the gym where all the different countries trained. We trained in private,' Cruz told me. The final was fought according to Cruz's plan. While Carruth's opponent, Juan Hernández, hadn't been beaten in over three years, he'd previously been a pupil of Cruz who knew his style intimately.

Carruth was a natural counter-puncher so the plan was to hold back and make his opponent come forward. Hernandez obliged and time and again was picked off by Carruth's powerful right hook. The Irishman would have been 11-8 ahead after the second round had he not been penalised three points for holding. Level going into the last round, the nation held its breath. In the last three minutes, the Cuban scored two. Carruth added five. He won his gold medal 13-10 and greeted the result with a frenzy of jumping that was both celebratory and cathartic.

On the morning of Carruth's gold-medal victory, Oscar De La Hoya became Olympic lightweight champion. He went to become a multi-millionaire global superstar, winning multiple world titles and being dubbed 'The Golden Boy'. Promoter Bob Arum predicted De La Hoya would earn €100 million in purses alone.

Despite his gold-medal status, Carruth hadn't been able to catch a break as a pro fighter. Eight years later, in early 2000, Carruth was planning to annex the WBC light-middleweight belt held by Javier Castillejo. With his career in the doldrums, the fight with Castillejo would change his life, for better or worse. And Carruth knew it.

'This fella is going to push me harder than anyone has in my life,' Michael said of Castillejo, 'El Lince' ('the Lynx'), who he was meeting in Madrid in March. 'He's going to headbutt me. He's going to hit me low. He's going to hit me with elbows. He's going to have twenty thousand Spaniards cheering him on. He's on his home turf. It's going to be war.'

Carruth was a soldier in the Irish Army before he became a professional fighter. He knew as much about the art of military engagement as the ancient Chinese strategist Sun Tzu. 'I'm ready to go to war,' he declared.

II

I'd caught the end of an arduous training session in Drimnagh Boxing Club, the war room that shaped Carruth's spectacular amateur career. As he wound down, Carruth revealed how he'd been worn down by inactivity and a succession of undercard fights in almost empty venues.

He'd set himself performance targets, trained hard and made sacrifices in his personal life. Not getting the important bouts he felt he deserved, he'd come close to retiring. His pro career depended on an unpredictable confluence of questionable business deals, unlikely promotional alliances and the vagaries of availability and fate. 'If complacency sets in for a fighter, for want of another word, you're dead,' he explained.

Although the contract for Castillejo hadn't been signed off on yet, Carruth was upbeat and ready to rock. 'This fella's a worthy champion. He took it off a good champion, Keith Mullings. He defended it three times. He's a tough boyo.'

Behind the scenes, promoter Brian Peters was arranging Carruth's training camp. 'Brian will spare nothing,' enthused Carruth. 'He wants this more than me. How many promoters do you see who are younger than the boxer?' He had a point. Baby-faced Peters, a publican from Dunshaughlin, seemed to be an enthusiastic overgrown schoolboy hobbyist who turned up at the wrong gig. Instead of working on the merchandise stall at a rock concert he found himself involved in the promotion of professional boxing. However, enigmatic Peters had the smarts of a seasoned three-card-trick man at a funfair and a knowledge of boxing and the business of boxing to rival a seasoned veteran.

The sparring partners he'd hand-picked for Carruth would cover all the important bases ahead of his world-title bid. Michael was happy. There was Jim Rock, Irish super-middleweight champion, Jim Webb, from Belfast, too. ('He's a mauler and a brawler.') And Keith Mullings was expected in camp. ('An old campaigner, a sly old dog and a tough spar.') Austin, Carruth's father, and two of Carruth's boxing brothers were going to work his corner. Gerry Storey from Belfast was being asked to come on board as cutman.

'There's going to be clashes of heads in this one. You need someone you can trust in the corner. I trust Gerry.'

Surveying his twenty professional fights with eighteen wins, Michael argued that he'd been robbed of a decision in the two losses on his CV:

> Gordon Blair in Scotland in '95, I battered him and then they gave it to him. It was a home-town decision. I justified it a year later. I took him out of it. All the boxing pundits had me winning by three rounds against [Michael] Loewe for the WBO world title. To me I'm unbeaten. This fellow [Castillejo] hasn't been stopped. He knows I'm an Olympic champion. He'll know he's in for a war.

Carruth's southpaw style frequently presented opponents with a problem. Eleven of his eighteen wins came by knockout. Boxers mainly jab with their non-dominant left hand. 'I'm right-handed,' he said. 'I should give the anaesthetic with the left hand but I give it with the right, which fools a lot of people. They don't realize how strong my right hand is until they're caught with it.'

It became clear that Carruth hoped his performance against Castillejo would be noticed by the critics. 'Sometimes I feel forgotten about by the media,' he revealed. Acknowledging neighbour Eamonn Coghlan's 1983 World Championship 5000-metres gold-medal win in Helsinki as an inspiration, Carruth said:

> I won the greatest thing in the world. The Olympic gold medal is the greatest of them all and I've one of them. I've a bronze medal from the World Championships as well. So winning the gold wasn't a fluke. But when you see you're ranked tenth in the all-time rankings in Ireland by certain journalists, you think, 'How can they put somebody ahead of an Olympic champion?' When you're still only thirty-two and you're not remembered for certain things …'92 was only eight years ago.

Twice an Olympian, Carruth had also boxed for Ireland in Seoul in 1988. A solid citizen, he was no Flash Harry. He didn't court celebrity or cultivate the aura of showbusiness glamour associated with many professional fighters.

'I boxed at ten o'clock in the morning Irish time,' he said, recalling Barcelona:

> I read that there were 880,000 television sets tuned in here to watch my fight. If you put two or three people in front of each of those

sets, and there was about four million in front of my ma's telly alone, then you say, 'How did people forget you?' Only five people on this island have won an Olympic gold medal. When people deliberately say stupid things about you, it hurts.

He didn't need to search for motivation ahead of his title fight. 'I'm classed as the underdog for this fight and I like that. I'm going to remind them I'm not dead. When I'm WBC champion I'll be flying into Dublin on 4 March with my belt hanging around me.'

III

Becoming the first Irish competitor to claim Olympic gold since Ronnie Delany won the 1500 metres in Melbourne thirty-six years previously was an historic achievement.

He claimed the top podium place at welterweight, and his teammate Wayne McCullough won silver at bantamweight. Adding to the romance of the story was the fact that Carruth been primarily coached throughout his career by his father, Austin, a wily – and witty – tactician.

In Ireland's first ever involvement in a World Cup tournament finals, Jack Charlton's team had reached the quarter-finals of Italia '90. The squad's homecoming remains the stuff of legend. Crowds thronged the route from the airport to the city centre. Carruth and McCullough arrived home from Barcelona in the middle of the night but, the following day, they enjoyed an open-topped bus ride down an O'Connell Street packed with cheering well-wishers. At the Mansion House they were officially welcomed home by city dignitaries. The Irish government announced that the former army corporal was being promoted to sergeant in recognition of his achievement.

Carruth found himself in demand. A newly acquired agent ensured the Drimnagh boxer was busy in the corporate world. 'I didn't spend weekends in my house for months,' he told me. He'd come home from the Olympics nursing two broken hands. Designed to protect the boxer's hands, not the opponent's head or body, even with the fists being properly taped beforehand, gloves aren't always successful in preventing disastrous finger, knuckle, ligament or wrist injuries. Carruth's injuries, which also included a damaged elbow, prevented him from training properly for months.

The period of inactivity weighed heavily on him. 'There was a comedown in not boxing again,' he admitted. 'There were nights of depression. I don't suffer from depression but I was getting low. I wasn't going to the stadium to see the boys boxing and I said, "Hold on, I need to get back into the ring."' Under pressure to decide on his future, he opted to turn pro and signed with London promoter Frank Warren. Fourteen months after his Olympic triumph, he made his professional debut winning a six-round bout on points.

Three years into his pro career, Carruth had challenged the previously unbeaten Michael Loewe for the WBO world welterweight title in Aachen, Germany, in 1997. He'd come close but lost by a majority decision. Not for the first time commentators made use of the caustic epigram coined by Henry Cooper's manager, Jim ('The Bishop') Wicks, 'You've got to knock them out to get a draw in Germany.' This proved to be Loewe's last fight. He retired with a record of 28-unbeaten, and later became a successful race-car driver like his father, Nicolae Leu.

Warren also had 'Prince' Naseem Hamed on his books. By comparison, Carruth's career didn't appear to have received the careful nurturing normally associated with emerging world champions. Following the defeat in Aachen, he stalled. He had just one fight in '98, a points win in Dublin. Then Brian Peters popped up and arranged three fights for Carruth in '99. He won all three by knockout. The new millennium was just a few weeks old as he considered the challenge in Madrid.

Carruth was acutely aware that, since Barcelona, teammate Wayne McCullough had gone on to win and stage two successful defences of his WBC world bantamweight title. By the time Carruth had his first fight for pay, McCullough had already fought, and won, ten times. The Pocket Rocket was operating at the highest level, fighting for world titles.

No one doubted Carruth's ability, courage or determination, but he needed to make up ground. Big, headline-grabbing title fights continued to elude him. Until now.

As we parted company, Carruth, ever the realist, added an unexpected caveat. There was the hesitant caution of a man confounded by the smoke-and-mirrors fandango of boxing promotion. 'This is all speculation still. Brian [Peters] could ring me tonight and say, "This is not on."'

IV

I sometimes wonder if I should have spoken more to my father about the boxers I met and the fights I'd been at. I didn't, of course, for fear of opening a door on a shadow world of painful memories. Besides, I was reluctant to revisit my early years of motherless anxiety, that bleak time when there was no hope. None of my friends or acquaintances cared much for boxing. The fights were something I went to alone. In hindsight, the currency that appealed to me most in boxing was hope. Hope is ingrained in boxers. 'I didn't win but I'll beat him in the return.' Curiously, at ringside I found a new family, a sodality of the knowing, a confraternity of the classless. People for whom hope wasn't an abstract theory. As Muhammad Ali said, 'If you even dream of beating me you'd better wake up and apologize.'

With less than two weeks to go to the most important fight of his career, Carruth received the phone call he secretly dreaded. His world-title fight with Castillejo was off. 'Hearing that tore the guts out of me.' The champion was said to have picked up an injury in sparring. Suspecting skulduggery, Carruth was furious: he diagnosed Castillejo's condition as 'a dose of yellow-itis'.

The capricious nature of professional boxing was alien to a man whose life in the army had been regimented and whose amateur career followed a preordained calendar of national and international tournaments. Freed from the demands of training camp and making weight, Carruth switched off. His heart broken, he considered his future. From being totally in the zone, his mindset switched from high to low. He put his feet up. His glorious opportunity gone, Carruth was less than razor-sharp when Brian Peters presented an alternative plan.

Peters had been busy. He'd landed a Saturday night Sky TV top-of-the-bill title fight for Carruth in London. Not a shabby alternative; it was the kind of showcase boxers craved. He'd be fighting Adrian Stone, a boxer from Bristol who'd been reared in New Jersey. At stake was the IBO world super-welterweight title, which, while not as exciting as the WBC belt, offered Carruth a route into the big time. 'This is my chance to get back into the limelight,' he told my colleague Karl McGinty. 'Where my own national TV stations wouldn't back me, Sky are going to tell the world that I'm still here. I firmly believe there's a pot of gold at the end of the rainbow.'

Carruth quickly assessed his opponent: 'Stone is not in my class.' It was of little concern that twenty-one canaries failed to come back from the mine after meeting 'The Predator' down at the coalface, where in just three of thirty-one fights he hadn't chopped out an early victory. Stone could punch.

V

Surrounded by officials and pressmen, Carruth was subdued. He looked drained. And worried. The weigh-in revealed he was two and a half pounds over the regulation weight, eleven stone (154 lbs). Stone was comfortable at 153 lbs. Officials explained they would allow Carruth on the scales again before the offices closed at 6 pm, giving him three hours to make the weight. When Michael left with his team, the consensus among the boxing pundits was that he hadn't a hope of shedding the pounds in the time.

The world-title fight was scheduled as the highlight of Sky's flagship Saturday night sports coverage. Such prime exposure was just what the Dubliner's stuttering career needed. But over the course of a few hours on a Friday afternoon, Carruth's golden opportunity turned to mush. Because he was overweight, Carruth's fight was rendered meaningless. In commercial terms, this was tantamount to committing professional suicide.

The pressure on Carruth had been immense but he'd blown it. With the Castillejo fight cancelled, Carruth stopped training and quickly returned to his walking-around weight. He weighed twelve stone when he'd been offered the Stone bout just nineteen days earlier. Desperation drove him to grasp this opportunity and, with it, the possibility of the bigger, more meaningful fights that could follow. He took the fight believing he could drop fourteen pounds in nineteen days and still be in top shape to meet the challenge of the heavy-hitting journeyman. It was a miscalculation.

Traditionally, boxing had been structured around the premise of eight different weight divisions – heavyweight, light heavyweight, middleweight, welterweight, lightweight, featherweight, bantamweight and flyweight. Gradually, more weight classes were added, resulting in more and more title fights. Seventeen weight divisions meant more opportunities for fighters. And, of course, more business. Not that Carruth was surveying the history of weight divisions in those torturous days preceding the official weigh-in as he strove to lose excess baggage to enable him qualify for super-welterweight, a division wedged between welter and middle that's sometimes referred to as junior middleweight. A crash diet had helped him shed five pounds in the twenty-four hours before weigh-in. It hadn't been enough.

When Team Carruth left the weigh-in to attempt the impossible, Gerry Callan and I repaired to a nearby hostelry, which we were told had been serving ale when Shakespeare was a lad. An entertaining companion and Irish boxing's unsung hero, Callan had kept the Irish Boxing Writers Association alive during lean times for the sport. Thanks largely to his efforts, emerging young talent received official recognition and the accolades they deserved. Callan's knowledge of boxing was prodigious. For years before the arrival of online search engines, Callan had self-published the encyclopaedic *Irish Boxing Yearbook*. It was not unknown during press conferences for promoters, trainers or boxers to consult with him on contentious stats or historic facts. His word was law.

After a sojourn in the Bard's alehouse, we caught up with other members of the press corps at a fashionable hotel, where we were joined by Irish super-middleweight champion Jim Rock, a colourful character who, away from the ring, offered 'knockout' deals as an entrepreneurial car dealer. Rock would be fighting for the Irish super-welterweight title on Carruth's undercard. Stories were swapped, great fights recalled and gossip traded. Arriving later, a smiling English boxing writer broke the ice by declaring, 'You Irish chaps must be happy with the news.' What news?

It had just been reported that a well-known Dublin criminal had been convicted for his role in the murder of investigative journalist Veronica Guerin. Those of us who had known Veronica as a colleague or friend nodded grimly. We'd attended her funeral and witnessed the anguish of her husband, Graham, and family. And saw the innocent bewilderment of her six-year-old son Cathal, who hadn't fully realized that he would never see his mother again. In London, Jim Rock's declamatory response surprised everyone. His outburst came with the revelation that he'd been shot by a relation of the crime boss some years previously. The newly arrived English boxing writer chuckled, remarking how the Irish couldn't resist telling tall tales.

Rock then indignantly recalled how when, working as security for a Dublin nightclub, he'd barred a patron who happened to be the son of a notorious gangland figure. Later that evening, a high-powered car arrived and three men approached Rock. One pointed a shotgun at him. Rock jumped and forced the gun barrel towards the ground. The trigger pulled, the double-barrel blasted both his legs. Clearly unconvinced, the English writer found the plot line highly entertaining. With that, Rock sprang to his feet in the open-plan lounge, dropped his trousers in public view and pulled up his boxer shorts to display unsightly scarring high on both his inner thighs. The room went quiet. The colour drained from the writer's face. Rock continued, 'The fucker was about to shoot me in the balls. There was blood everywhere. They drove off and left me to die.'

We raised a toast to Veronica before returning to the offices of the BBBofC (British Boxing Board of Control) where Carruth returned looking even more gaunt. He'd managed to drop one and a quarter pounds, but was still overweight. Officials agreed the fight would go ahead but if Carruth won he couldn't claim the title.

Later, as I approached the door of the York Hall for the fight, a London cab pulled up and Carruth and his father got out. As he ascended the steps, the former army sergeant's demeanour suggested someone who was going back, none too optimistically, for the results of a serious medical examination. By failing to make the weight for a televised title fight, Carruth had sabotaged his pro career. What was impossible to gauge was the extent of the damage done. I couldn't imagine how Carruth's mindset could be right for this bout, which, even if he won, would mean nothing. With a growing sense of alarm, I realized I was witnessing a sporting tragedy unfold.

The bout was a parody of a title fight. Stone imposed himself from the first bell and landed meaningful shots on Carruth's face at will. With his opponent in control, Carruth had no answer to the punishment he was taking. It was an impoverished performance by the Dubliner. Under heavy ordnance, he looked exhausted and disoriented. He'd have been running on empty if he'd had the energy to move his feet. His flimsy guard was an exercise in futility. He lost each of the first five rounds and was cut, bruised and dazed as he returned to his corner. His experienced coach was a realist. With his son slumped on his stool like a drunk at closing time, Austin knew there was no point in sending him back into the roiling abyss. He waved off the fight. It was over.

The crowd had left and the TV crew were de-rigging when I spotted a lone figure attempting to make her way through the lines of chairs. It was

Carruth's wife, Paula, on crutches and pregnant. She was anxious to be with her husband. Gingerly, I escorted her around the chairs and up the narrow stairs to the dressing room where, through a fug of saline aroma and regret, we stepped into a private world of desolation. I've been at wakes that were more cheerful. Sport's loneliest place is the loser's dressing room.

An old stained washbasin, doubling as a receptacle for a pile of bloodstained towels, lent the room the ambiance of a backstreet Victorian dentist's surgery. Despite the gravity of the situation, a battered-looking Carruth, his face displaying a patchwork of multi-hued weals, the badges of his defeat, was courteous and stoical. 'The proper Michael Carruth wasn't out there tonight and I'm to blame for that. I kidded myself for this fight, thinking I could lose weight, get in and fight him.' He made no excuses. Much later, in a lengthy jeremiad, we heard about the effects of his struggle to shed the necessary pounds. His leg muscles began to cramp during the bout. His hands throbbed with pins and needles and his back went into spasm. 'I was so dehydrated, my lips had begun to crack. I didn't know my left from my right.'

He was involved in a second fight that night. A shouting match with angry promoter Frank Maloney, one of the power brokers in English boxing. The punishment he'd taken in the ring was matched by the ferocity of Maloney's criticism. 'Carruth was a disgrace to the sport and he has cheated on the public,' the promoter thundered. 'If it was up to me, I'd take his licence off him.' As tempers flared, Carruth chucked a chair at the promoter. There was no need for sanctions. Michael Carruth, Olympic gold-medal winner and Irish national hero, had enough of the vagaries of the professional game. His logistical miscalculation was an embarrassment not a crime. A few days later, he quit professional boxing.

Awarded the belt, Stone went on to successfully defend it three times. Writer George Plimpton once told a story of how King Levinsky, a journeyman heavyweight, was fond of saying, 'Joe Louis finished me. In one round that man turned me from a fighter to a guy selling ties.' Things were looking sweet for Adrian Stone until he landed a bill-topping world-title fight with Shane Mosley in Caesars Palace. A series of clubbing rights and an explosive left hook in the third round left Stone staring at the ceiling through vacant eyes. By then, his career as a fighter behind him, Michael Carruth was in Dublin selling life-insurance policies.

4
THE PHANTOM PUNCHER

'One punch can change a fight.'
Bernard Dunne

I

'PROTECT YOURSELVES AT ALL times …' Referee Terry O'Connor looms like a giant over the super-bantamweights who stare balefully at each other.

The bell rings. Twenty-nine seconds later, a punch that causes a world of trouble hits its target. A clubbing right hook crashes into the side of Bernard Dunne's head. It's followed by a sharp left that comes up, venomous and terrifying, from the deep. Dazed, Dunne tumbles backwards and lands on his arse. He takes an eight count. In his corner, Harry Hawkins is screaming like a man who can see the roof caving in.

For the next forty-six seconds, Dunne impersonates a haystack in a tornado. Caught by another savage right, he's on the canvas again. Another mandatory eight seconds plus a few extra moments of respite as the referee exhorts him to raise his gloves for protection before waving the fight on.

Under a furious onslaught, Dunne is rudderless, a canoe floundering in the wake of a battleship. The punches rain down. Disoriented and pawing against a tidal wave, he slumps to his knees. It's over.

Bernard Dunne's world has been turned upside down. Less than halfway through the first round, he's lost his European title. The crowd packed into the Point Depot are shell-shocked. But at least they know where they are. The glazed look in the former champion's eyes indicate he hasn't a notion. Nothing registers other than an instinctive urge to cover up and punch back against an offensive that has that swept him off his feet three times in a minute.

With shocking ferocity, Kiko Martínez, who'd been a model of politeness and diplomacy since he arrived from Valencia, unleashed the sort of merciless, barbarous assault that made Mike Tyson the most dangerous fighter on the planet.

II

Martínez had entered the ring first. Seated at the ring apron, next to the second with the spit bucket in the Spaniard's corner, I noticed how, as he climbed between the ropes, the Spanish fighter had the flushed look of a man who'd just fought a few rounds in the car park. He was fully switched on.

Dunne and his manager, Brian Peters, valued the noisy intervention of a partisan crowd. 'It has to be like walking into the Colosseum and everyone baying for blood,' the champion said earlier in the week. Ahead of the biggest fight in his career, they kept Martínez waiting. After what felt like a very long time, Dunne's familiar introductory symphonic flourish rumbled through the arena. 'O Fortuna' is the strident opening movement of Carl Orff's cantata *Carmina Burana*. It had long come to be associated with the berserk underside of bacchanalian excess. When Ray Manzarek of The Doors recorded the piece, he described the Latin lyrics as 'the work of renegade monks'. This was not a window into a cloistered, celibate lifestyle; it was a celebration of orgy and excess.

I looked up at Martínez as he paced his corner like a caged lion. He glanced down and our eyes met. His gaze was chilling. Instead of unsettling him, this calculated display of disrespect had hardened his resolve. And the object of his ire and indignation had yet to make his appearance. It was then I knew Dunne was in for a rough night.

Orff's Grand Guignol treatment of medieval poetry isn't exactly a party singalong so, to fully engage the crowd, Dunne's actual ring walk was to the rousing strains of 'The Irish Rover', a time-honoured ballad of exorbitant intemperance delivered by the twin-pronged attack of The Dubliners and The Pogues. I understood the emotional impact and power of the song full well, having once hammered out its message with both groups when I deputized behind the kit for the Pogues' drummer in Dublin.

The blood was up. The scene was set. We were in for a fight. Then, eighty-six seconds after the opening bell, it was over. Expectation had crash-landed. We had a new European champion.

The arena was emptying out. As Dunne, battered, bewildered and remorseful, was led back to the sanctuary of the changing room, the words of the evening's opening fanfare revealed themselves as an esoteric incantation.

'*O Fortuna, vellum luna state variabilis … immanis et inanis, rota tu volubilis, status malus… mecum omnes plangite.*'

'Oh Fate, like the moon, you are always changing … monstrous and empty, you whirling wheel, you are malevolent … everyone weep with me.'

III

Bernard Dunne's professional career was almost derailed before it began. He had an impressive amateur record. Of his eleven national titles, three were at senior level. He boxed 130 bouts and lost just 11. He had never been defeated on home soil. Having agreed to sign with London promoters Frank Maloney and Panos Eliades, Dunne discovered that he had a cyst on his brain.

Following tests, informed medical opinion believed its size and positioning meant it wasn't dangerous. Despite dismissing it as 'the size of a pea', Dunne believed the BBBofC would most likely deny him a licence to box so he switched his focus to America.

When Dunne had quit the amateur code, boxing enthusiast Brian Peters, who was involved as co-promoter of some major events including the Steve Collins–Chris Eubank and the Wayne McCullough–José Luis Bueno title bouts, had been anxious to manage his professional career. But the young fighter from Neilstown had considered the Dunshaughlin publican small fry.

However, with his career prospects floundering, Dunne was happy to grab the lifeline Peters threw him in 2001. Straight away, Peters took a crucial, career-defining initiative. He introduced Dunne to Los Angeles-based coach Freddie Roach. Boxing out of the famous Wildcard Gym, Dunne caught the attention of Sugar Ray Leonard who signed him to his new promotions company in 2002. Two years later Leonard's company ceased operating: Dunne was ready to return home, bringing with him a wealth of boxing knowledge and a record of fourteen unbeaten fights.

Brian Peters had a plan. He knew that Dunne wouldn't be allowed to fight in Britain, because of the earlier medical ruling. The promoter's strategy was to attempt something that had never been achieved before. With Peters directing operations, Bernard Dunne would become the first Irish boxer to be crowned world champion from the small island he came from, a country without the tested infrastructure that professional boxing demands. It was an audacious concept. So many things could go wrong, but the promoter had an ace up his sleeve. The national television station, RTÉ, had expressed interest in showing Dunne's homecoming bout live. This was to prove the bountiful promotional aid that primed an explosion in boxing's popularity.

In boxing, as in showbusiness, timing is crucial. As Emanuel Steward once said, 'No matter how good a fighter is, he won't make a name for himself until he's on television … and he won't make any money either.' Bernard's homecoming coincided with changes in RTÉ's Sports Department. New boss Glen Killane believed in boxing's potential to attract viewers. Dunne was a local boy made good in America. The viewing figures for his first bout at the National Stadium were impressive. RTÉ was pleased. A vicious left hook to the body in the fifth round destroyed Jim Betts. Game over. Dunne was triumphant. The television viewers liked what they saw.

Following three more wins in 2005 and another two in 2006, Dunne prepared to meet a tough former American youth champion, David Martínez. From Albuquerque, New Mexico, Martínez had been raised by his mother when his father was in prison. Nicknamed 'El Finito', Martínez was fighting to make something of his life. If Dunne got through this fight unscathed, he was in the frame for a shot at a European title.

A week before the bout I visited Dunne at the home he'd bought, close to his parents in Neilstown. His record had grown to twenty unbeaten pro wins, twelve by knockout.

In the States, Dunne was a TV commentator's dream. 'I've been called "skinny", "scrawny" and "a choir boy" on national television in the States,' Dunne said. 'That's what they liked about me. A skinny white kid getting in with Black guys and solid Mexican guys with plenty of muscles. But I'd knock them out. They couldn't believe that I was doing it. Commentators joked that I was "the phantom puncher".'

Dunne fitted in. 'I was never a stiff upright boxer,' said Dunne, who'd been boxing since he was five:

> I was always good at slipping and ducking and rolling punches. As a kid I was watching tapes of Sugar Ray and Mike [Tyson]. I loved Mike in his prime. His upper-body movement was fuckin' phenomenal. Perfection. He slipped to the side and hook! That's what knocked you out. If you see it coming you can react. It's the surprise and the speed that knocks a guy out.

Dunne insisted he wasn't looking past Martínez at a possible European title fight. 'You've got to be on your game every second of every round, because one split second …'

He reminded me of his bout with Ukrainian Yuri Voronin, a fight he'd won on points, but not before he gave us a fright. 'I dominated him for nine rounds and in one momentary lapse of concentration, he nailed me. I didn't see that punch coming. BANG! When it hit me I thought, "Where the fuck did that come from?" It only travelled about six inches. One punch can change a fight.' The damaging shot, early in the final round, caught Dunne behind the ear and staggered him. He survived a major scare that night, but he hadn't forgotten it.

Nevertheless, the question of a European belt couldn't be ignored. If he maintained his progress, Dunne hoped to have a title fight in Dublin. His concern was that business deals might scupper the idea.

Business regulations are more convoluted and elastic in the fight game than in other professional sports. Fighters are frequently shocked to discover their take-home pay is much less than expected. And they're the lucky ones who get the lucrative fights. Most fight on the undercard for chicken feed and have to cover the expenses of coaches, training camps, sparring partners, medical fees and so on. The business of arranging a big-money fight can often be torturous, with any number of interested parties positioning themselves for a slice of the gross.

As we chatted in their compact kitchen, Dunne's wife, Pamela, prepped fresh veg for the evening meal. Bounded by rough breeze-block walls, the grass in the small back garden looked unkempt. Bernard wouldn't be drawn on financial matters. In seven days, he'd meet a man who intended making the question of a lucrative title-fight academic.

Dunne was relishing the occasion. 'The atmosphere at the National Stadium is fuckin' phenomenal,' he said. 'I've been in venues all over the world at some really big fights and I've never experienced anything like it. It's amazing.'

IV

Shortly before the start of World War II, Ireland's Minister for Defence, Frank Aiken, opened a newly constructed 17,000-square-foot venue on Dublin's South Circular Road designed to be the HQ of the IABA, an association dedicated to fostering the Olympic sport of amateur boxing. The 2000-seater National Stadium was the jewel in the Association's crown when it hosted the European Championships in 1939. It remains the only purpose-built amateur boxing stadium in the world and hosts tournaments at all age levels throughout the year.

As a child, I overheard my father and his friends marvel at how thrilling it must have been for boxers to walk up the steps at the National Stadium. When I eventually got to the venue, I was confused to find it was built on flat land. There were no steps to the entrance. Although I subsequently headlined concerts at the venue in the 1970s with Horslips, it wasn't until, at one of Leonard Gunning's Celtic Clash promotions, when I followed a boxer from the changing room into the arena that I realized what my father's friends had been referring to. The changing rooms are situated beneath the sloping arena floor and to approach the ring, the boxers must walk up a short flight of steps. They emerge on a passageway in the middle of an indoor amphitheatre surrounded on all sides by cheering spectators, the ring below is bathed in white light and the air is heavy with thunderous noise and expectation. Oddly, I'd never noticed this as a musician, having been completely focused on the performance ahead. Years later, I recognized the same psychological state in many boxers at the venue. Total concentration. No distractions. In the zone. Ready to rock.

The hooded figure of Bernard Dunne walked up those steps and appeared through a cloud of smoke, as if from a subterranean cavern, to meet David Martínez. The visiting American was quickly revealed as unprepared for the full range of Dunne's capabilities. Dunne soon began displaying the choreography of an exhibitionist. Martínez received a painful education and the American's corner called him ashore in the eighth round.

It was Dunne's last time fighting in the National Stadium. Peters was taking the show to a bigger stage. The old Point Depot in Dublin's docklands was booked for November. Dunne would contest the EBU (European) super-bantamweight title against Esham Pickering (29-4). Dangerous as Pickering was, a greater threat was presented by the coach who trained him in Sheffield. An inspirational figure, Brendan Ingle was a Dubliner who'd emigrated from recession-blighted Dublin in 1958 when he was eighteen. He had hoped to get a job in the Sheffield steelworks. Seven years later, he was fighting for money. He won the first of his thirty-four fights in the Manchester Free Trade Hall in October 1965. He was eighth in the rankings when he quit in 1973. By then he had embarked on a career as a coach.

Having guided Prince Naseem to the top, he was keen to repeat the journey. Pickering was his current project. The returning emigrant had every incentive to mastermind an upset. 'Bernard is a terrific fighter,' acknowledged Brendan. 'But we're here to win.' Brendan knew that European champion Esham Pickering had a world-title fight in his sights.

Dublin had changed dramatically since Ingle's departure. Disputes in the drugs trade had resulted in an escalation of gang violence. The year 2006 saw an unprecedented spate of murders. Twenty-two people were gunned down in those twelve months. Signs on the wire-mesh fencing surrounding the Point Depot alerted customers to strict body searches: 'All patrons please be advised that all dangerous weapons will be confiscated.'

This was a major event and Dunne's manager, Brian Peters, had developed a slick promotional machine, which brought a touch of glitz to his fights. The Dubliner's ring walk had become the essence of theatrical experience, an eagerly embraced moment of mutual obligation and participation for Dunne's growing legion of fans, one that facilitated a unique communion of spirits, all in the service of blood sacrifice. With the home crowd as his worshipful congregation, Dunne was anointed chief celebrant in the glorification of aggression.

For Dunne's first fight at the bigger venue, Peters was determined to match the occasion with a memorable ring entrance for the homeboy. When discussing presentation ideas, he asked if I could recommend an uillean piper. Irish pipers had been considered a dangerous threat to England's interests during the sixteenth and seventeenth centuries. Many were imprisoned or transported to penal colonies. Having first incorporated the pipes in rock 'n' roll in the early 1970s with Horslips, I knew a variety of talented players. Assuming the promoter needed someone to play '*Amhrán na bhFiann*', I suggested my friend Sean Óg Potts, whose father had been in The Chieftains. But it wasn't the national anthem Peters had in mind.

Balcony seating on three sides of the venue helped create a bear-pit atmosphere. While Pickering waited in the ring for Dunne to arrive, the crowd gasped as a boxer in black dressing gown, with a black snood masking his face, appeared on the steps of a balcony just a few metres above the ringside. It was former Olympian Paul Griffin impersonating Dunne. With the crowd and Pickering already distracted, the emotive, high swirling sound of the pipes pierced the boisterous atmosphere and a sweeping spotlight found a lone piper seated on the steps of the balcony on the opposite side of the ring. It was an outrageous piece of jiggery-pokery which set pulses racing and added to the entertainment value of the event on TV.

In the ring, neither fighter gave an inch. Dunne used his lethal left jab to pulverize Pickering's nose. If he didn't break it in the second round, he certainly did in the third. Pickering came back strong. Dunne stayed in the driving seat. After twelve high-tempo rounds, Dunne won on a unanimous decision. He was now European champion, unbeaten in twenty-two fights.

I left my seat at the ring apron with my shirt and jacket sprayed with Esham Pickering's blood.

V

Dunne successfully defended his title twice before meeting Kiko Martínez in what was his third title fight in five months. Not an ideal itinerary but, unlike in other professional sports, a fighter's aspirations frequently play second fiddle to the demands of commerce.

The pressure on Dunne to take such an important fight again so quickly came when Bran Peters found himself at a disadvantage. As the new manager of Martínez, Belfast businessman Pat Magee became a powerbroker, much to Peters' chagrin. A joint promotion was agreed.

With the Point Depot due to close for a lengthy restoration project, the fight needed to be scheduled for August. Just eight weeks on from a gruelling twelve-round fight against rugged Norwegian Reidar Walstad, and with business negotiations a further distraction, Dunne's recovery and preparation to fight the mandatory challenger weren't ideal. Despite the carefully choreographed ring walk, the night quickly turned sour.

Those eighty-six seconds of cataclysmic action were ruinous for the Dublin champion. From being on the verge of a lucrative world-title fight, Dunne's defeat saw him slip down the rankings and out of contention. The emotional devastation was immense. Andy Lee, who'd had his first pro fight on Irish soil on the undercard, accurately described the doleful atmosphere, saying, 'It was like somebody had died.' The shock result had scuppered outline plans for a million-dollar world-title fight for Dunne in Croke Park.

With a depleted press corps, I waited for Dunne to appear for the obligatory post-fight press conference. At the back of the room stood boxing coach Pete Taylor, wife Bridget and their daughter Katie. Chaperoned at every big event by her father, the emerging young amateur star was getting to experience every aspect of the sport she would come to dominate.

Enveloped in an aura of *matière obscure*, Dunne arrived. His world had collapsed in on itself, crushing his hopes and dreams. What tears he had had been left behind on the floor of the shower stall. Though vanquished and with future uncertain, he remained unbowed, ruefully admitting, 'I just got caught with a shot I didn't see coming and that's it.' Remorseful for having let his followers down, he vowed he would come back stronger. Dunne had been severely punished for a momentary lapse of concentration. The slightest complacency in the ring can be bad for business. It can also be injurious to your health.

Master of ceremonies at the briefing, Brian Peters, did his best to keep air in the tyres. 'We haven't seen the last of Bernard Dunne,' he promised, as weary reporters pushed their chairs back and made for the exit.

VI

The humiliation of his defeat by Kiko Martínez was followed by a period of reassessment for Bernard Dunne. With coach Harry Hawkins and manager Brian Peters, a new road map was planned.

In 2008 Dunne had wins in three testing fights against rugged fighters from South America and was showing the benefits of hellish sessions with the Ireland rugby squad's strength and conditioning coach, Mike McGurn. Dunne was determined to never again be bullied by a stronger opponent.

As Brian Peters explored options for Dunne, it was clear that neither the new European champion Rendall Munroe or Martínez were willing to challenge the newly promoted WBA world champion Ricardo Cordoba, who'd knocked out twenty-one of the thirty-four opponents he'd beaten.

Ranked eleventh by the WBA, Bernard Dunne was way down the list of possible challengers. Anyone who'd seen him capsize against Martínez was unlikely to be worried by Dunne. But the Dubliner was a box-office attraction in his home town. An easy money fight for the champion, perhaps?

On Christmas Day Peters signed a contract for March 2009. Cordoba's agent, Richard Dobal, didn't wish to seem too eager. 'I'd seen Bernard sparring with Manny Pacquiao at the Wild Card Gym in Los Angeles a few years back. Seeing a skinny white Irish kid holding his own with Pacquiao, who back then was one of the baddest men in the world, is fresh in my memory.'

Dobal was confident Cordoba would win. He wasn't alone. Frank Maloney, who managed Rendall Monroe – who'd beaten Kiko Martínez twice – didn't rate Dunne and aired his belief that Brian Peters was 'leading him into an execution'. Dobal, however, wasn't about to risk damaging ticket sales. 'The great Hank Kaplan, the world's foremost boxing historian, would dismiss a first-round knockout,' he declared, talking up Dunne's challenge. 'It means nothing. Anybody can get caught cold. Talk to me about a ninth- or tenth-round knockout. That's significant.'

Shouldering bitter disappointment in the aftermath of his Martínez defeat, Dunne's professionalism and humility showed he had the strength of character required to one day reclaim his European title. But make the jump to world champion? Given the depth of talent at the top of the division, that would require a superhuman effort.

Nineteen months after his 86-second catastrophe, Bernard was set to fight the Panamanian southpaw they dubbed 'El Maestrito' ('The Master') for a WBA belt.

The O2 Arena was a reconfigured Point Depot. It now held over 9000 customers, which made for twice the bedlam when MC Mike Goodall announced, 'The time has come.' A few hours earlier Ireland had won an historic Six Nations Grand Slam win in Cardiff and the home crowd delivered a lusty version of '*Amhrán na bhFiann*'.

His face smeared in grease, Dunne looked confident as the fighters were introduced. The opening round saw both men in a hurry to open hostilities. With the champion measuring his range, a sharp left hook to the chin from Dunne in the third round caught him off guard. He teetered across the ring, fell and bounced backwards, his shoulders hitting the lower ropes. Quickly back on his feet, he took the eight count before Dunne tried to finish him off. The bell ended the action.

As Dunne landed shots in the fourth, the crowd raised the noise level. They sensed an early win for the Dubliner. A clash of heads opened a cut above Dunne's left eye. Cutman Benny King stemmed the red tide. In the fifth round, as they went toe to toe, a huge arcing right from Cordoba saw Dunne briefly sink to his knees. He took a mandatory count of eight. And still both men appeared reluctant to take a backwards step. In another fierce exchange, Dunne shipped another crushing right that dropped him on all fours. He beat the count but everyone knew that if he went down a third time in the round Cordoba would be declared the winner. He looked disoriented as, ducking and weaving, he tried to hold on to his opponent. In the final seconds he covered up and weathered a ferocious street-fighter onslaught. Those forty seconds of hard-learned survival tactics earned sixty seconds of vital restoration work.

At the break, his corner was a hive of industry and then, bruised and blood-splattered, Dunne went back to work knowing he needed to win his rounds to win the fight.

By the eighth, some of those closest to the action believed they could see signs of fatigue creeping into the champion's stance. But Dunne looked equally drained. Both men strained to find reserves they weren't sure they had. In the tenth, Cordoba continued to press forward, unleashing bombs.

They were shovelling fuel into an open furnace now. This was an epic, full-throttle, winner-take-all punch-up.

In the eleventh, seeing he was having some success, Cordoba's coach urged him forward. There was so much action, so many clinches and such a blizzard of punches thrown, it felt as if the space-time continuum was fundamentally altered. Poised on a knife-edge at the centre of a hurricane, this fight could go either way.

Dunne tattooed Cordoba with punches. The Panamanian keeled over. Bravely, he wouldn't stay down. Dunne came in with more punishment. Left, left, right, left ... the blows put the champion down a second time. But still he refused to capitulate. He still remained a threat. That was until a powerful right shook him and a follow-up left put him down for the third time in the round. This time he wasn't getting up. The bell was just one second away as Canadian referee Hubert Earle waved off the fight.

Dunne sank to his knees in exhausted relief. He was the victor. Waves of adrenaline broke through the ramparts of fatigue and kept him buoyant long enough to thank his team and, aware of the emotional turmoil his mother and wife had just endured, he added, 'And Happy Mother's Day to every mother out there.' Ricardo Cordoba was taken to Beaumont Hospital. Running repairs were carried out on Dunne who required ten stitches in one of the cuts. 'There were a lot of people writing me off,' he said. 'But I did believe I could win the title.' He was champion of the world.

Later he visited Cordoba in hospital and sat with him through the night.

VII

Earlier, while Dunne had been warming up, local hero Jim Rock won on points against Alessio Furlan at middleweight. It was Rock's last fight and he retired with a remarkable record. He'd won Irish national titles at four different weights in a fourteen-year career.

I recalled seeing him eight years earlier. With pro boxing in Ireland a rare commodity, I accepted an invitation to attend an event at Dublin's Burlington Hotel that was billed as 'Punch-and-Munch'. Thanks to the ever-helpful Gerry Callan, I got enjoy a memorable experience, promoted by Welsh promoter Paul Boyce in tandem with Brian Peters.

Black-tie boxing dinner events, which combine fine dining, a champagne reception, cabaret performers, a number of pro fights and an after-party, tap into the corporate hospitality market, providing an opportunity for networking in a convivial, intimate dinner-show setting. At the Burlington, the well-upholstered, predominantly male clientele loosened their cummerbunds and bow ties as the evening wore on. For the first time since Derry southpaw Charlie Nash successfully defended his EBU European lightweight title in this Burlington's Banqueting Suite in 1980, pro boxing was coming home.

It was an evening of sweat, cigar smoke and posh perfume. While patrons tucked into the prime roast sirloin of beef, in a rich sauce of tomato, herb and malt whiskey, the pain game played out in front of them. As the last of the bombe pralines were being polished off, MC Mike Goodall announced grandly, 'Gentlemen, please be upstanding for a serious moment.' With glasses were raised, I couldn't escape the echoes of history, and the atmosphere of an earlier era of prize-fighting events in private members' clubs in eighteenth and nineteenth centuries, when England's George IV, a noted boxing enthusiast and sometime promoter, would have had his good health extolled.

When light-middleweight Richard Inquieti hit the canvas for the first time in the opening bout, patrons sensed they were in for a treat. A journeyman underdog in the opening fight on the undercard is not the place you want to be in boxing. From Nottingham, Inquieti had seventeen fights that year and lost sixteen of them. He was on the canvas again when the bell ended the bout but managed a purposeful swagger as he was lead to the changing room.

By then some chaps in the crowd were pledging their undying love for the card girls. The card girls are an integral part of any fight night, but in keeping with the stylish dress code of 'Punch-and-Munch' there were no bikinis to be seen. Low-cut LBDs replaced hot pants.

Boxing legend Brendan Ingle lead out Jason Collins, a fighter from Sheffield, before a procession fronted by a tricolour announced the arrival of Jim Rock. On a four-fight card, this was the main event. It was late. Emotions were running high. In a neutral corner, referee Emile Tiedt was caught off guard when through the ropes came a wild-eyed wannabe champion. Dishevelled, with bow tie askew and shirt hanging out, the burly fight fan with spreading moustache lurched into a lap of honour, acknowledging the slurred cheers of the crowd. It was after midnight. He'd supped well and was incapable of controlling a Pavlovian response to the brassy strains of Rock's booming ring-walk fanfare, 'The Pink Panther Theme'. Tiedt and MC Mike Goodall waited diplomatically until, exhausted by his endeavours, the walrus lurched back to his seat.

As waiters scurried back and forth with bottles of champagne and trays of creamy pints, the feeling was that, for some present, life couldn't get much better than this.

Irish super-welterweight champion since he beat Allan Gray in the York Hall, Bethnal Green, twelve months previously, Jim Rock had won the Irish super-middleweight title in 1999. A successful businessman in the motor trade, Rock fought for enjoyment. A tough nut who knew how to fight, he presented as the 'Pink Panther' in shocking pink shorts.

Against Collins, Rock did what Rock does. He coiled himself into an impenetrable shell, making himself difficult to hit, and doled out punishment. Collins didn't back down. He stood his ground. By the fifth round there was blood around Rock's left eye and spattered across Collins' fluorescent green trunks. The sixth and final round had the crowd out of their luxury seats. This was the real deal. In the centre of the ring, both boxers resembled out-of-control windmills. As many shots missed as landed. At the final bell, the crowd was exhausted. But they roared their approval. In referee Tiedt's judgement, Rock dominated every round and had his arm raised.

VIII

For Dunne's epic world-title win against the bookmakers' favourite Cordoba, coach Harry Hawkins had judged the preparation and tactics to perfection. Irish boxing was on a high, with several fighters poised for a shot at major titles. The tools of Dunne's trade, his title-winning fists, were bruised and painful, and his face had a few cuts. But they'd heal. 'The world is his oyster,' declared Brian Peters, who was already eyeing the mouth-watering prospect of a title defence on 'main street Las Vegas'.

The plan was for Dunne to cash in on his world-champion status by fighting a couple of lucrative voluntary title defences in Dublin before meeting the WBA mandatory challenger, Poonsawat Kratingdaenggym from Thailand, a man regarded by all in the division as extremely dangerous. As Dunne waited for his cuts to heal, Belfast promoter Pat Magee again entered the picture.

Just as he'd done previously with Kiko Martínez, Magee signed a representative deal with Poonsawat. Attempts at delaying the Thai fighter's mandatory title challenge failed. As a result, there would be no high-earning voluntary defences for Dunne. Instead, in September the much-feared Poonsawat and his team flew to Dublin. *Ring* magazine ranked Poonsawat at No. 3 with Dunne trailing at No. 6. The Dubliner knew he was in for a brutal inspection of his capabilities.

Eleven days away from his title defence, Dunne rang from his training camp to pay tribute to Darren Sutherland, the Olympic bronze medallist whose death had been reported the previous day. 'Darren was a brilliant talent. He'll be a huge loss to Irish boxing and to his family and friends. His death puts everything in perspective.'

As we spoke, Bernard revealed nothing of the behind-the-scenes haggling between promoters. He was under no illusion how tough the defence of his belt was likely to be. Days earlier, he'd told me, 'This guy has been sitting in the mandatory position for over eighteen months. He's phenomenal. He's very aggressive with a constant work rate. It's going to be a hell of a fight.'

When I got to watch Poonsawat working out in a Muay Thai gym in Stoneybatter after he arrived in Dublin, I had to agree with Dunne. Known in Thailand as 'The Little Tank', Poonsawat drew gasps of admiration from the gym's regulars as he rifled off a repeated series of high-speed power punches with left and right. Following a brief display of his kick-boxing skills, I got to speak to the visitor and his interpreter. Compared to the volcanic destructive presence I'd just witnessed in the ring, Poonsawat's eyes suggested inner calm. Had he a plan? As inscrutable as Sherlock Holmes in an opium den, he smiled and replied, 'To stay in the ring.' Fighting was his vocation. 'When I'm fighting I forget everything else,' he said. 'Everything is quiet.' Clearly he had meditated on the upcoming encounter. 'I respect Dunne's heart,' he said softly. 'Don't forget, Dunne's chin is suspect. I am confident my power will make the difference.' It was the most gentle pre-fight threat I'd ever heard. But one I felt compelled to take seriously.

Arriving at ringside in the O2 Arena, Poonsawat dropped to his knees at the foot of the metal steps that led to his corner. Head bowed, he prayed to his ancestors. As we were to discover, someone up there was listening. Short though it was, the fight wasn't one for the squeamish. Dunne's left jab operated like a well-oiled piston in the opening round as the visitor pressed forward in search of his target. Round two saw Dunne continuing to work behind his jab and put together some eye-catching combination punches. But Poonsawat just rolled forward, weaving, bending, swinging hooks and loading up on clockwork body shots any time he got near the champion.

Dunne's hit-and-move plan was working well until midway through the third round when Poonsawat connected with a pile-driving left hook. Dunne slumped face forward. Meeting the eight count, he looked stunned. Suddenly the ring had become a terrifyingly claustrophobic space. With his head pushed into Dunne's face, Poonsawat eagerly ran through a repertoire of close-range shots hoping to finish early. Dunne fought back but another lightning-flash blink-and-you-miss-it lump-hammer left fist sent him down a second time, limbs flailing like a marionette whose strings had been cut.

The Thai fighter unleashed a monsoon of granite rain. As stationary as Nelson's Pillar in O'Connell Street before the lads arrived with the gelignite, Dunne received another of Poonsawat's thunderous left fists to the side of the head. BOOM! Down for a third time in the round, Dunne's dreams of making his next title defence in Las Vegas lay in rubble. The medics quickly surrounded his frail body. As blood trickled onto the canvas, someone put an oxygen mask on his face. His hard-earned WBA belt was destined to travel east.

IX

Five months after the Poonsawat fight, Dunne held a press conference. Brian Peters wasn't present. The mood was sombre. Flanked by his coach, Harry Hawkins, Dunne announced, 'It's time for a new challenge. I'm twenty-five years boxing. I've loved every minute of it but it's time to do something else with my life.'

It can't have been an easy decision to make. Dunne was in his prime. There could have been a few more big paydays for him. 'I don't want to continue boxing,' he explained. 'I don't need that challenge anymore. I put twenty-five years in. Thankfully I've still got some brain cells left in my head.'

As Dunne spoke, Hawkins looked crestfallen. 'I was in Belarus with Bernard at the European Championships in 1988 when he was only a child,' he recalled:

I had a part in the negotiations when Bernard went to America. We stayed in touch. When he came back and asked me to train him, we brought everybody along on a fantastic journey. He's made the right decision because you need to have a hunger in this game. There are lots of guys in the world fighting for their breakfast.

The Dunne–Peters axis had brought big-time boxing to Ireland with such regularity that the sport began to thrive and membership of the Boxing Union of Ireland more than quadrupled in a few years. 'The success of boxing at this time is a lot to do with Bernard Dunne,' said Hawkins.

It wasn't his second defeat in thirty professional fights that ended Dunne's love affair with boxing. Nor was it the physical punishment endured in training or on fight night that wore him down. We had to wait until he published his autobiography to read the reality some of us had suspected. 'The ugliest side of the sport is not the brutality,' he revealed. 'It is the mental torture inflicted upon fighters by those who have never so much as swung a fist at their own shadow... the promoters ... along with the managers, they are the ones that control boxing and it is these people who will leave a sick feeling in your gut.'

5
DAZZLER

'The fear of losing was greater than the will to win.'
Darren Sutherland

THERE'S NO ROOM FOR negativity in boxing. You've got to be positive.

In hindsight, when Brian Peters declared, 'This is a golden era in professional boxing' at John Duddy's homecoming press conference in Dublin in 2007, it wasn't just hype. It was prophecy.

But Peters was no soothsayer. An astute promoter, he was aware of the talent swelling the ranks of the amateur game. When we'd discussed his plans for 2010, he took a moment to reflect on the previous twelve months. 'A world champion [Bernard Dunne] and two European champions [Matthew Macklin and Paul McCloskey] last year, it wasn't bad going, was it?'

Peters put together a bill for February that would feature four Irish title fights. A national title gives a fighter a boost in the international rankings so there'd be plenty at stake at Dublin's National Stadium when Cavan's Andy Murray, recovered from a broken collarbone, took on Dublin terrier Oisín Fagan in an Irish lightweight decider. Other appetizing fights included heavyweights Coleman Barrett and Colin Kenna, brother of Ireland footballer Jeff. Patrick Hyland would defend his featherweight title against Mickey Coveney. And Dubliner Anthony Fitzgerald was set to contest the super-middleweight belt with Lee Murtagh. At a press conference in the Brazen Head to announce the event dubbed the Civil War, Brian Peters was in full effect. 'These boys are great,' he trumpeted. 'They're the next generation. This brings it to a new level.'

Irish pro boxing was on a roll. Mel Christle, President of the Boxing Union of Ireland, was understandably enthusiastic. 'It's being predicted that 2010 will see an explosion in professional boxing,' he said. 'I've no doubt that Ireland will play its part in the resurgence of boxing on the European and world stage. These four fights are all highly competitive, fat-free championship fights.'

An executive from the state broadcaster RTÉ underscored the developing success story. 'We started off tentatively enough,' he began. 'But then Bernard [Dunne] did a whole lot for the sport. He had two big figures. Over 600,000 and 700,000. What that did was like the rising tide lifting all boats. Andy Lee and Matthew Macklin did tremendously well too. The figures have been rising.'

Peters chimed in. 'Almost one in every two watching telly watched Bernard.' Encouragingly, those viewing figures were purely domestic. They didn't include crowds watching in pubs.

There had always been boxing talent in Ireland. It took until 2003 for amateur boxing to move with the times and set up an elite High Performance coaching system. After years of operating on a shoestring budget and relying on the goodwill of volunteers, Irish boxing quickly began to show the benefits of substantial funding by the Irish Sports Council.

As the IABA looked towards qualifying boxers for the 2008 Olympic Games in Beijing, High Performance Director Gary Keegan knew what was required. 'Unless you're more scientific about preparation, you're going to be left behind,' he told me, explaining the computerized testing rig he'd installed in the gym at the National Stadium. The data being fed into the system meant that Irish boxers could be benchmarked against the top four boxers in the world in every weight division. At the time, the High Performance Unit monitored fifty-two youth, junior, senior male boxers and Katie Taylor. Across all levels, Irish boxers competed in twenty-eight international programmes per year.

Of course boxers aren't robots. A nanosecond of carelessness in a boxing ring can lose a fight. Ireland's Head Coach Billy Walsh, a former Olympian who'd won seven national senior titles, knew the sport intimately. Working alongside experienced coach Zaur Antia, a Georgian who relocated to Bray, Walsh's shrewd analysis and ability to adapt under pressure began to get results as the High Performance team polished the rough diamonds created by a network of coaches in clubs around the country.

A year before the 2008 Beijing Olympics, Ireland hosted the 5th European Union Boxing Championships. Irish captain Kenny Egan, Darren Sutherland and Roy Sheahan all won gold. Cathal McMonagle and Carl Frampton both claimed silver. Billy Walsh told me, 'When we started this programme we wanted to have competition for all the places in the team. We're beginning to create that now.'

I

They booed champion Darren Sutherland in 2008 the night he beat Darren O'Neill in what was their third Irish senior middleweight final in a row. Also at stake in the bout, dubbed 'the Battle of the Darrens', was Olympic qualification.

While Sutherland had previously been denied the title by Andy Lee and John Duddy, his hat-trick victory wasn't well received by a section of the crowd in the National Stadium. Many mistook his confident attitude for arrogance.

Boxing has a cruel way of mocking romantics. Within a few weeks of his win, Sutherland failed in his Olympic qualification bid. There were tears. However, one last qualification opportunity remained open to him at a tournament in Athens in April.

No boxer ever tried as hard to convince me of his talent as Sutherland did. Articulate and personable, his favourite topic was his single-minded fixation on training, his understanding of the science of boxing and the precision of his blueprint for success. It occurred to me that the person he was attempting to convince was himself. Sutherland didn't do things by half. As Kenny Egan recalls, on the only occasion he roomed with Sutherland when the team were in training camp ahead of the World Championships in Chicago in 2007, he woke from a deep sleep to the staccato sound of a skipping rope cracking on the floor. It was Sutherland, with his earphones on, going through skipping exercises at 4.30 am.

Before Athens, Sutherland told me earnestly:

The World Championships was a nightmare. The fear of losing was greater than the will to win. I do sports science and they say, 'Focus on the controllables.' It's an airy-fairy comment but it's simple. All I can do is me. I train every day. I live right. I eat right. I don't drink. I don't smoke. I don't go out clubbing. I'm a professional in my approach. I'm my worst critic. I set very high ambitions for myself.

Sutherland had a passionate sense of vocation. 'I can't wait to get out there. Look at Carruth. He got the very last spot when he qualified for the Olympic Games and he won a gold medal. I'm ready. I'm a crazy man. I'll give it everything.' It was clear that Sutherland was devoting as much energy to banishing self-doubt as to perfecting his skills.

Four wins in Athens sent him to the Beijing Olympics where two decisive victories took him into the semi-final. Irish hopes were high ahead of Sutherland's meeting with James DeGale (GB). Four years older than DeGale, Darren (26) had beaten the southpaw four times in five previous fights. Ominously, DeGale's one win against the Dubliner had been in the qualifiers in February. The fight had been close, 23-22.

An Olympic bronze medal assured, Sutherland gave a lacklustre performance. DeGale had learned how to deal with Sutherland's power. He got ahead in the first and, using nimble footwork, went into the final round with an 8-2 lead. It ended 10-3. It was perplexing. Sutherland had been in brilliant form. Even team captain Kenny Egan was disappointed. 'He looked good enough for gold,' he says in his autobiography. 'He should have beaten DeGale. He was too happy with being in a semi-final.' The St Saviour's club man was oddly buoyant. 'My career is only starting,' he announced. 'That was my last amateur fight.' DeGale went on to win gold.

Two months later, Darren Sutherland signed a three-year management deal with Frank Maloney. The London promoter, who'd supervised the careers of four world champions, Lennox Lewis, Paul Ingle, Scott Harrison and David Haye, believed Sutherland would become his fifth.

Having first worked with promoter Frank Warren, who survived being shot twice by a masked gunman in 1989, Maloney got past the gatekeepers of global boxing promotion through guiding Lennox Lewis. As Lewis picked up titles, everyone wanted to deal with Frank. A feisty personality was packed into the diminutive 5 ft 2 in frame that became an easy target for industry banter. 'Maloney's so superstitious he won't walk under a black cat,' was Micky Duff's artfully studied quip.

With the practised ease of a vaudeville illusionist, Maloney conjured up images of a glorious future for Sutherland at a packed press conference in Dublin City University (DCU), Sutherland's old college. 'I look forward to taking him to Croke Park in front of 80,000 people,' he declared. The dream hypnotized 'the Dazzler'. 'A world-title fight in Croke Park,' he mused. 'The last person there was Muhammad Ali in 1972. You've got to think big. That's what I like about Frank.'

The man they called 'No Baloney' Maloney, was on form. 'Boxing is desperately looking for a superstar,' he announced.' Sutherland is going to go all the way to become a major world champion.'

Sutherland would box at super-middleweight and his first fight since losing to James DeGale would be screened by Sky Sports. Frank believed the TV channel's early investment was a further endorsement. 'They've never done this before,' he enthused. 'This is the future.'

The only fighter I've ever met who said 'pardon', Darren's charisma lit up his first press conference as a professional. The vibes were good. But I had to ask the question that nagged so many Irish fight fans. Professional boxing champions need to possess a killer instinct. Was Darren Sutherland too nice to do what is necessary? Feathers ruffled, he responded tartly, 'Anyone who had met me in the past, before my profile became this big, and they didn't know I boxed, they said, "I can't believe you're a boxer. You're too nice." When I get into the ring, I'm like a pit bull. If I smell blood I go in for the kill.' Suddenly, this wasn't just a happy-clappy homecoming. This was Sutherland's future we were talking about. His private dreams. 'It's very hard to describe it,' he continued. 'I love to fight. Outside of the ring I hate confrontation. But in the ring, I like to be right in the centre of it.'

Did he feel he left a gold medal behind him in Beijing? 'No, I don't,' he retorted. 'I achieved everything I set out to achieve. I wanted to win a medal and do the best I could and that's what I did. No regrets.'

Sitting at his left arm, Frank Maloney offered a considered rationale. 'I don't mean to be rude but amateur boxing is not boxing,' he said. 'It's like sword fencing. Darren's style obviously wasn't suited. I'm glad he didn't get a gold medal. It might have been a lot harder to sign him.'

II

'Please spit in buckets.' The handwritten sign was pinned to the wall of the Fight Factory, a spartan gym located above the Lord Clyde pub among the tower blocks down by the Thames in Deptford.

The pilgrim route ran through these parts centuries ago. But Chaucer, the geezer who wrote *The Canterbury Tales*, wouldn't recognize this unforgiving urban landscape. We were on London's Murder Mile and I was there with another pilgrim of sorts. A man in search of salvation. Darren Sutherland was working on becoming champion of the world. This brutal environment was where he was taking his first steps.

He had work to do. It was just a few weeks before his pro debut against Bulgarian Georgi Iliev. Glistening after a skipping session and a series of warm-up routines, he climbed into the ring with sparring partner, Matthew Thirlwall, a rugged pro who'd won sixteen of his nineteen bouts.

Sutherland had been in London for almost a month, training with Brian Lawrence, the coach who'd guided the success of Ian Napa. He believed he was on his way to becoming world champion. Nobody had told Matthew Thirlwall. The gutsy middleweight, who KO'd three of his last four opponents, soon found out. The hard way. Sutherland dropped him in the second round and, in the next round, blood began pouring from Thirlwall's pulverized nose. This was what fighters call 'quality sparring'. Both boxers gave it all they'd got. Sutherland proved too powerful. Too relentless. His jab was fast, accurate and punishing. After five bruising rounds, the sparring ended. But the workout wasn't over. Both boxers got stuck into the punch bags and Sutherland then got back into the ring for a few rounds of pad work with Lawrence. Surveying the scene with satisfaction, Maloney declared with a flourish, 'You're looking at the start of a masterpiece.'

Sutherland's trainers had been finding it difficult to get sparring partners for the Dubliner. The word was out. Sutherland did damage. Light heavyweight Joey Vegas had been forced to cancel an upcoming bout because of badly bruised ribs following his stint with Sutherland. Maloney had to go to Manchester to find willing opposition. 'Dynamite' Carl Dilks was a super-middleweight with an unblemished eight wins. From Sutherland's perspective, these were happy problems. He was on his way to the stars.

Ambition is cheap. But Frank Maloney knew about boxing. He was convinced. 'I believe Darren can surpass Lennox's earning,' he claimed over breakfast in a café near his office, a discreet converted mews. So how much did Lennox Lewis earn as world champion? 'A hundred million would be a quick estimate.'

Maloney was living in leafy Chislehurst. Boxing promotion had made him rich. He'd swum with sharks and repelled all attacks, even the fury of Don King, a promoter once memorably described by my one-time housemate author Jim McNeill as having 'a smile that somehow never reaches to his eyes'. When King, who'd served time for stamping an employee to death, failed to get a slice of the Lewis action, he branded Maloney 'a pugilistic pygmy' and 'a mental midget'. Pausing over his healthy option in a local café, Maloney made sure I was paying full attention before predicting, 'Darren will become the richest sportsman in Ireland.'

What did Maloney see in Sutherland? What does it take to become a world champion? Plates pushed back, the pugnacious potentate counted on manicured fingers: 'Dedication, commitment, enthusiasm and the willingness to learn.' Sutherland, he insisted, was one of the most dedicated he'd seen.

As if on cue, Sutherland and his coach arrived. The young Dubliner sat at a separate table and opened a Tupperware box of nutritious ingredients he'd prepared earlier. Happy for me to join him, he spoke with the zeal of a convert. 'The first time I laced up the gloves, it was all for this. This is just a start.'

As we chatted, Sutherland admitted he was having to adjust, saying, 'It was a shock to get one-on-one training because I was so used to training in a squad environment.' He was now having to cope as a sole trader.

Those who knew him, knew that Sutherland had dedicated his life to boxing. Even when he'd been out of the game with an eye injury as a youngster, he'd never stopped thinking about his next bout. That injury, received when a gloved thumb pushed his eye back in his skull fracturing his eye socket, had been potentially life-changing. 'For six months I was in the dark, literally,' he told me. 'The doctors didn't know how I would respond.

It was a hard time for me. It made me reassess things. I went through many emotions. Depression and feeling sorry for myself to then having hope and clinging to that hope and developing a never-say-die attitude.'

III

College students, male and female, created a giddy prom-night atmosphere for Sutherland's pro debut. That Rendall Munroe was defending his European title or that Kiko Martínez was also on the undercard seemed of little consequence. The students were there for 'the Dazzler'.

While attempting to navigate the sprawling DCU campus in the winter fog, I encountered an elderly woman who, like me, was lost. It was Maureen, Frank Maloney's Irish mother. Together, we found the venue. Frank's mum had a lively personality and, yes, she was pleased her son had signed an Irish boxer to his company. But he was working too hard, she complained.

Sutherland's fight lasted a mere two minutes and forty-two seconds. His opponent didn't stand a chance against the finely tuned machine.

Two months later, Sunderland was back in Dublin drumming up business for his second pro fight, a six-rounder against Belarus journeyman Siarhei Navarka in Wigan.

Four months into his career as a full-time pro, Sutherland's earlier wide-eyed exuberance had been replaced by a new realism. 'There's no secret formula, no quick fix,' he said. 'I was used to being the fittest on the Irish national squad. I thought I'd get in and spar ten or twelve rounds no bother. But it takes time. So far, the maximum I've sparred is eight rounds and that's pretty intense. You come out thinking, "How do these guys do twelve?"'

Although he posed the question, Sutherland already knew the answer. His coach, Brian Lawrence, had been drumming into him the importance of being patient and how putting in the groundwork was all-important for a long-term career. 'The only way you're going to get to box at championship level is to put in the time in the gym,' Sutherland explained. He could see how Ian Napa had progressed. 'He's banging out fifteen rounds on the bag,' he said with awe. 'The other day he did eighteen rounds and he's still jumping around full of energy. After eight I'm breathing out my arse.'

There was a hint of disappointment in Darren's voice. Realistically, the dream of fighting for titles was still a long way off. Logically, he understood that. Emotionally, it was something he was trying to come to terms with. He'd put his degree in sports science at DCU on hold while he'd set out in pursuit of his professional boxing ambitions and, intellectually, understood the dynamic now in play. 'By the end of the year I hope I'll be ready,' he said.

He had a third-round win in Wigan. The following month he told Irish-boxing.com, 'I'm twenty-seven this week. I still feel twenty-one or twenty-two. I live a good life so I can have a long career. I don't want to be a flash in the pan. I'll have another four fights between now and Christmas and after that I'll be ready.'

Two months later, he stopped an opponent in the fourth round and in June his adversary at York Hall also withered under the power of his punches. In seven months, Sutherland had four knockout wins to his credit. Each fight had been scheduled for six rounds. He had bypassed the four rounders that many new pros acclimatize with. Maloney was pleased with his progress but Sutherland's fourth win came at a price, an aggravating cut high on his right cheek. A fight scheduled for Sunderland in July had to be scrapped.

IV

Monday, 12 September 2009 was the start of what promised to be a busy week for Frank Maloney, a man dealing with a number of pertinent business concerns. He'd been at ringside in Brentwood on Friday night when his fighter John McDermott lost on points to Tyson Fury. The decision enraged Maloney, who suffered serious chest pains at the venue.

Having met Sutherland for dinner on Saturday, Maloney knew his fighter had a problem. His suggestion to meet on Sunday didn't suit the boxer. On Monday Maloney drove to Bromley to collect him. When there was no reply, he left and later returned with an assistant and let himself in. That's when he found Sutherland hanging from a radiator. The police were called. Just after 3 pm, paramedics pronounced Sutherland dead. Maloney collapsed and was taken to the Princess Royal Hospital where it was discovered he'd recently suffered a heart attack. Doctors inserted stents.

News of a sudden death is always difficult to accept. Sutherland's family, friends, supporters, the wider boxing community and the general public were stunned. Tributes poured in. Describing Sutherland as 'a phenomenal talent',

Barry McGuigan said. 'He would have become a world champion.' James DeGale, who'd defeated him in Beijing, described him as 'an excellent fighter and a true gentleman', adding, 'It's a tragedy.' Everyone at St Saviours was shocked. 'He was here a few weeks ago, bright and laughing with the young lads,' said club secretary Martin Power. 'He didn't seem under pressure and was glad to be home.'

The police said they weren't treating Sutherland's death as suspicious. A post-mortem examination stated that he had died from asphyxia as a result of suspension by a ligature.

In the immediate aftermath of receiving the shocking news, it was difficult to write a newspaper article about Sutherland who, the first time I met him, was playing slick R'n'B on the boom-box speakers he was wiring up in his car. He appeared not to have a care in the world. For the opening sentence of my report, I reluctantly drew on a truism from the fight game. 'The most devastating punch in boxing is the one you don't see coming.'

In Greek mythology, the warrior Achilles, noble, brave and swift of foot, 'the breaker of the battle-line' as Homer described him, was said to be invulnerable. But he had a little-known weakness. His mother, Thetis, had dipped him in the river Styx to make him less than mortal. As she held him by his left heel, it hadn't been touched by the sacred waters. And so it was that, just as victory at Troy seemed certain, an arrow fired by Paris, and guided by the god Apollo, hit the fatal spot. They had found his weak point and the dark night of death descended on him.

Darren Sutherland was buried in a graveyard in Navan, just a few miles from Tara, home of the ancient High Kings. It's said that the clay in those parts holds its secrets close. Warrior secrets. As his distraught parents, Tony and Linda, struggled to come to terms with their loss, their disbelief gave way to anger. 'A lot of questions need to be answered,' said Tony. The family requested a second post-mortem.

Hired by the family, Professor Jack Crane, state forensic pathologist for Northern Ireland, raised the question of possible third-party involvement in Sutherland's death. It was revealed that, when he was found, his wrists had been tied together behind his back. Dismissing the initial post-mortem as 'wholly inadequate', Prof. Crane's report stated, 'The presence of a ligature, even if only loosely tied around the wrists, raises some concern about the possibility of a third party.' Of concern too was the lack of description of the ligature found around Sutherland's neck and the manner in which it was knotted. The description of marks on his neck was also deemed to be inadequate.

A year after his death, Sutherland's body was exhumed and a second post-mortem conducted. A further eighteen months later, during a four-day inquest at Croydon Coroner's Court, a picture emerged of Darren, living alone, anxious and stressed because a cut, caused by a clash of heads, had become infected. Dr Natasha Haugh said she had seen Sutherland twice for his infected eye cut and once for bouts of insomnia. Describing him as 'a worrier', sports therapist Heather Pearson told the court that the boxer had phoned her three days before he died. 'He was very worried about this injury,' she said. 'He sounded a bit more panicky than normal, but I just thought he was making a mountain out of a molehill.' It was revealed that, five days before his death, accompanied by his mother, Darren had consulted psychologist Michele Roitt. Her assessment was that the boxer was suffering from depression, a conclusion disputed by his mother.

Also revealed at the inquest was how a number of documents and notes had been recovered by the police at the flat. Others were later found by the family and also by a private investigator hired by Frank Maloney. These were handed to the police. In a second statement to police, the promoter revealed he'd seen a note addressed to himself, which hadn't been recovered. A question remained over the whereabouts of that mysterious note. Investigating officer Detective Sergeant Lee Dunmore said: 'A number of documents were gathered up and placed on the table. I take responsibility if something was left. It shouldn't have been and I'm not seeking to justify it in any way.'

A handwritten list, which outlined the negative aspects of quitting boxing, had also been found in the flat. It had been written by Sutherland's friend Declan Brennan as the pair discussed the implications of Sutherland retiring. It was read in court. The list was stark:

£75,000 + VAT to Frank.

Give car back.

Give flat back. £100,000 a year in salary lost for the next two years.

Frank will destroy you and your family in the media.

They will hunt you down, take photographs of you and do articles about how you fucked up.

He will destroy you for the rest of your life and he'll be right, you were given a God given talent.

You think you feel bad now you just have no idea how bad it's going to get.

I will help you if you help yourself.

Declan, your pal.

Det. Sgt Dunmore, who claimed he had 'no doubt' that Sutherland killed himself, stated, 'It is apparent from the statements obtained from friends, family and medical professionals that he was experiencing a crisis in confidence in his boxing ability, the financial implications that would arise should he breach his contract, and (also) sleep-related issues.'

Darren had been messaging on Facebook into the small hours the night before his death. We'll never know how dark it became for him before dawn. Or the extent of the misgivings that enveloped him as he contemplated the wound on his face. Sutherland chose boxing to prove he could be the best. A hero of his time, this was his quest. In sport as in life, it's impossible to tell when we might face the big critical moment; when we might face the sternest test. While there's much we can't gauge, it's clear the tyranny of his ambition haunted him.

'A coroner in contemplating such a verdict has to be satisfied beyond reasonable doubt, not only that the individual did an act unaided, but also must be sure that he fully intended that it should end his life,' said coroner Roy Palmer, delivering his verdict. 'Here I am persuaded that there is sufficient doubt to make me hesitate to return a verdict of suicide.'

Frank Maloney would later tell journalist Alan Hubbard, 'It looked like they were trying to say Darren killed himself because of Frank Maloney ... I had nothing to be ashamed of ... The memory of finding him hanging there in that flat will be with me forever.' The following year, Maloney retired from boxing after thirty years' involvement, saying, 'My heart is no longer in the sport that I loved so much.'

6
BIG BANG

'It's going to be a test of who can recover the quickest when they get caught with a big bang.'
Willie Casey

BOXERS HAVE TO BE delusional. Just consider the parade of aspirational fighters who came with ambition but were viciously beaten by Mike Tyson in his terrifying prime. Not all fighters aspire to becoming a world champion: some are happy to take the pain and earn a few quid. But the majority want to prove they're the best, to acquit themselves with dignity. Very few boxers become world champions.

There are career goals to aim for. Moving from four-round fights to six rounds, to eight, to ten and then, the real test, twelve rounds. There are area titles, national titles, continental titles, intercontinental titles, international titles and, ultimately, world titles pointing the way like mileage markers. Each sanctioning body has its own ranking system. The higher up the pecking order, the bigger the pay day.

Ambitious fighters treat each bout as the most important fight in their career. It's not unusual to hear a fighter, after winning a particularly difficult fight, be it four rounds or twelve, say, 'That was my world-title fight.'

I

In boxing, the interface between entertainment and pain is often reflected in a fighter's nickname. The Executioner, the Hitman, Bonecrusher and Iron Mike will tell you a lot more than Bernard Hopkins, Tommy Hearns, James Smith and Mike Tyson. Willie Casey was simply 'Big Bang'. In the argot of the boxing fraternity 'a banger' is a puncher with devastating power. Limerick man Casey was a boxer whose USP was delivering bombs of knuckle and bone packed in hard leather.

Casey had flitted in and out of the amateur scene until Dublin coach Phil Sutcliffe noticed that when Casey hit someone, he hurt them. After just four pro fights, Casey travelled to Toronto to fight unbeaten Canadian champion Tyson Cave. Casey stopped the southpaw in the eighth round. His profile raised by the win, Casey was asked to replace an injured Wayne McCullough in the Prizefighter series in London. Added to make up the numbers, he blasted his way through to the trophy and a cheque for €37,000. It was a useful payday for Willie, who was married with four children.

The year 2010 proved to be a defining year for Big Bang. Following two more wins, he landed a shot at the European title. For his eighth fight in ten months, Casey was set to challenge European super-bantamweight champion Kiko Martínez ('La Sensación') who, three years earlier, had downed Bernard Dunne.

Brian Peters skilfully persuaded La Sensación to defend his European title against Casey in the University of Limerick Sports Arena, with the fight screened live on Irish television. Casey envisaged a raucous bloodthirsty atmosphere. 'My crowd goes mental,' he enthused.

Commentator and former Olympian Mick Dowling was excited by the prospect of a Casey and Martínez fight. The eight-times Irish amateur champion said, 'It's two guys who can box and two guys who can mainly fight. On paper, this is one of the best fights we've seen here for a long, long time.' At a press conference to announce the contest, when Martínez explained that a couple of earlier losses had been due to illness, Casey laughed in his face: 'I'm hoping Kiko will be fit this time because I don't want any excuses afterwards.'

It was impossible not to be charmed by Casey's personality. A member of the Travelling community, he was reared on a halting site with eleven brothers and sisters older than him. And another eleven younger than him. He was used to a rough-and-tumble life, but was the first of the twenty-three siblings to complete the Junior Cert. In his final school year, he took a job as a welder. Sacrifice and ambition were dominant traits in Casey's make-up. His game plan wasn't secret. 'We're going to be boxing and fighting and brawling. It's going to be a test of who can recover the quickest when they get caught with a big bang.'

Martínez looked bored as questions were raised about whether Casey was a suitable title challenger ahead of Dublin's EU super-bantamweight belt holder Paul Hyland, who was present. Casey didn't hold back. 'Paulie is good enough to fight for the European title. He should have already fought for it. If I win it, I'll give him a chance otherwise he could be stuck.'

Hyland was one of three talented brothers all coached by their father, Paddy Hyland Snr, who bristled at Casey's analysis. 'Let's not worry about where Paulie Hyland is stuck,' he replied. 'We offered to fight Bernard [Dunne]. We offered to fight Kiko. I guarantee Paulie Hyland will be fighting for a world title within a year and a half. Paulie would box anyone.' Having heard enough of this local squabble, Martínez intervened. 'There's only one real champion here and it's me,' he declared. 'There's only been one real super-bantam champion in Ireland. That was Bernard Dunne and I beat him.'

Lines from Patrick Kavanagh's poem 'Epic' hung in the air:

'… Homer's ghost came whispering to my mind.
He said: I made the *Iliad* from such
A local row. Gods make their own importance.'

II

The capricious nature of prize-fighting was highlighted when a rib damaged in training put Martínez out of action two weeks before the fight. Displaying some nifty footwork, Brian Peters persuaded the European Boxing Union to allow Martínez to vacate the title on the understanding that the Spaniard would get first shot at the new champion – either Casey or mandatory challenger Paul Hyland. The scene was set for a historic night for Irish boxing; the first time ever that two Irish challengers met to contest a European title.

After six years as a professional fighter, Hyland embraced his sudden change of fortune with enthusiasm: 'I'm ready for anything.' With automatic ranking in the WBC top ten also at stake, the build-up began. Asked if he'd be nervous meeting Casey in front of his Limerick crowd, Hyland reminded his inquisitors, 'I went to Naples and won the EBU EU belt (118-112). That was a hostile environment.'

In winning a title on Italian soil, Hyland succeeded where Steve Collins had failed. Regarded by some as Bernard Dunne's understudy, the fearless EU champ was part of a Hyland boxing dynasty that stretched back to Hyland's great-grandfather, Patrick 'Whack' Finn, a former Irish champion. Boxing out of the Golden Cobra, their father Paddy Snr's project, the three Hyland siblings, Eddie, Patrick and Paul, could count a total of nineteen All-Ireland and twenty Dublin amateur titles between them.

Working with strength and conditioning coach Joe Clifford, Hyland told me, 'My defence is great. My reflexes are good. I'm starting to increase my punching power.' While Hyland was expected to display superior skills against Casey, opposing coach Sutcliffe predicted his pride would ensure he'd front up to Big Bang.

In front of a strident, partisan crowd, Hyland glided through a busy opening round, commanding the space like a practised choreographer as Casey swung wildly. He answered a vicious Casey uppercut with a couple of well-executed body shots. The high tempo continued into round two. When stung by a Hyland left hook, Casey responded with a barrage of punches.

By round three, with Casey's followers in full voice, it became obvious that Hyland was being sucked into a brawl. Casey began to dominate. A warrior impulse saw Hyland jettison his game plan in favour of a tear-up. In the fourth, a series of heavy lefts over the top reduced the Dubliner's cognitive powers and, sensing a stoppage, Casey pursued his quarry like a rabid dog worrying sheep. Hyland's credentials received rigorous scrutiny. With punches raining in from all angles, and Hyland incapable of replying, referee John Keane stopped the fight. Casey was ecstatic. His parents, wife and children invaded the ring. Lifted aloft, he was champion of Europe. Looking on, Kiko Martínez cautioned, 'You've only borrowed the belt.'

The following morning, I sat opposite Willie and his wife in the hotel dining room as, fresh-faced, he tucked into a hearty full Irish. The pair could have been mistaken for a couple of newly-weds on a weekend break. Beaming like a Sun King, Willie was monarch of his domain. I took a mid-morning train back to Dublin.

The Sunday papers would bring me up to date on current issues on the journey. Ireland was still reeling from the financial crisis of 2008, the banks were in disarray, emigration figures were at their highest since the 1980s, the Taoiseach had sounded drunk on an early morning radio interview and the International Monetary Fund was at the gates. We were living in uncertain times.

The carriage remained empty until a young fair-haired chap took a seat across the aisle. A soundscape artist, his latest project was a commission for a ballet company. I had just completed some notes for an RTÉ music DVD that featured tracks I'd recorded with Horslips in the National Stadium in the 1970s. 'From what seems like aeons ago,' I wrote, acutely aware of how, having shunted my life as a musician into a siding, I was now a busy journalist, travelling to cover breaking-news stories at home and abroad and reporting on major sporting events. Familiar with each other's work, the artist and I chatted about ambient music and the aesthetics of some contemporary composers.

At a stop somewhere in the Midlands, the door slid back and a burly, dishevelled man appeared. Throwing a plastic supermarket bag on the seat in front of me, he barked 'Mind that' before barrelling up the train towards catering. Every other seat in the carriage was empty. I eyed the bag with suspicion. Arriving back, he plonked his steaming takeaway tea on the table between us along with a handful of tiny cartons of milk, a small mountain of sugar sachets and several long wooden stirrers. Removing his hoodie, he revealed a frayed T-shirt as soiled as his sweatpants.

'Where are you coming from?' he demanded.

'Limerick.'

'What were you doing there?'

'I was at the fight.'

'Oh yeah. Did the knacker win?'

'Willie Casey won. He's European champion. He beat Paul Hyland.'

66

'I used to go to the XYZ Gym,' said the big man, brightening up. 'The coach showed me how to punch properly. Plant my feet. Twist my fist as it landed. Punch through to the back of the head. Make a punch do damage. But then they said I couldn't come back.'

'Why?'

'Because I was too violent. They said I didn't have any discipline.'

After a short pause, the interrogation recommenced. 'What were you doing there?' 'How come you know my old coach?' 'Are you involved in boxing?' The questioning was relentless. And tedious.

I explained I wrote about the sport. A dark cloud flitted across the mountain.

'Do you write about crime?'

This was becoming an irritation. I had to shut down the nonsensical questioning. It was risky but I leaned in. 'What the fuck would I be writing about crime for?'

'Fair play, man. Fair play.'

Following a pause, he announced gaily, 'I hear it's all kicking off in the Joy.'

He then launched into a soliloquy about gang violence in the historic jail on the North Circular Road. Was he acquainted personally with prison system?

'Yes.'

What had been his sentence?

'Twelve years.'

I nodded. 'Serious, so.'

'Armed robbery.'

The ease with which a complete stranger embarked on a conversation that veered worryingly close to incipient violence was somewhat disconcerting. While his willingness to converse may have stemmed from years of confinement or from the reputation Dubliners prize for being entertaining conversationalists, I didn't discount the possibility of chemical enhancement. Either way, there could be no backing out now. We rolled on.

There had been an attempt on his life in prison. While he was holding a tray, someone had come from behind and slit his throat with a shiv. He leaned back in the seat and displayed a livid weal that stretched from under his ear to about a millimetre from the trachea. Had the windpipe been severed, death by choking and suffocation would have followed.

'Thirteen stitches,' I ventured.

'No. Fifteen.'

He pulled up his shirt to allow me inspect a discoloured gash on his ample stomach.

'Four stitches,' I suggested.

He nodded approvingly. 'Four outside and four inside.'

'I assume you elbowed your assailant,' I ventured.

He had done. And then snatched up the shiv which had fallen from his attacker's grasp. His aggressor lay on the tiled floor clutching a broken jaw. Although blood was spurting freely from the big man's sliced throat, his attacker's face and head presented a target.

Suddenly, grabbing the wooden stirrers, the big man began to violently stab the tabletop in front of me in a kinetic and guttural demonstration of rage and retribution. By now, across the aisle, the ballet composer, his face deathly white, had shrunk in his seat. He looked as if he was about to throw up.

Thankfully, my travelling companion hadn't killed his adversary. Amid the blur of stabbing action, splashing blood and splintered teeth, other inmates dragged him off but not before the shiv had penetrated his opponent's face several times. Perhaps relieved that he wasn't a convicted murderer, my friend proceeded to regale me with stories from the frontline of crime. Some about individuals whose names seemed familiar from reports in tabloid newspapers. Others who were the supporting cast in epic sagas of impropriety.

As we approached Dublin, he fell into a meditative silence for a few minutes before remarking wistfully, 'Fair play to Casey. European champion, eh. Maybe I should have stuck with the boxing.'

III

What doctors call 'blunt-force trauma' was Willie Casey's speciality. If Casey hits you in the head, things go dark. Casey's unique gift propelled him, in record time, to an Irish title, a European title and, then, a shot at a world title.

Coach Phil Sutcliffe explained why, with just eleven pro fights to his credit, Casey had accepted the world-title challenge on offer. 'Everyone has underestimated Willie so far,' he said. 'How many world-title fights do we put on in this country? We believe Rigondeaux is not unbeatable.'

Guillermo Rigondeaux's name struck fear across the division. The Cuban fighter they call 'El Chacal' ('the Jackal') knew more about the art of boxing than Big Bang could ever begin to imagine. He'd won Olympic gold twice, had been world amateur champion twice and national champion seven times. He'd won an astonishing 243 amateur bouts. Having blazed a path through the pro game in just seven fights, he was determined to hold on to his interim WBA World super-bantamweight belt. The fight was set for March 2011, four months after Casey's European title win.

One of those who turned up at a pre-fight event was Francis Barrett, the first Irish member of the Travelling community to represent his country in the Olympic Games. At nineteen, he carried the Irish flag in Atlanta in 1996. A trailblazer, Barrett had learned and perfected his winning techniques in the Olympic club in Galway where coach Michael 'Chick' Gillen was a benevolent presence. Away from the gym, Barrett trained in an open-fronted steel shipping container parked in Hillside halting site on the outskirts of town. At a time when they didn't have either electricity or running water on the site, this austere metal shell with a punchbag hanging in it became young Barrett's personal theatre of dreams.

In Atlanta, he had a spectacular win in his first bout but then came up short against a Tunisian boxer who eventually claimed bronze. Barrett's story was beautifully painted in Liam McGrath's documentary film *Southpaw*, billed as 'the real life drama of one man's fight against all the odds'. I met the Olympian shortly before the film came out. Francis was training for the Irish National Championships at the time. In North London, he and his wife, Kathleen, lived happily with their two children on a halting site within sight of the IKEA towers. Francis was working for Oughterard man Dennis Curran's Barhale Construction company. 'Dennis gives me time off with pay to train,' he said.

The several trophies on display were just part of a bigger hoard. 'Me and the brothers have three caravans in Ireland,' Barrett explained:

And they're full of trophies. Over here I have about forty. I gave Kathleen's mother some and my uncle, and Chick [Gillen] and Louie [Luigi Leo, his London trainer] and Dennis. It's great to have them. We live on the same bay as Kathleen's mum. She made a bit of room for us in her bay. She gives me a call every morning for work.

Work was digging trenches, erecting steel, shifting materials and driving vans. This was followed each evening by training at the Trojan Police Amateur Boxing Club in Harlesden. I watched as he attacked the pads held by wily ring mentor Phil Pierson. 'I'm looking for the gold, same as everyone else,' he said. With qualification for the 2000 Olympics his immediate goal, Barrett didn't want to discuss the options of turning pro. But he confided, 'There's a lad I beat a couple of years ago who Barry McGuigan expects to be the next world champion. I gave him a count in the second and third rounds. I beat him. I know that if I ever go pro I'll win a world title.'

Barrett was also acutely aware of the many obstacles that could impede his progress. A few months earlier at the Multi-Nations Championship in Liverpool, he'd gone into the competition knowing that he'd broken his hand a week earlier. 'I split the bone in two places hitting the pads,' he told me. He kept his injury secret and defeated the European champ before losing narrowly to the Russian world champion when the hand packed in during the fight.

Other dangers lurked much closer to home.

Barrett and his father had been confronted by members of a rival Traveller family who insisted the Olympian fight their bare-knuckle champion. When Barrett refused, he and his father were attacked with knives. The case had been widely reported but hadn't yet gone to court. 'I'm letting the law deal with that,' said Francis:

> I said I wasn't getting involved in street fighting. They started throwing punches and next thing, the knives came out. They stabbed my father twice in the chest and three times in the arm. They stabbed me in the head. Thirty-five stitches I got. When all the other Travellers heard what happened to me they said, 'Street fighting is not Francis's game. He can't get involved in that.'

A few months later, in the Galway Circuit Court, two members of the McDonagh family were found guilty of assault and sentenced to three years in prison. Both sentences were suspended on condition that the men refrain from fighting, never carry weapons or travel in a vehicle in which weapons were present.

Barrett didn't make it to Sydney. He boxed his way to the national light-welterweight final and was winning 7-4 going into the final round. The judges gave his opponent, Seanie Barrett from Cork, that round. Francis lost, 9-8, and didn't get to fight for Olympic qualification. He turned pro instead and had seventeen wins in twenty fights. In 2004 he became EBU EU super-lightweight champion. As a pro, he fought just once in Ireland, on the undercard of Bernard Dunne's fight with Jim Betts.

Those were homecoming fights for both Dunne and Barrett. While Bernard went on to make history, Barrett, disillusioned with the business, retired after his next fight. Ahead of Willie Casey's big night, he was a picture of positivity. Having a member of the Traveller community fighting for a world title was something to celebrate.

IV

Casey's favourite fighter was Mike Tyson. He admired what Iron Mike had achieved and lamented his mistakes. Tyson gave careful consideration to how best to dispatch an opponent and described his technique as delivering punches 'with bad intention in a vital area'. After demolishing Jesse Ferguson, one of thirteen opponents he defeated in 1986 on his way to the WBC heavyweight title, he explained, 'I try to catch my opponent on the tip of the nose. Because I want to punch the bone into the brain.'

Under Phil Sutcliffe's guidance, Big Bang worked on getting maximum value out of a punch. He and his team knew what was needed to beat El Chachal. 'Rigondeaux will be the hardest puncher he's faced,' said Sutcliffe. 'He'll be physically strong but a couple of shots can change the game. He likes to come forward. If he comes forward at Willie he'll be getting hit. He's elusive but no matter which way he goes, he'll be getting a few clatters.'

As I spoke to the coach, a sweat-drenched Casey sat alone in the corner of the gym, unwinding the bandages from his fists. It had been an arduous morning. Working on the heavy bag. A session with the speed bag. There'd been gruelling rounds of sparring with a parade of fresh, fit and dangerous boxers, most of them national champions. One tough training partner, Robert O'Gorman, had once broken one of Floyd Mayweather's ribs. 'Willie's had over 160 rounds of sparring,' said his coach. 'We've tried to put every scenario into different rounds.'

Guillermo Rigondeaux was managed by Irishman Gary Hyde, a Cork promoter who represented several Cuban fighters. Imposing heavyweight Ismaikel 'Mike' Perez had been his first Cuban signing.

Hyde had spotted the talented Perez, a product of the La Finca academy in Cuba, at an amateur tournament in England. Convinced he was world-champion material, Hyde travelled to Cuba, located Perez's village, offered his services as manager and put plans in place to orchestrate his defection. A covert mission was duly devised. Gary knew that if he could dodge the spooks and the military and get the boxer outside the twelve-mile offshore limit, he'd be in the clear. International waters. Simple, eh? As legend has it, months later, receiving a prearranged signal, Perez said goodbye to his family, travelled to the coast and swam offshore after dark to a waiting launch manned by Mexican traffickers. Out at sea, he was transferred to a bigger boat, which headed towards Mexico evading patrols. Another change of boat followed but a storm in the Gulf forced their smaller craft away from the coast for days. The traffickers had run out of food and water by the time they could land their human cargo.

In a cartel safe house on Mexican soil, Perez was held under armed guard. Becoming increasingly impatient, the smugglers threatened to shoot him. The lines remain blurred. The client had become a hostage. Perez wasn't going anywhere until the silver-tongued Cork diplomat met their demands. Ransom or reward? I'm not sure how you'd term the sizeable chunk of cash that changed hands. Hyde saved the day. And a deeply worried Perez his life.

The good news continued with a first round KO in the Neptune Sports Arena in Cork on his debut as a pro fighter in January 2008. I was at ringside in Limerick when he repeated the round one KO trick in his second fight. Six wins later, I was present when he went into action on the undercard of the Andy Lee–Mamadou Thiam fight. Following a forty-eight second first-round stoppage win, Perez came back to the ring for a second fight on the same night. This time, it took until the third round for the human steamroller to send another journeyman in search of medical attention. In London in 2011, with three wins in one night, Perez, who by now was dubbed 'the Rebel' after his adopted county, Cork, won the international Prizefighter tournament clinching the deal with a spectacular forty-two second knockout of Tye Fields in the final.

His fight against unbeaten Magomed 'Mago' Abdusalamov in Madison Square Garden in 2013 for the WBC United States heavyweight title proved a career changer for the Cuban who was unbeaten in nineteen fights. Abdusalamov, known as the Russian Tyson, had won his eighteen pro fights by knocking out every one of his opponents. The battle of the two big punchers was an appetizing contest. Both fighters had a mega payday in their sights, a title fight with world champion Wladimir Klitschko.

Perez broke Abdulalamov's cheekbone in the first round when his forearm connected with his face. As the fight continued, Abdulalamov broke a hand. And an orbital bone. There was a cut above his left eye, which required stitching. During the ten rounds he was on the receiving end of 312 punches. Perez won the fight. Looking battered, his 6 ft 3 in opponent was assessed by doctors at the venue. Although Abdulalamov complained that 'inside' his face was hurting, no one spotted signs of neurological damage. He was paid his $40,000 fight fee and allowed to leave. His team used ice to reduce the swellings. But all wasn't well. Outside the venue, he collapsed on the street. Rushed to hospital in a taxi, he was placed in an induced coma and operated on. Part of his skull was removed to allow doctors treat internal bleeding and blood clotting on the brain. He then suffered multiple strokes and became incapacitated. He lost the ability to speak, required round-the-clock care and never recovered.

Abdusalamov's fate took its toll on Perez, who was back in Ireland before he learned of his opponent's misfortune. To cope with the anguish, Perez began drinking heavily. He later admitted, 'That fight changed my life.' From having won his first twenty fights, he drew one and lost two of his next four tests. When he fought Alexander Povetkin in Moscow, he was knocked out for the first time in his career.

The last time we met, the kid who'd arrived in Ireland with hope and big dreams had been replaced by a careworn warrior attempting to regain control of his career. Focused on the future though he was, somewhere in the half-light, uncertainty and demons still lurked.

When Gary Hyde expressed interest in signing Guillermo Rigondeaux, Mike Perez obliged by establishing contact on his behalf.

Hyde brought his highly rated Cuban client to Dublin to contest the WBA interim World super-bantamweight title decider with Willie Casey at City West. The showbiz ballyhoo of the weigh-ins didn't faze Casey who insisted, 'I've no nerves. It's time for action.' Tyson Fury, imposing in a leather overcoat, was among the fighters lending him moral support.

In Rigondeaux's corner was 2003 Hall of Fame trainer Ronnie Shields, who'd worked with both Evander Holyfield and Mike Tyson. 'We have to take Willie's momentum away from him very early in the fight,' he said. Casey knew it would be a tough night. 'A double world champion with over 400 fights with only a couple lost, if we were to meet in the amateurs he'd beat me a hundred times over,' he said. 'But he's in my game now. My training pushed my body way beyond all human levels. Now I'm going to give him a piece of it and see how he likes it.'

On the left side of Willie's chest, where we like to think our heart is, there's a striking portrait with the inscription, 'In loving memory of Paddy'. The tattoo is Willie's tribute to an older brother who died a couple of years earlier, a victim of the drugs epidemic that swept Limerick. Willie knew the catastrophic damage the drugs trade was doing to his city, his community and his family. He hoped his example would show kids that life wasn't a dead end.

By the time of the Casey–Rigondeaux fight, rival Limerick gangs had been feuding for a decade. As the death toll mounted, the Gardaí developed more robust in-your-face methods of policing. Arriving at City West for the fight, I expected a heightened level of police security. As I stepped out of a taxi beside a hedge, I was startled to come face to face with a man in a black ski mask brandishing a sub-machine gun. It was a member of the Armed Support Unit (ASU) whose cover I'd inadvertently blown. He was just one of an extensive squad of tooled-up cops staking out the venue in anticipation of a gang war.

The atmosphere was feverish as referee Stanley Christodoulou gave the fighters their final instructions. Casey's jab had snap. Alert, he moved forward with purpose. But Rigondeaux quickly asserted himself and exposed the frailties of Willie's claim. My abiding memory of the fight is Casey's facial muscles convulsing in agony from a body shot so destructive it instantly engulfed Big Bang in a sea of pain. The Cuban's uncanny ability to create such moments of crisis made the ring inescapably claustrophobic.

Rigondeaux revealed himself as a perfect fighting machine. A vicious predator, he was capable of sensing opportunity and exploiting any identified weakness with ruthless efficiency. Almost halfway through the first round, with Casey winded and still in pain from the body shots, an accurate left uppercut toppled him to the canvas. Breathing deeply, Casey gamely sprang back up. There was to be no reprieve. The Cuban pursued his quarry, connecting with a left hook that carried TNT. Casey's senses imploded and he fell over, his head cradled by the lower rope. Unsteady on his feet, he went back to war. But where was the enemy? Rigo blew in like a Force 5. Fearing Casey could be seriously hurt, the referee intervened. After two minutes and thirty-seven seconds of measured fury it was over, the crowd silenced.

Already accustomed to sharing the ring with her male counterparts in the IABA's High Performance gym and benefiting from her father's commitment to her cause, Katie Taylor had got to spar four rounds with Rigondeaux days before the fight. It proved a learning experience. Taylor was awestruck. The Cuban proved so elusive she said it had been like trying to hit a ghost. There had been nothing spectral about the sledgehammer left that Rigondeaux ripped into the body beneath Casey's right elbow. It was a substantial and crippling punch. The Cuban's performance was impressive but not to him. 'I've had better days,' he snorted dismissively afterwards. There was no warmth in his eyes when we were introduced by Gary Hyde. No hint of sentiment or diplomacy. Nor was there small talk about the fight. 'It's business,' he said curtly.

Casey never did get to bring the WBA belt to his late brother Paddy's grave as he'd hoped, but he did go on to have seven more fights, including a win against Jason Booth in Sunderland for the vacant WBO Inter-Continental super-bantamweight title. In September 2014, on the undercard of the Carl Frampton–Kiko Martínez world-title fight at the Titanic Centre, Belfast, he bowed out of boxing, saying farewell with a trademark sixth-round knockout win.

7
GOLDEN
GLOVES

'Every time I'd get hit in the ring I'd think, "Why am I doing this,
getting hit in the head?"'
Seamus McDonagh

I

BOBBY CASSIDY, the Long Island southpaw who fight fans knew as
'Irish', lit up cards on the East Coast in the 1960s and 70s. As a kid, Cassidy
grew up with an abusive, bullying stepfather. Regular street fighting led him
to court and, eventually, the boxing gym. Later, young Cassidy would spar
Sugar Ray Robinson and Emile Griffith, the first fighter to break his nose.

With a powerful left hook, Cassidy was a contender. But the night in
January 1974 when he fought the biggest fight of his career, a title-fight
eliminator, he blew it. On the undercard of the second Muhammad Ali–Joe
Frazier fight, he wasn't in good condition. With his marriage on the rocks and
an arrest for bookmaking dogging him, Cassidy was drowning his troubles.

Ill-prepared from drinking instead of training, he was stopped in the third round. A notorious boozer, Bobby became a regular bar brawler. That was until he KO'd a 6 ft 6 in bouncer and two of his acolytes in a saloon. The victim was a respected figure in the Hells Angels so the heat was on. His life in danger, Bobby needed to get a grip. And he did, eventually becoming a respected coach.

Cassidy's son, Bobby Jr, wrote *Kid Shamrock*, a gritty stage play based on his father's story. When I was introduced to the author, he was enjoying the success of the play's early run in New York. The man who starred as the troubled fighter in that initial run was Seamus McDonagh, an Irish boxer from County Meath who, for a brief golden spell, had been torchbearer of the tradition of handsome Irish fighter in the halls of New York. As I would come to know, McDonagh could all too readily convey the emotional import of Cassidy's line, 'I was only nine years old. I wished I was dead.'

McDonagh isn't the only Irish fighter to play the part. John Duddy is another who has starred in the role, describing the play as being about 'a guy who picks himself up after boxing and makes something of his life'. Both McDonagh and Duddy knew their way around a ring. And knew about survival. Born in England, McDonagh and the family first moved to Mulhuddart and then to Enfield, County Meath, where he spent the 1970s. His boxing apprenticeship had been tough. 'As a child, nine years old, we sat in the back of the car as dad patrolled the neighbourhood looking for the biggest, baddest kid he could find,' explained McDonagh. 'The gloves came out, were laced up and the punching began. That was terrorizing.' His father, Jim, a boxing fanatic, then set up a boxing club with a couple of local men and told his four sons they'd become world champions.

Seamus put in long hours of training. 'There was nothing to do in the town, only drink or play football,' he says. Soon he and a younger brother, John, began dominating the county schoolboys championships. Next they won provincial titles. Seamus lost his first All-Ireland championships when he was twelve. It was a learning experience. Soon afterwards, he was matched against an older boy, Barry McGuigan, in a local tournament in Meath. Having seen young McGuigan box previously, Seamus had noticed how Barry stopped an opponent with a right to the body so he kept his elbow tucked in defensively and won the bout on points. From there he went on to win three national Juvenile titles and two youth championships. When he was eighteen, he won a national Junior light heavyweight title.

In 1981 his father moved again. This time to Chicago, taking Seamus and his brother John with him. John won a Golden Gloves title there and, at the third attempt, Seamus too became a Golden Gloves champion, knocking out his five opponents on his way to winning the heavyweight division in New York. Muhammad Ali made the presentation. 'Ali looked at me wide-eyed in disbelief and said, "You won the heavyweight division?"' McDonagh would recall. 'I was just 190 pounds. He was twice my size.'

From there the obvious move was to try out the professional scene. Soon he was on a roll, winning fourteen of his seventeen pro bouts by way of knockout. He packed a power punch, had an indestructible jaw and his fights were big box-office attractions. Stars were queueing up for seats at ringside. You'd see Mickey Rourke there. Matt Dillon. Donald Trump. Politicians, sports stars, TV stars. All the East Coast glitterati. McDonagh became a celebrity. 'People were asking me to make movies and everything,' he recalled when we spent an afternoon together along the way. Today, not everyone would readily remember that Seamus McDonagh came just one fight away from boxing immortality.

'In April of 1990 I got offers to fight Mike Tyson, George Foreman and Evander Holyfield,' he told me nonchalantly, a mischievous glint in his eye. These were elite world-class fighters. I needed to remind myself that I wasn't talking to Larry Holmes, Frank Bruno or Riddick Bowe. The guy smiling at the memory had the smouldering looks of a matinee idol and the smarts of a graduate with an honours degree in English literature. Yet somehow Seamus McDonagh had found himself challenging the champion, Holyfield.

When Holyfield defeated Carlos de Leon in 1988, he added the WBC title to the WBA and IBF titles he'd already won and became the first undisputed and undefeated cruiserweight champion of the world. After that fight, he moved up to heavyweight. By the time he met McDonagh, he'd already made short work of five heavyweight challengers. McDonagh's father cautioned against taking the fight, arguing it was too soon. McDonagh listened dutifully but rejected the advice.

'I didn't like fighting,' he insisted. He didn't have to do it. Nonetheless, being a stubborn romantic, he accepted the challenge. 'I was only a cruiserweight at about 200 pounds,' he recalled. 'They were talking $25 million if I beat him. So I could not not take the fight. I took it.'

It was a fight that New York wanted to see, a showcase with the sense of an old-fashioned Hollywood script about it. The handsome, heavy-hitting Irishman, who'd won a Golden Gloves title by knockouts all the way, punching his way to the stars at the Atlantic City Convention Centre on Friday, 1 June 1990.

'It was for the WBC Continental Americas title,' explained McDonagh. 'You could compare it to the heavyweight championship of the world. I did better than Tyson and Douglas [against Holyfield]. He knocked out Douglas in three rounds. Tyson quit. I didn't quit.'

There was a lot of pressure on the young Irishman's shoulders. The night before the bout, his phone rang. It was Norman Mailer calling to wish him well. McDonagh had come a long way from Mulhuddart.

Despite having boxed in Madison Square Garden, the scale of the event was overwhelming. He was led into the ring by bagpipers. The buzz was intense. He attempted to get himself focused but failed. 'Physically I was in great shape,' he said. 'But mentally I wasn't prepared at all. The bell went and I came out for the first round and I couldn't walk. I was thinking, "Jesus Christ, let me get out of here."'

A cruiserweight, programmed by an atavistic code and confronted by the world's number one heavyweight, McDonagh did what came naturally. He smacked Holyfield with a left hook. He reckoned it hurt Holyfield. But if it did, the champ didn't show it. Undefeated Holyfield (twenty-three wins, nineteen KOs), a glistening specimen of finely tuned muscle, was at the height of his power. 'He hit me on the shoulder and knocked me down in the first round but I got up and said I was okay,' said McDonagh with a clarity that suggested it had just happened the previous evening. 'In the fourth round I hit him with a great right hand. The whole place stood up. Donald Trump came to my dressing room after the fight. He still comes over to say hello whenever he sees me.' McDonagh can laugh at it now.

Evander Holyfield went on to fight Mike Tyson in 1996. He stopped Iron Mike in the eleventh round in Las Vegas. The rematch the following year is regarded as one of the most infamous fights in history. Don Turner, Holyfield's coach, predicted, 'Tyson's character is going to let him down. Evander will expose his limitations.' Neither Turner nor anyone else could have foreseen the savagery with which Tyson underscored his reputation as the Baddest Man on the Planet.

Frustrated by Holyfield's bullying tactics and, accidental or otherwise, head clashes that resulted in cuts to both of his eyes, Tyson spat out his mouthpiece and sank his teeth into Holyfield's right ear, biting off a chunk. Despite the lump of bloodied flesh and gristle landing on the table in front of one of the judges, Tyson wasn't disqualified. This was a multimillion-dollar showcase event. Vegas, baby. The show must go on. Despite Holyfield's distress and the unsightly bloody mess, following hurried consultation, Tyson had two points deducted and the fight resumed. Then, in a clinch, an enraged Tyson bit Holyfield's other ear and chaos ensued. Tyson was disqualified and the fight abandoned amid ugly scenes. 'It doesn't show no courage to foul to get out of the fight,' commented Holyfield later. 'Fear causes people to do the easy thing.'

Holyfield fought his last fight in 2011 but didn't officially retire until 2014 when he was fifty-one. The only four-time winner of the heavyweight title, he'd earned an estimated $350 million. Yet at the time of his retirement, he was bankrupt. 'If you're a professional fighter, you're on your own for everything.'

II

One definition of a truly brave person is someone who knows fear and refuses to be dominated by it. McDonagh has fought the fear all his life. Courage has been his watchword.

'Every time I'd get hit in the ring I'd think, "Why am I doing this, getting hit in the head?"' he told me. 'And I boxed for seventeen years.' It's often impossible to unravel the tangle of gnarled blood roots that stretch far back in family history. McDonagh's grandfather, Patrick McDonagh, hailed from the village of Cultrasna, Kiltimagh, in County Mayo. He'd worked in construction in New York city – one of the team that erected the Empire State Building. He was tough. It was part of family lore that he'd been at the fabled Long Count Fight between Jack Dempsey and eventual winner, world heavyweight champion, Gene Tunney in Chicago in 1927. Patrick McDonagh would have been urging on Tunney whose mother and father both came from the Kiltimagh area.

McDonagh recalled his fourth-round knockdown by Holyfield: 'I lay on the canvas ... I wasn't hurt and I was totally conscious but I was thinking, "If I stay here it'll all be over." There was so much mayhem and madness.' Did he stay down for the count? Of course not. 'I couldn't stay down.'

'I was up at eight but he [the referee] illegally stopped the fight,' protested McDonagh, as aggrieved now as on that clamorous night in 1990. It went down as a technical knockout. No disgrace. 'I did good in the fourth round,' he said. 'And just got caught with a left hook. Then I was running around with a rake of money.'

'At the time I fought Holyfield, I needed two classes to qualify for my degree,' he recalled ruefully. 'I wanted to win the title and graduate as champion. But it didn't work out.' His next bout was his last. McDonagh was back in Atlantic City a year after the Holyfield fight. 'I was training with Joe Fariello, one of Cus D'Amato's prodigies,' he said. 'At twenty-seven years old I learned how to box. But I overtrained for the fight [against former Texas State champ Jesse Shelby]. A headbutt in the second round and I fought in a blackout for eight rounds.'

McDonagh was living with his girlfriend on the West Side of Manhattan. 'I woke up the next morning and I was battered,' he recalled when we met:

I don't remember the fight. I was supposed to fight for the title next fight so it was a real big let-down. I was black and blue. My hand was broken. I had black stitches. Black eyes. A broken nose. Everything. A mess. I was a suicidal kid when I was eleven. I tried to kill myself with pills at twenty-one. I woke up the morning after that fight and my girlfriend, Renee, had gone to college and I thought, 'Well now I can kill myself.'

'What kept me alive?' McDonagh anticipated my question. 'I thought, "Now I can drink like I wanna."'

Twelve months later he was struggling to quit drinking when fate intervened. Dublin actor and director Jimmy Smallhorne, who became the first Irish director to have a film in competition in Sundance with *2by4*, spotted Seamus in Manhattan and introduced himself. 'We were in rehearsals for the play *Bobby Sands MP* at the Irish Arts Centre,' recalls Smallhorne. 'Nye Heron, great-grandson of James Connolly, was directing and he was saying the prison wardens we had were all too skinny. We needed convincing heavies to play the part.' Invited to audition by Jimmy, McDonagh was hired and fell in love with acting.

'He played a prison warder and every night he came out and grabbed me by the balls and threw me up against the wall,' said Smallhorne. 'I was stark naked because Bobby had refused to wear prison clothes. We had to work hand to hand. A few times Seamus missed the cue and caught me. It was very painful. Seamus loved acting. It was at a point in his life where he was struggling to decide what direction he should go.'

Critics and audiences were impressed by the depth of expression he'd brought to the role of the young Bobby Cassidy in the first run of *Kid Shamrock*. The sharp edge of Cassidy's life experience was something he could readily relate to. McDonagh was a reluctant boxer. 'Whenever I got in the ring I'd think, "Why am I doing this?"' he told me. 'I had the same thought doing the play. There was only me on the stage. It's the same fear.'

In 2011, with Smallhorne directing, the play was set to be staged at Atlantic Theatre II. 'I thought, "Why can't we get boxers to play the other roles?"' McDonagh said:

'What about Duddy?' At the time, John was getting ready to fight Andy Lee for 100 grand [American dollars]. We also got in touch with Gerry Cooney [world heavyweight contender], who said he'd like to do it but changed his mind, saying, 'I'm too nervous, man. I might forget my lines.'

Smallhorne had a boxing ring erected in the middle of the stage. 'The play is really about alcoholism,' he explains. 'You knew that Bobby Snr and Seamus were in recovery. It was very moving.'

Duddy joined rehearsals and fitted in. But there was another surprise for Smallhorne:

Duddy said, 'I'm pulling out of the fight [with Andy Lee].' I said, 'But you'll be losing out on $100,000.' He said, 'I don't mind. I love this. I don't want to do that fight.'
He turned down 100K. He said, 'I love this acting.' When John told me, I said to him, 'You make sure everybody knows that you're not doing this for Jimmy Smallhorne. You're doing this for yourself.' I was shitting myself. We were rehearsing and I was waiting for some big Italians to come in and give me a punch if people were losing money on gambling.

Duddy suited the role of Cassidy the young fighter. He'd experienced the highs and lows of being a pro and had become disillusioned with the discipline. 'I'm just glad I got out while I still had one or two brain cells left,' he told Mark Gallagher. Duddy's new-found acting ability impressed my friend George Kimball, the boxing writer and arts commentator, who described him as 'almost astonishingly competent, delivering his lines (in a New York accent) with a flawless ease'.

Jim Rock & Michael Carruth (Exhibition bout, Dublin, 2007). (Credit: Aidan Walsh)

Esham Pickering & Bernard Dunne (Dublin, November 2006). (Credit: Aidan Walsh)

Eamon Carr & Darren Sutherland (Dublin, 2008). (Credit: Aidan Walsh)

Georgi Iliev & Darren Sutherland (Dublin, December 2008). (Credit: Aidan Walsh)

Paul Hyland & Willie Casey (Dublin, October 2010). (Credit: Aidan Walsh)

Paul Hyland & Willie Casey (Limerick, November 2010). (Credit: Aidan Walsh)

Patrick Hyland, Keith Whelan, Martin Rogan (Dublin, 2010). (Credit: Aidan Walsh)

Rafael Sosa Pintos, referee Emile Tied, Matthew Macklin
(Dublin, December 2009). (Credit: Aidan Walsh)

Tyson Fury (Belfast, August 2018). (Credit: Ricardo Guglielminotti)

Tyson Fury & Francesco Pianeta (Belfast, August 2018).
(Credit: Ricardo Guglielminotti)

Pete Taylor & Katie Taylor (Dublin, 2009). (Credit: Aidan Walsh)

Katie Taylor (Wembley, London, October 2022). (Credit: Tom Cockram)

Katie Taylor (Wembley, November 2016). (Credit: Ricardo Guglielminotti)

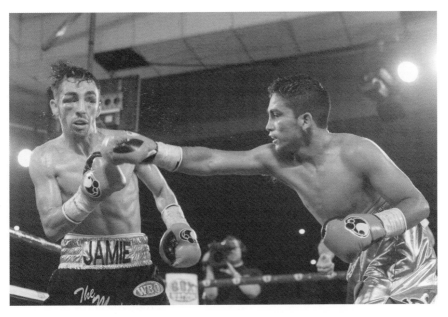

Jamie Conlan & Junior Granados (Dublin, July 2015).
(Credit: Ricardo Guglielminotti)

Chris Avalos & Carl Frampton (Belfast, February 2015).
(Credit: Ricardo Guglielminotti)

Andy Lee (Limerick, July 2008).
(Credit: Aidan Walsh)

Floyd Mayweather & Conor
McGregor (London, 2017).
(Credit: Ricardo Guglielminotti)

Jamie Kavanagh (Dublin, February 2016). (Credit: Ricardo Guglielminotti)

Meanwhile, McDonagh was frequently doing meditation during rehearsals. Smallhorne recalls, 'If there was any artistic conflict, Seamus would sit down and put a towel over his head and meditate. People would be worried that maybe he'd come out then and punch someone. But he was a lovely guy.'

'Performance' is a word boxers regularly use. 'I performed well tonight.' 'I didn't give a good performance.'

The discipline of theatre, an environment where senses are heightened, where it's necessary to be ever alert on stage, where the actor is in control while simultaneously being controlled by something other, some force outside and beyond, proved a rewarding discovery for McDonagh and Duddy.

American composer David Amram has said that Miles Davis went to small-hall boxing shows 'to watch the boxing and to see the courage and loneliness of what it's like to be doing that'. Davis found boxing inspirational.

Art is a form of knowledge. Like a great jazz gig or evening of theatre, the shifting intricacies of a boxing match can be mind-blowing. Spectators can leave an arena feeling their perception of life has been radically altered. In performance something transcendental can happen.

III

These days, Seamus McDonagh reaches out to fighters struggling to cope with life away from the ring.

'Having it all just taken away can wreck your life and your head,' he advises. 'We need some way to deal with post-traumatic stress disorder. Keep talking to somebody. I was given the twelve steps and they are a way to express it all – the disappointments, the rage and whatever else – on paper. Don't let it stay in your head.'

Recalling his years as a boxer, McDonagh noted a little-known statistic. 'I've been knocked down twice in my life,' he says. 'When I was eleven years old, Peter Reynolds put me down in the gym at the back of Jimmy Gorry's petrol station in Enfield. It was a flash knockdown. And Evander Holyfield knocked me down. They were about seventeen years apart.'

Looking back on life as a fighter, McDonagh reveals, 'When I finished boxing, my mother, who was always supportive, said, "You won't know your life now." She saw how much of a terror it was in my life. I don't know what it's like to not have trauma. But I'm glad I did it.'

8
IRON MAN

'I've seen too many fighters get badly damaged.'
Martin Rogan

DANNY X was our hero.

He lived nearby and boxed in national tournaments. He even got to represent his country. This was a really big deal to us youngsters in the bleak 1950s. Because our families were friends, it felt as if I had skin in the game.

Being described in the press as 'a KO specialist', Danny had unofficially become our representative, as notable as any local politician or inter-county GAA player. I'd heard he was tough and destructive in the ring but had been too young to see him box in his prime. On the one occasion I got to watch him fight, it seemed that, unafraid of being hit, he simply relied on hitting harder and more often.

At a time of national economic paralysis, forced emigration and cultural stagnation, Danny was one of a few people whose example showed how, if we fought with courage and determination, we could ultimately emerge victorious.

While Danny was collecting accolades, I was setting an unenviable record among my classmates. No one else had spent as much time in so many different hospitals. My mother being ill, my father was no longer assisting the local sports-mad curate who'd set up a boxing club as a community initiative. When my mother died, the spectre of the orphanage loomed as my father fought to keep his young family together.

The gang of older delinquents I hung out with lived for the weekend when they'd travel to different towns for street fights. It sounded exciting but I was still in short trousers. Before I got to tag along, my relatives staged an intervention. That's when I was shipped off to boarding school, a uniquely alien environment for an at-risk juvenile with personal issues.

Former Basque soldier turned Jesuit priest Ignatius of Loyola once said, 'Give me a boy until he is ten and I'll give you a man.' Iggy was on to something. A few years in the Diocesan college proved transformative.

While on school holidays, I was shaken by a newspaper headline. 'Trail of Blood on City Street'. The story concerned a bloke who'd been sentenced to penal servitude for life for having beaten someone to death. It was Danny. Homicides weren't frequent back then so the case dominated the headlines. Respected by his peers in boxing, and from a respectable family, Danny had somehow slipped through the cracks. Months of sleeping rough and drinking cheap wine in alleyways and at camp fires on waste ground had led to petty crime, violence and, ultimately, incarceration. Something had gone tragically wrong.

I

I was still just a nipper the time, with my father, I saw Danny fight. The heavyweights had come in towards the end of the night. Enormous men. The bigger of the two was a huge, fleshy individual with thick legs, muscular arms and a head that looked like it was carved from granite. I couldn't imagine how the shorter boxer, who looked a lot lighter, might survive.

When the bell tolled, the two men advanced, snorting loudly as they threw punches that smacked the other's gloves. Close to ringside, the thud of their boots on the canvas floor was deafening. The referee, who attempted to pull them apart when they clinched, looked puny in contrast to these lumbering leviathans. As they huffed and puffed, the primitivism of the big men held me enthralled.

Appearing to snuggle tight to his opponent during the third round, the smaller man swung a sharp-right hook that connected with the giant's jaw. I'd seen bombed buildings collapse on the cinema screen and that was all I had to compare it to. A tall building of bone and blubber, the big man wobbled and then keeled over with such a resounding crash I thought the floor of the ring would shatter.

I gasped and looked to my father for a response to the intensity of the spectacle, the premonition of disaster and evocation of ruin that had just played out in front of us.

'A glass chin,' he said.

II

Former world champion Eamonn Magee had his gimlet gaze fixed firmly on the tableau playing out after the weigh-in. 'He has him,' he snarled, like a proud owner of a greyhound at a coursing meeting as the hare squeals in terror.

I looked over and saw the 6 ft 5 1/2-in frame of Olympic gold-medal winner Audley Harrison towering above Belfast taxi driver Martin Rogan. 'See,' urged Magee aggressively. 'He won't look him in the eye. Rogie has intimidated him. He's going to cause an upset.'

What is it about the big men that fascinates so much? Jack Dempsey, Jack Johnson, Gene Tunney, Joe Louis, Rocky Marciano, Muhammad Ali, Joe Frazier, Mike Tyson and so many others. The boxing heavyweight championship has long captivated the general public and held spectators around the globe spellbound in a manner denied any other contact sport.

Here, both fighters were surrounded by a constellation of officials, journalists and hangers-on. But Rogan continued to stare balefully at the local superstar, the man he was due to fight the following night in London's Docklands. Harrison attempted to appear oblivious. Back from his base in Los Angeles, he was on a mission to land a world-title fight. 'I've fought loads of fighters like Martin Rogan,' he said dismissively. 'The difference will show on the night. People will see why I'm special.' Promoter Frank Warren believed Harrison's counterpunching would cope with Rogan's aggression. 'If he delivers in the ring, then I'll get him that world-title fight he so craves,' he promised.

'D'ya see the look in his eyes?' Rogan demanded of me when the hustle and bustle died down. 'He wasn't expecting me to be this big. But I put the frighteners on him when we squared up. He knows now that I'm going to beat him.' Rogan was spoiling for a fight. He'd have been happy to go there and then. 'He's not that tall when he steps out of those stupid-looking high-heel shoes he's wearing,' he sneered.

On the night of the fight at the ExCeL Arena, I went to wish Rogan well and discovered a scene like the set of a dystopian sci-fi film. The dressing room where Eamonn Magee and coach John Breen were supervising Rogan's warm-up was an abandoned office space at the end of an upstairs corridor. The Belfast fighter had just one fight the previous year. A fight he'd won in the second round. Before meeting Harrison, he'd had three Prizefighter bouts, each just three rounds. It wasn't ideal preparation but Rogan had sparred with Magee, a southpaw. Being schooled by an ex-champion, described by his biographer Paul D. Gibson as 'a truculent, temperamental, dangerous, depressive, paranoid alcoholic', had the desired effect on the novice heavyweight. His face a grotesque mask that conveyed a disarming mix of comedy and savagery, Rogie didn't require motivating. The upbeat presence of Irish promoter Brian Peters added to the aura of confidence being generated. Soon we were joined by well-wishers Matthew Macklin and his brother Seamus. In a game of fine margins, Rogan's determination received a timely psychological boost.

An official arrived. Showtime.

'Let's go,' urged Peters.

Someone else took up the call. 'Right, let's go.'

A psychic charge rippled through the room. There was going to be a fight.

Bringing up the rear as the team trekked down the deserted corridor, my adrenaline was pumping. The longest, loneliest ring walk in history must have added to Rogan's chagrin because soon he was pacing the canvas like a bad tempered Rottweiler ready to tear an intruder apart.

Harrison arrived with pomp and bluster. He and his cornermen were resplendent in flash black and gold-trimmed Everlast tops with A-Force logos.

The local press corps became more engaged. Having lost two title challenges, Harrison had yet to convince. On the face of it, this seemed like a routine 'keep busy' scrap with an unproven journeyman. A Grub Street reporter dutifully enquired, 'What's that top Rogan's wearing?'

'It's the County Antrim GAA senior hurling team jersey.'

'Hurling? What?'

I attempted to explain. But was interrupted by his colleague enquiring about the legend *An Siamsóir* on the back of bucket man Eamonn Magee's shirt.

'It's the Irish language,' I replied. 'Rogie's known locally as "the Entertainer".'

Unconvinced, the Londoners eyed me sceptically. Despite having won the inaugural Prizefighter series, it was his only claim to fame: Rogan was regarded as a novelty act.

Adopting the stance of a street fighter, Rogan's objective was to get inside the pawing reach of the Olympian while avoiding the threat of a gumshield-rattling left hook. It was roughhouse. Harrison found his range and began to inflict damage. It looked as if the more experienced fighter would control the bout with his 6 ft 5-in frame and southpaw jab. Though battered, Rogan remained unbowed. He kept coming forward. It was a bizarre scenario. Willing to brawl, with craggy head and flattened nose, features that would see him come up second in a beauty contest with a dump truck, the trouble-seeking Belfast man laughed between punches. The line from the *Rocky* movie – 'It ain't about how hard you hit, it's about how you can get hit and keep moving forward' – was being played out for real.

Though seeming reckless and naive, the tactics worked. Soon Rogan was rocking Harrison with powerful uppercuts, shots to the head and excruciating body blows. As his shots landed, Rogan seemed to grow stronger. In the sixth round, he stunned his opponent with a meaty right hand and followed up with an array of punches that were only partly smothered by the hulking figure draping himself around Rogan's arms. Magee's advice to unleash the uppercut paid dividends in the seventh. Soon the London fight fans joined the underdog's supporters in singing 'The Fields of Athenry' and 'Olé Olé Olé'. The 37-year-old visitor found extra pep in the final rounds.

Desire versus experience. Fighting spirit versus technique. The result hung in the balance going into the final stretch but Rogan fought like a man possessed. His performance upset the odds and confounded London's jingoistic boxing elite. At the final bell, his arm was raised. No one disputed the decision. Martin Rogan, taxi driver, part-time actor and late bloomer, now had the attention of the heavyweight division.

Rogan's victory in one of the most exciting fights of 2008 was sensational. 'The odds were stacked against me,' he told me. The shots he took in the first round were, he claimed, part of a scoping exercise. 'It's better to know early what somebody has,' he said, grinning. 'I got the head chewed off me by John and Eamonn for doing that. They were hard and troubling punches and I dare say they would have put a lot of people down. But I knew from that round onwards that I was going to whip it into a higher gear and go for it.'

Rogan couldn't have been more elated if he'd just lifted the Liam McCarthy Cup in Croke Park. I asked about the jersey we wore on his ring walk. 'I played for Antrim Under 18 and Under 21,' he explained. 'My brother Ger played for Antrim senior team for thirteen years. He played in the All-Ireland final against Kilkenny in '89. It was my chance to wear the Antrim jersey. That's the sport I grew up with and came from into boxing. Even my socks were Antrim socks.'

Breen and Magee were beaming. They'd called it right. Peters was chuckling. A sense of mischief was trumped by genuine elation. This had been a notable victory against the odds. 'One of the papers called me a journeyman,' snorted Rogan. 'But there are not many journeymen out there who'll have eleven straight wins, five by KO, beat the Olympic gold medallist and beat the Commonwealth Games gold medallist [David Dolan]. If I'm only a journeyman then I'm a hell of a journeyman.'

He wasn't to know it that December night but, having captured the public imagination, Rogan was set to galvanize Belfast with a further string of spirited performances, inspire a new generation of young pros and help reconnect the gritty old shipbuilding city with its deep-veined boxing identity.

III

After his win against Harrison, outsider Rogan was matched with European champion Matt Skelton in Birmingham for the Commonwealth heavyweight title. With just two losses in twenty-four fights, durable Skelton had never been stopped.

The fight looked to be going Skelton's way, until a right from Rogan created a gaping wound over the champion's left eye in the fifth round. Displaying an allegiance to his trademark mob-handed brawling style, the Belfast man piled on the pressure, stunning Skelton in every round. The frantic energy expended seemed to sap Rogan's resources. He was landing more punches but Skelton's carried power. In his corner after the tenth, he told John Breen, 'I'm knackered.'

When it looked as if lack of experience was going to deny him, Rogan found a way. Pushing through Skelton's jab, he hit the target with another big right in the eleventh round and, with Skelton reeling, unleashed a bombardment that put him down. The sight of him wobbling back to his feet keyed another furious onslaught from Rogan and convinced referee John Keane to intervene for the last time. Rogan was the new Commonwealth champion.

Instead of a European title fight next, the 37-year-old had to defend his new belt. His opponent, Sam Sexton, a 25-year-old from Norwich, had a similar pro record. On the positive side, Rogan was headlining at the Odyssey Arena in his home town. The former taxi driver was now a box-office star.

Sexton's jab had bite but Rogan, with a wall of noise behind him, ushered his man on to the ropes and strafed him. A looping right fist that rattled Sexton in the sixth was followed by a flurry of pain-inflicting punches upstairs and down. Breaking in a clinch, Rogan displayed an inflating bruise under his left eye. 'Low lie the fields of Athenry,' chorused the crowd in the seventh as a doctor was called to inspect the injury. Cleared by the medic, Rogan went back to work. Stalking his quarry, he misjudged the speed of Sexton's punching and walked into a thunderous shot. Miraculously, he withstood its numbing qualities and saw out the round.

With the swelling around his eye still a topic of concern among the officials, Rogan went into the eighth round knowing time was running out if he was to finish the job and hold on to his title. So he did what he does best. He came out swinging and sent Sexton careering around the ring. As the man from Norwich backed into a corner; he was pursued by Rogan, who fired off solid body shots and uppercuts. The referee pulled them apart yet again. But Sexton, having spat out his gumshield, dropped his hands by his sides and stood, like a toddler in playschool, looking open-mouthed at pretty patterns on the canvas floor. Unbelievably, instead of delivering the *coup de grace*, Rogan gestured to the referee to rescue his hapless opponent. And he did. But he didn't stop the fight. Instead, with Sexton's gumshield returned to his mouth and immediate danger averted, the punching resumed. Briefly. Seventeen seconds remained on the clock when the doctor was again called by the ref to examine Rogan's vision. This time the fight was called off. And Sexton, who seconds earlier was one punch away from concussion, was crowned the new Commonwealth champion.

Months later, I'm standing in front of Belfast City Hall when a flash, high-end BMW jeep draws up and a voice commands, 'Hop in, big man.' I climb on board and am soon cruising a topography of streets familiar from years of bleak news bulletins; Castle Street, Divis Street, Springfield Road. A decade earlier this journey would have been impossible without encountering intimidating police and army checkpoints.

My driver, Martin Rogan, knows these streets well. As a kid he'd seen a neighbour being blasted by a loyalist gunman. In Belfast, a city with a proud boxing tradition, Rogan has become an unlikely sporting ambassador. 'It makes me feel great because there's been so much division,' he says. 'I was born and reared just off the Falls Road. The night of the Sexton fight I had people from every corner of Belfast and beyond coming to give me their support.' As recognizable as a block of basalt from the Giant's Causeway, Martin is greeted warmly by folk from both sides of the cultural divide.

A fellow said to Rogan, 'You speak well on television and I feel you represent me.' 'Thanks very much 'cos I do fight for everybody,' replied Martin.

'That's good because I'm from the Shankill Road,' said the man.

It's clear that Rogie the Entertainer is the People's Champion.

Warming to this theme, Martin continues:

The people on the Shankill Road are just the same as me. There's people come over from America and say, 'I'm American but I'm Irish-American.' If that's what they class themselves as, then okay, let's seek to find peace. If boxing can make a difference, I'll do everything I can to get people thinking in the right direction. People on the ground can do more than people in Stormont or anywhere else.

I'm here to talk to Rogan about his upcoming rematch with Sam Sexton but the longer I'm in his company the more insights I gain into the late-vocation heavyweight. Over coffee, I hear about his childhood on one side of the Peace Line in Belfast.

'I don't want my children coming through the divisions I've seen [while] growing up,' he says:

> With explosions going off and you with your mates trying to guess where the explosion was. Then you hear gunfire and you're trying to guess where it was. You'd have to wait to hear the news to see who got it right. To me that's a very sad way to grow up as a child. Trying to pinpoint the sound of gunfire and explosions. And lying in bed hearing shouts from grown men in the middle of the night and wondering what's going to happen. Always waiting on an explosion or gunfire. I don't want any child, Protestant or Catholic, to have to grow up in that. No one deserves it.

Rogan explains he'd taken up boxing just seven years earlier. Few amateur clubs were willing to welcome a hulking Gaelic hurler with zilch boxing experience who probably thought ringcraft was a jewellery shop. 'People were sniggering that I was clumsy,' says Rogan. 'But in my heart I knew I was going to do this. I ended up with "Nugget" [Gerry] Nugent at Immaculata. He worked with me very hard.' In the space of four years, Rogan won Ulster titles, a national senior title, captained the Ireland squad and boxed in Olympic qualifiers. Then he turned pro. He'd lost just one of his thirteen pro fights – to Sexton – and is intent on redressing a wrong.

Genial to a fault, Rogan explained his loss against Sexton at his post-fight press conference, saying, 'I've seen too many fighters get badly damaged and I didn't want to be part of that.' Although worried that it might be like throwing dynamite into Mount Vesuvius, I ask again how he let the Commonwealth title slip away from him. Did chivalry cost him dearly?

'The referee was a total disgrace,' thunders Rogan. 'When the guy turned his back on me and held onto the ropes, I thought the fight was being stopped. Only a coward spits out the gumshield. The referee brought the sport into disrepute.'

Rogan fails to explain exactly why he didn't just wallop Sexton and finish the fight. Whether through compassion or inexperience, his failure left fans and pundits confused. 'People have been saying that I was never going to win that fight no matter what,' he insists, becoming agitated. As we cruise down the Falls Road, there's nothing to be gained, and possibly everything to lose, in forcing Rogan to face the harsh reality of his decision not to have finished off Sexton, so I change the subject. Three months after that fight, Rogan began working with a different coach, Paul McCullagh. 'One loss was enough,' he reasoned.

The rematch didn't go well for Rogan. After four rounds, things were evenly balanced but, in the fifth, a clash of heads opened an ugly cut above his eye. Hampered by a recurrence of the neck injury that had caused the fight to be postponed until November, Rogan shipped enough punishment in the sixth to persuade his corner that he needed rescuing. This second defeat by Sexton didn't spell the end for Rogan. There were more paydays to follow. And Rogan would play a part in a storyline that even Hollywood might deem implausible.

History frequently gets rewritten; events ignored or conveniently overlooked. However, it cannot be denied that a fighter who won an Irish national heavyweight title took just seven more fights to establish himself as undisputed champion of the world, lifting belts that had previously been the property of such greats as Muhammad Ali, Joe Frazier, Mike Tyson and Lennox Lewis. Sadly, it wasn't Martin Rogan.

Following a couple of wins in 2010, which were followed by a year of inactivity during which he played the part of a bodyguard in *Keith Lemon: The Film*, Rogan came back to headline at the Odyssey in a tilt at the BUI Irish heavyweight title. His opponent was Tyson Fury, a 23-year-old fighter with a 17-0 record, who'd won both the British and Commonwealth heavyweight titles in 2011 but vacated the lot to contest the Irish title.

By now Rogan was rebranded as 'the Iron Man' because of a titanium plate that had been inserted in his neck following a persistent injury. He'd had just two fights in two years but, at forty, this was an opportunity to make history.

'I can fight,' he said. 'No one comes to this city and tries to take my place.'

9
THE GYPSY KING

'I'm in fight mode. Kill mode.'
Tyson Fury

WHEN YOU STRIP IT all away – the glamour, the romance, the flash, the braggadocio, the sentiment – what prize-fighting boils down to is blood and money. Pain, snot and pieces of silver.

Vast wealth can be earned fighting for world titles. So when someone proves handy with their fists, there's always going to be someone – a gym rat, a hustler, a conman or a coach searching for a big ticket – to assure them they can go all the way, become King of the World.

People have long been fascinated by divination. Over the centuries, people given to oracular utterances were feared, tortured or burnt at the stake. They were outsiders. In the popular imagination, Gypsies and Travellers were believed to have the power to read the signs and intuitively glimpse the future. Whether hokum or holy writ, the extended Fury family subscribe to the belief. It's said that Uriah Burton, a legendary English bare-knuckle fighter who it's claimed beat two opponents at a time, declared that a son of a marriage between members of the Burton and Fury families would one day gain renown as a fighting man.

When John and Amber Fury's second child was born three months prematurely, he weighed just one pound and had a slim chance of surviving. Legend has it that, watching his frail newborn baby struggle to survive, the father of the vulnerable infant, sensing a family fighting spirit that stretched back through generations of bare-knuckle fighters, was moved by the urging of ancestral voices to proclaim, 'He's going to be called after Mike Tyson.'

Fury Snr continued with a profound prediction. 'And he'll be the heavyweight champion of the world. It is his destiny.'

I

In 2012 a 23-year-old Tyson Fury was being considered for a shot at the world title. The fighter protested, 'Wladimir or Vitali Klitschko can wait because winning the Irish heavyweight championship means everything to me. I'm a real Irish warrior.'

Having boxed for Ireland as an amateur, Luke Tyson Fury was upset when he was dropped by the IABA because he couldn't officially document his Irish roots. Although born and raised in Manchester, Tyson identified as 'a fighting Irishman'. 'My father was born in Galway, along with the rest of my father's family who are from the west of Ireland,' he explained. 'My grandmother on my mother's side was born in Belfast, Nutt's Corner. People who know me know I've been back and forward to Ireland for a long, long time.'

There were plenty of dissenting voices, including an irate Mike Perez who spoke out when the Fury camp claimed he had turned down a fight. 'Why would I not want that fight?' he responded. 'It's easy money and a chance to make a lot of people happy by knocking him out and shutting his big mouth.' Addressing Fury directly, Perez went on, 'Put your money where your mouth is and make a real offer.' Upping the ante, Cork's 'Rebel' Cuban blasted, 'It takes more than wearing a GAA jersey for five minutes, or sticking a tweed cap on your head, to become an Irishman.'

When Andy Lee testified that Fury was his cousin and Lee's father presented a sworn affidavit declaring that Fury's grandmother was Irish, the Boxing Union of Ireland accepted Tyson's bone fides and gave permission for an Irish title fight with Martin Rogan. It still rankled with Fury that lack of official documentation had denied him a shot at Olympic qualification. 'I always knew I was Irish,' he declared. 'It hurt me deeply. When I knock out Martin Rogan and get the Irish title, it will be like winning the gold medal at the Olympics.'

Fury wasn't shy about sharing his grandiose notions. 'Never before has a fight like this taken place on Irish soil between two proud heavyweight warriors who never say die,' he announced. 'The ultimate Irish warrior was Cú Chulainn. Rogan and I will decide who is the rightful heir to his throne.'

When he fought in Ireland on the undercard of Bernard Dunne's last fight in 2009, Fury had already won seven of his eight pro fights by stoppage. Against a Czech journeyman who'd won just four of thirty-one fights, referee Emile Tied scored Fury a 60-57 win over six sluggish rounds. In mitigation, Fury had broken his hand when he punched the top of his opponent's skull.

Before meeting Rogan three years later, Fury notched up wins against more difficult opposition including a unanimous decision over twelve rounds for the Commonwealth title against Derek Chisora. In Detroit, Kronk Gym guru Emanuel Steward had spotted a diamond in the rough when Fury trained with him for a month. 'Tyson may look sloppy at times but he always manages to win. He has the size to cause any fighter problems.'

Ahead of meeting Fury in Belfast, Rogan dismissed the seventeen-year age difference saying, 'He probably expects me to rush in. But I have a Plan A, B and C.' Fury also had the advantage of weight, height and reach. Initially David performed well against the visiting Goliath. But Fury caught Rogan unprepared by cunningly fighting in a southpaw style. It's uncertain which letter of his alphabet of game plans Rogan was on when Fury sank a thunderous left into the liver and kidney interface in the fifth round. Gasping for oxygen, his distressed nerve-endings transmitting waves of pain, Rogan attempted to fight on but his corner had seen enough.

An impassioned Tyson Fury declared, 'I've got a Manchester accent but all my family's from Ireland. When people discredit you and say you're not something that you are, it's hurtful.' There was a lot of emotion in the room as the big man set the record straight. 'I've wanted to explain this for a while,' he said:

I should have gone to the Olympic Games in 2008. I was finished with boxing but I kept getting letters from the Irish Amateur Boxing Association saying, 'Come over and we'll send you to a qualifiers.'

So I went over and boxed in America for Ireland and I knocked out Maurice Byram. I went to Poland and I knocked out the Polish champion. So I'd already boxed twice for Ireland. In the All-Ireland [Championships], I got a bye to the final and was going to fight some Russian kid. But they said he was Irish and I wasn't. There was a lot of politics going on. I was bitter about that. It upset my family and my dad. I'm born in Manchester but I'm Irish heritage. I trained for this belt like it was the unification fight for the world title. This means more to me than any world title.

The Irish title in the bag, Fury had six more fights in three years before he travelled to Düsseldorf to contest the multiple world titles held by Wladimir Klitschko in 2015. By then he'd developed into a credible challenger, far removed from the earlier plodding behemoth who'd seemed woefully short on skill but high on resolve and brute strength.

His transformation owed a great deal to the coaching nous of his uncle Peter Fury, whose first fight in charge was the one against Rogan. When Tyson's father, John, was absent at Her Majesty's pleasure, it fell to Peter to cast a paternal eye on the young fighter. Initially Peter recommended Brendan Ingles' gym in Sheffield. Eventually, Tyson asked Peter, who coached his own son Hughie, to take charge. Efforts were made to eliminate basic mistakes from Tyson's technique. They worked on perfecting his jab with both left and right fist and they worked on conditioning. The key was controlling Tyson's weight. From there they built up his strength and stamina. Speed and footwork were two further areas for development. Fight by fight, changes in the fighter became more obvious. The one unique factor that wasn't eliminated from his repertoire was the bare-knuckle fighting sensibility that formed the core bedrock of the ethos Fury brought to the ring.

Building a career requires patience, strategy and the gift of timing. Knowing who to fight, and when, is an essential cornerstone of successful career development. Relinquishing his Commonwealth and British titles in order to contest the Irish title was both a positive psychological boost for Fury and also a shrewd piece of business.

Britain's Olympic bronze medallist David Price reacted furiously, claiming that Fury vacated the titles to avoid him. 'He's a coward,' he blasted.

Two more wins in 2012 saw Fury add to his titles. In July he met Vinny Maddalone to dispute the WBO Inter-Continental title but not before he and his team had a bizarre run-in with the Dutch police while travelling to his training camp near the Belgian border. Arrested at gunpoint, Tyson and his crew were brought to a police station and quizzed by detectives searching for a murder-robbery gang. After eleven hours, they were released but their clothing was retained for forensic examination. 'They apologized and gave us flip-flops and paper sheets to wrap ourselves in so we could walk back to the car,' explained Tyson. 'We got our clothes back three days later.'

Fury duly stopped Maddalone in the fifth round. By now he was telling anyone who'd listen, 'I'm going to be the first Irish heavyweight champion of the world.'

In December he was back in Belfast for a WBC title eliminator against Kevin 'Kingpin' Johnson, an American who'd lost just two of thirty-one fights. Johnson was adamant. 'I'll beat Fury so bad he'll want to retire.' The fight went the twelve rounds. All three judges scored Fury the clear winner.

As the new year dawned, coach Peter was satisfied with his nephew's progress. 'Tyson is developing into a serious world-class fighter,' he said. 'The hard work's been done. He just needs polishing. We're hoping to take a world title in 2013.' His timeline seemed optimistic. Tyson was still rough around the edges. True, he'd lost the flabby belly, his footwork had improved and his punching had more poise and purpose but, coming from such a low-skills base, there was still plenty of room for improvement.

II

For an IBF title eliminator with Steve 'USS' Cunningham in New York in April, Peter and his promoter Mick Hennessy set up training camp in Ottawa-Gatineau in Canada. Things didn't go according to plan as Tyson quickly knocked out two of his four sparring partners and new fighters had to be found. Peter was upbeat. 'Tyson is hard to prepare for,' he said. 'Because everything he does is different in every fight.'

Peter wasn't at ringside in the Theatre at Madison Square Garden for the Cunningham fight. A prison record resulted in the denial of a US visa. Without the calming influence of the zen master in his camp, Tyson dialled up the rhetoric. Unabashed, he taunted the former cruiserweight champion at the pre-fight press conference, asking how much it would cost to have his Twitter account details printed on the soles of Cunningham's boots. ''Cos I want to pick up more followers around the world,' he explained. 'I hit him. He hits the floor. Tyson Fury hits New York.' On a roll, Fury continued, 'I'm going to retire you Steve. I'm tall, dark, handsome and super-sexy. I'm the best fighter on the planet. I'm going to hurt you, seriously.'

Fury's brashness antagonized many neutral American observers. They cheered loudly when, early in the second round, Fury naively left himself open to a powerful overhand right, which put him on the floor. But the big man clung on and from there used his forty-four pounds weight advantage to wear his opponent down. In the fifth round, referee Eddie Cotton deducted a point from Fury and cautioned him for use of the head. It became a brawl with Fury spoiling, holding and liberally using his forearm. In the seventh, he connected with a series of uppercuts that sent Cunningham crashing to the canvas.

In celebration, Fury entertained the crowd with a croaky blast of 'Keep It Between the Lines', which had been an early hit for country star Ricky Van Shelton. 'And I said, daddy, oh daddy, are you sure I know how. Are you sure that I'm ready to drive this car now ...' At the time, his father John was two years into an eleven-year prison sentence which had been handed down by Judge Michael Henshell at Manchester Crown Court. Former bare-knuckle fighter 'Gypsy' John pleaded for leniency, saying, 'I'm worried about my son. His boxing career is on the line.'

The court heard how a twelve-year grudge, which began over a bottle of beer while on holiday in Cyprus, erupted at a car auction when John (46) confronted Oathie Sykes (44) saying, 'I'm the best man here in the auction, I'm the best man in the country. What about me and you finishing that fight?' Fury grabbed Sykes in a headlock. 'He was pushing his hand in my face,' Sykes testified. 'It was his finger, it went in my eye, in the corner and he wouldn't stop, he was like gouging and poking and twisting and poking, all of a sudden I heard this sound, a clicking like, a popping noise and when he took his hand away I realized blood was in his hand, a lot of blood.'

'After that he tried to take my other eye,' claimed Sykes. 'He tried to blind me, sir, not once. He tried to blind me, twice.'

In his defence, John claimed it had been 'a fair fight between Travelling people' but that Sykes' family members had joined in. In his view, the injury occurred accidentally when, having bitten him, the victim pulled his head away. 'If I was going to do what he said I done to him it would have been a lot worse than that,' he argued. 'I'm a not a feather-duster man.' The judge found Fury's evidence 'entirely unconvincing' and, with a distraught 22-year-old Tyson viewing from the gallery, imposed a custodial sentence.

Without uncle Peter in his corner for the Cunningham fight, Tyson reverted to his earlier gung-ho style. Disappointed, Peter tweeted, 'That wasn't him last night – I give it two out of ten. This is what happens when I'm not there. He did nothing of what we've been doing in the gym. Flat-footed. No upper-body movement. Tyson is temperamental and needs guidance otherwise he goes in to fight.' Tyson looked a long way from being a credible world-title challenger.

When Peter came to Dundalk three months later for son Hughie's fight on the undercard of Anthony Fitzgerald and Eamonn O'Kane's BUI Irish national middleweight headliner, he was in a more positive frame of mind. A high-profile fight was on the cards for Fury with David Haye. In 2011 Haye had lost over twelve rounds to Wladimir Klitschko so this would be a good yardstick to measure Fury's progress. Haye possessed a deadly punch that had dispatched twenty-four of his opponents.

As his son Hughie limbered up in the changing room under his father's penetrating gaze, the bristle-haired coach told me, 'These are all dangerous 50-50 fights now. David Haye has explosive power, good boxing skills, good movement. Tyson's on a world level. I've said we want the 50-50 fights. David Haye's a world-class fighter. But Tyson's ready.'

In his seventh fight of the year, eighteen-year-old Hughie had a fifth-round win in Dundalk. Peter indicated his son was a work in progress, saying, 'We're not interested in quick KOs. I want Hughie in difficult fights. He needs to get the rounds to learn how to survive.'

Tyson was there that night too. He climbed into the ring after Hughie's win to serenade a bemused crowd. Over the years, I'd been in Tyson's orbit on a few occasions. We'd shared a few pleasantries after fights or at press events. He'd seemed reserved and tentative, an outsider. A tall youth (at the age of fourteen he was already 6 ft 5-in), he was finding his place in society.

When he arrived at the venue in Dundalk, the now 6 ft 9 in 25-year-old giant responded favourably to well-wishers seeking autographs or selfies. As he joined a group of us, a photographer merrily snapping away called Tyson to stand beside me for a quick photo-op. Tyson obliged but, as he adopted the traditional boxer pose of making a fist for the camera, something mercurial happened.

In a flash, horse-nostrilled, mouth quivering and bug-eyed, his great hulk towered over me. This warp spasm display went way beyond the customary knuckle-flashing act of faux aggression that seems obligatory in these situations. I'd worked with enough talented actors to realize this wasn't play-acting. The man's eyes revealed something I hadn't witnessed in him before. As fleeting as sudden cloud-shadow darkening the moon, I glimpsed the presence of demons. For a hair-trigger instant, I felt the fear. Here was a human engaged in a struggle with a supernatural force. What dark world existed in the depths of those eyes? Was it one he'd spoken of to journalists, where a child had witnessed his parents screaming and hitting each other? The one where just four of his mother's fourteen pregnancies survived? The one that believed the devil is strong and the end near?

There was danger in that moment. Danger that Fury might succumb to the Serpent of Evil with its venom of hatred, destruction and despair. Danger a sinister Mr Hyde might disprove the jovial Dr Jekyll's public image. The entertaining man-child afforded me sight of a manic, knife-edge persona. I'd heard about his bingeing on junk food, bouts of depression and flashes of suicidal thoughts but assumed it was exaggerated. However, in this instant, a heartbeat away from tipping into full-on berserker state, I came to understand this family man's volcanic capacity to become an unpredictable natural hazard. A real and present risk to others and, more realistically, to himself.

Given the unstable nature of the raw material he was working with, it was evident that Peter was doing a remarkable job shaping Tyson's erratic talent. Impressed by the coach's gravitas, stoicism and cold-eyed pragmatism, I'd described Peter in print as 'a man set to become the Alex Ferguson of British boxing'.

My assessment of his man-management and coaching skills was made before I learned that Peter had previously been branded 'Mr Big' in an illegal amphetamine distribution business in the north of England, a vast criminal enterprise with an international reach, and had been jailed for ten years. Or that he'd received a further two-year sentence in 2008 for money-laundering and had been forced to pay almost £1 million to the authorities. Clearly Peter was someone with a logistical brain and the ability to get things done. During his involvement in the sharp edge of criminality, Tyson's uncle had encountered many who were to die horrible deaths or mysteriously disappear. Against this stressful environment, where life and death situations were, as he described them, 'normal procedure', coaching errant boxers seemed kindergarten stuff. Somehow Peter had gone from being 'one of Britain's most feared crime lords' to a venerable philosopher of boxing.

Despite his busy schedule, Peter obligingly took my calls. In a training camp in Belgium ahead of the proposed David Haye fight, he explained, 'There are no distractions. We're strictly business.' With fifteen KOs in twenty-one wins, his 25-year-old nephew was still unbeaten. Unfortunately, injuries forced Haye to pull the fight. And a rescheduled event.

In February 2014, after ten months without competitive action, an impatient Tyson knocked out Joey Abell in London. Apart from an arson attack on cars at his home when Tyson was away in training camp, 2014 had begun well. However, tragedy lay ahead. Tyson's uncle Hughie, his coach early in his career, who'd been in his corner for the Derek Chisora fight in 2011, broke his leg and suffered head injuries in a freak accident while unhitching a caravan. A blood clot developed and caused a heart attack. While Hughie lay in an intensive care ward, Tyson's wife, Paris, had a miscarriage. In October, Hughie died. The postponed European title fight with Derek Chisora went ahead the following month.

III

Some would say that the influence of the Situationist International reached its zenith during the punk rock era in the 1970s when theories forwarded by a group of social revolutionaries in the 1950s found expression in the sloganeering and designs of a wave of anarchic bands intent on challenging established norms. It's unlikely that Tyson Fury was familiar with the thinking of French philosopher Guy Debord or the principle of *détournement* – subverting the system and hijacking media culture. But when Tyson appeared at a Derek Chisora fight press conference with his mouth crudely taped in protest at having been fined £15,000 by British Boxing Board of Control, it looked like he'd either been reading Debord's *The Society of the Spectacle* or leafing through Sex Pistols' designer Jamie Reid's old sketchbooks.

The governing body had fined Fury for an intemperate outburst on a televised conference. 'I don't give a fuck how many women and children are in the audience,' he thundered. 'I'm in fight mode. Kill mode. If you don't like the station, change the channel, bitch. This is my show. I do what I want.'

By then, Tyson was adept at making headlines on the sports pages. He was also reaching a mass audience on Twitter where he branded himself 'the Gypsy King' and had developed a questionable gift for taking trash-talking to new depths of toxicity.

The first fight with Chisora had gone the distance. Switching to a southpaw stance on his coach Peter's instructions in the second fight, Fury dominated proceedings, controlled the tempo and picked off Chisora as he came forward. While Chisora's increasingly disfigured face showed the sustained punishment he was taking, Fury didn't overextend himself. 'Play with him like a cat playing with a ball,' advised Peter. 'Confuse him. Don't rush into anything.' The fact the contestants were wearing gloves added a veneer of civility to what was otherwise a violent and barbarous confrontation.

The fight ended prematurely when Chisora's corner refused to allow him to continue after the tenth round. Promoter Mick Hennessy was happy to announce that Fury was now mandatory challenger for Wladimir Klitschko, saying, 'The big fight's on.'

World-title fights are a big deal. Once upon a time, there was one true heavyweight world champion. Over time, various regulatory bodies sprang up or broke away and sanctioned their own champions. A title fight for the WBA (World Boxing Association), IBF (International Boxing Federation), WBO (World Boxing Organization), IBO (International Boxing Organization), Lineal and The Ring heavyweight titles ranked as the biggest deal of all.

Wladimir Klitschko, dubbed 'Dr Steelhammer', had dominated the heavyweight scene for a decade. He'd fought in a record-breaking twenty-seven world-title fights. It took months for a deal to be completed. In the meantime, Fury kept busy with a fight in February 2015 against Christian Hammer. The Hamburg-based Romanian hard man had taken a few notable scalps but he lasted just until round eight against Fury's clinical wrecking plan. Fury believed he had God on his side. 'Without God, what have we got?' he asked. 'I'm battling within good and evil every single day of my life.'

The build-up to the world-title fight presented Fury with a global platform and he responded with a series of extraordinary lurid trash-talking outbursts. Dressed as Batman in London, he proceeded to insult the champion. 'Tyson, at times, is not stable in the mind,' said uncle Peter. 'That's what makes him such a good fighter because he's unbalanced.'

Fury's pronouncements became more extreme and controversial. He told sports journalist Oliver Holt: 'There are only three things that need to be accomplished before the devil comes home. One of them is homosexuality being legal in countries, one of them is abortion and the other is paedophilia. Who would've thought in the 50s and early 60s that the first two would be legalised.' Later in the interview he told Holt, 'To be honest with you, I know Klitschko is a devil-worshipper.'

'Wladimir, and all these rock stars and singers and these famous people, it's common knowledge that they are all involved in a cult group of Satan worshippers,' he continued. Klitschko's response to Fury's theories was diplomatic. 'He is bipolar,' he said. 'He has mental issues, for sure.' Although Tyson had talked himself into becoming the most reviled boxer in Britain, it was difficult not to see him as a court jester, a self-created Lord of Misrule.

The fight that went ahead in the 55,000 seater Esprit Arena, Düsseldorf, on 27 November 2015, wasn't one for the thrill-seekers. But it was a fascinating duel; the experienced champion versus the unpredictable upstart. Remember the old Cus D'Amato adage, 'Fighting is 90 per cent mental and 10 per cent physical'? The mind games employed by both sides beforehand ensured this would be both a masterclass in tactics and a supreme test of character.

The psychological warfare wasn't confined to Fury's foul-mouthed outbursts. The Klitschko camp deployed a few tricks of their own, including presenting Fury with gloves which proved unsuitable and also layering sheets of spongy foam under the ring canvas to sap his energy. Threatening to cancel the fight, Peter Fury had a new floor laid just hours before the doors opened. There was also a stand-off when the Fury camp discovered Klitschko had his hands wrapped without official supervision. The challenger had an important psychological victory when Klitschko had to have his gloves and tapes removed and redone with a Fury representative present.

From the opening bell, Fury sought to make his four-inch reach advantage count. His jittery, taunting approach dissuaded Klitschko from committing to an anything decisive. With Peter advising him to use the double jab, Fury displayed nimble footwork to stay out of range and land the more eye-catching shots.

Switching to southpaw in the third round, Fury teased Klitschko, inviting him to punch by putting his hands behind his back and sashaying in front of him like a cobra judging when to strike. Heading into the fifth round, the mongoose-and-snake game continued. Fury was landing the jab. The champion's thunderous right hand was his concealed weapon. Fury appeared happy to dance in and out of range. A clash of heads resulted in a cut under Klitschko's left eye.

By the end of round six, there was very little between them. But Fury had done more than survive. He'd frustrated Klitschko who appeared hesitant. That frustration was to increase when Fury inflicted another cut, this one above Klitschko's left eye. By now, Fury was benefiting from his height and reach advantage. Klitschko, who had won sixty-four fights, hadn't lost in eleven years. In the eighth round, he began to land some of the unfussy shots that had worn down lesser opponents.

Fury's eccentric style seemed to mesmerize Klitschko. But in the ninth, the champion rocked Fury by landing a laser right on his jaw. Quickly pulling himself together, Fury retaliated, catching Klitschko with a sweeping left. By the tenth, it was obvious that Fury's unpredictable roughhouse style presented a riddle Klitschko was unable to solve.

The eleventh round brought some explosive action with Fury throwing wild punches from awkward angles. The confused Klitschko eventually got caught by a series of solid lefts. There was blood seeping from a cut over his right eye as the referee cautioned Fury and deducted him a point for punching the back of Klitschko's head.

That left Klitschko just three minutes to save his multiple belts. And he fought with a savage intent that had been absent for most of the fight. Would the judges be swayed by the home fighter's record and reputation? As the scores were being tallied, Fury's father, John, recently released from jail having served four years of his eleven-year sentence, climbed into the ring to embrace his son. Tyson prayed.

MC Michael Buffer called out, 'We go to the score cards. César Ramos scores it 115 to 112. The same score from Raul Caiz Sr, 115 to 112. And Ramon Cerdan scores it 116 to 111. All three scores, for the winner by unanimous decision ...' The full message was lost in the roars from the Fury entourage. They'd heard enough. Tyson Fury was champion of the world.

With the deposed champion looking stunned, Fury serenaded his wife with a few verses of the Aerosmith ballad 'I Don't Want to Miss a Thing'.

Peter Fury had masterminded Tyson's remarkable victory and haul of world-championship belts. The victory had come against the odds despite Peter having calmly outlined his plans to me in a Dundalk changing room two years earlier when he predicted with steel-eyed certainty, 'It's Tyson's time.'

Crowned King of the World, Fury failed to cope with the pressures of celebrity. Overcome by depression and self-loathing, he hit the bottle and snorted cocaine. His weight ballooned to twenty-eight stone. Adding to his troubles was the revelation in June 2016 that tests, carried out in February 2015, showed positive for the banned steroid nandrolone. He denied the charge. In September, Tyson tested positive for cocaine. The following month, his boxing licence was suspended.

In 2017, hit with a two-year ban for doping, he claimed it was because he'd eaten uncastrated wild boar. The ban was backdated. After two years in his personal wilderness, he began to get his act together. When he re-emerged, he had dropped his uncle Peter as coach and split from dedicated promoter Mick Hennessy. Tyson completely overhauled his business arrangements and, two years after defeating Klitschko, signed a new deal with MTK Global in November 2017, joining a growing client list that included Billy Joe Saunders, Carl Frampton and Michael Conlan. 'We feel honoured he has chosen MTK Global to help guide him through what promises to be the most exciting phase of his illustrious career,' announced MTK's Paul Gibson, welcoming Fury to the company, which had been founded a few years earlier as MGM (Macklin's Gym Marbella) by Matthew Macklin and Daniel Kinahan, whose suspect family business empire was said to have been structured along the lines of the Italian mafia and was the focus of expanding investigations by Europol and other international crime agencies. While it was acknowledged that Macklin had no involvement in organized crime, MGM had been rebranded using the boxer's professional nickname, 'Mack the Knife'.

'It's fantastic news for the sport,' said Gibson, the company's global director. 'In many people's eyes Tyson is still the man in the heavyweight division.' The world champion was now being advised and guided by his new friend, Daniel Kinahan.

10
TORNADO

*'This is the acid test. I beat this guy and look good doing it, that's me
on the way to becoming world champion.'*
Matthew Macklin

FIGHTERS FOREVER STRIVE TO create a stronger, more resilient,
more efficient version of themselves. Some even implement demanding
psychological practices – cognitive restructuring, functional analysis,
mindfulness and so on – in their quest for self-improvement. For many,
confronting their frailties on a daily basis can be the toughest fight of
all. For some, time can prove more cruel than combat. There is no Senior
Tour for boxers. But age isn't always an impediment for musicians. The
Rolling Stones' drummer Charlie Watts, who died aged eighty in 2021,
was still laying down the beat until shortly before his death. When, having
reconvened after decades apart, I recorded with the old band, a lifetime's
experience enabled me to pare performance down to the essentials and still
pack the requisite punch. Too often, when a fighter has mastered much
of what there is to know about their profession, time ties their bootlaces
together and laughs in their face.

I

Less than four years into his pro career, Matthew Macklin won the vacant Irish middleweight title on the night of his twenty-third birthday in 2005. A fifth-round knockout took his record to 14-1. With a mother, Kathleen, from Tipperary and a father, Seamus, from Roscommon, Macklin, born in Birmingham, had spent enough time in Ireland to play inter-county hurling for Tipperary at all levels up to Under 21.

Four wins later, for his British super-welterweight title bout with Jamie Moore, Macklin struggled to make weight. The fight, which resembled two desperate men engaged in a death struggle in a phone box, had been ferocious. Coming to in an ambulance Macklin's first thought was, 'Am I dying?'

That occasion was the first time Macklin met Dublin boxing fan Daniel Kinahan, son of convicted drug dealer Christy Kinahan, the boss of a growing international crime group that came to be known as the Kinahan cartel. Won over by Kinahan's collegiate personality and enthusiasm for boxing, and undeterred by his family background or criminal acquaintances, Macklin and the Dubliner became friends. They set up Macklin's Gym Marbella together, a venture which provided Kinahan with a bridgehead in the sport. Signing more and more fighters, MGM became an attractive one-stop shop for many aspiring champions, providing management and promotional services as well as state-of-the-art training facilities.

With Brian Peters as his manager, Macklin began to fight more regularly in Ireland. For nine years, from when he KO'd Darren Rhodes in Dublin in August 2007, Macklin took us on a warrior journey, illuminated by some of the most thrilling and bloody attractions sport could devise.

Back in Dublin in October 2007 to fight Alessio Furlan, Macklin had Ricky Hatton working his corner alongside trainer Billy Graham.

Hatton could be heard above the din. 'Hook off the screw shot,' he shouted during the eighth round. At ringside, I thought Macklin hadn't heard Hatton when suddenly he unleashed a damaging two-fisted assault, which helped clinch a win by stoppage. Later, I asked him about Hatton's advice. 'There are a lot of things you don't hear because you're concentrating on the guy you're fighting,' he said. 'But I heard that and thought, "Yeah, maybe it's there." Ricky's never far off the mark.'

Two months later, Macklin was with his friend in Las Vegas for Hatton's fight with Floyd Mayweather. The fight got the full-on promo treatment in Sin City with giant plasma screens along the Strip blasting out ads, casinos doing a brisk trade in Hatton–Mayweather merchandise and HBO screening a four-part documentary 24/7. Over 30,000 fight fans flew in to support Hatton and over a million in the UK paid to watch it on cable TV.

When I spoke to Macklin in Vegas, he was buzzing. 'It's big time,' he said in awe. 'It makes you think, "This is what I want to achieve."' Macklin was ambitious, realistic and pragmatic, with an analytical business brain. He'd studied law at university. 'You can be clever at exams but not necessarily a clever boxer,' he said, explaining Hatton's talent for disguising his punches. 'He's a clever fighter.'

Macklin watched a parade of superstars, from Sugar Ray Leonard to David Beckham, visit Hatton's dressing room to wish him well. Part of his friend's ring-walk entourage, he watched the officials in action. He soaked it up and filed it away. 'This is where I want to be,' he told me. When Elvis Presley was King of Las Vegas, he had a logo on his private Convair 880 Jet with the letters 'TCB' set in a lightning bolt. The logo stood for 'taking care of business'. Las Vegas was the equivalent of finishing school for Macklin.

Back in Dublin in March to headline at the National Stadium against the experienced Arizona-based Mexican Luis Ramón Campas, Macklin had a new coach in tow, legendary American fighter Buddy McGirt. 'I always like the way Buddy McGirt got Arturo Gatti boxing more and got him back to using his jab,' he said. 'I had neglected my long-range skills.'

A former world champion, Campas had won 91 of 102 fights. He'd cut John Duddy to ribbons in New York eighteen months previously. Campas had fought the best. 'They will see a real fight,' he predicted. 'I guarantee that.'

Macklin had success with his jab. Happy to trade, 'Yori Boy' Campas showed power in his shots, leaving a neat bruise under Macklin's left eye. At the final bell, referee Emile Tiedt scored it 98-95 for Macklin.

The British middleweight title was now in Macklin's sights. Reigning champion was Wayne Elcock, also from Birmingham. With Joe Gallagher now in his corner, Macklin combined skill with intensity and caught Elcock with a right over the top in the third round that rattled him. A ferocious follow-up onslaught halted proceedings. 'I'm proud to be British champion but that's not my level,' Macklin declared. 'I'm world class.'

Targeting the vacant EBU European middleweight belt next, Macklin met former European champion Amin Asikainen (26-2, 16 KOs). Hatton, who'd signed Macklin to a promotions deal, believed his friend was en route to a world-title fight. Given the Finnish fighter's heavy hands, this promised to be a humdinger. No one, Asikainen included, foresaw the expertly timed explosive left hook that Macklin delivered to his opponent's jaw in round one. While he made it to his feet, Asikainen looked bewildered. He was shortly sent crashing with a right hook. The referee stopped the fight. 'Now we can gain some momentum,' said Macklin bullishly.

II

'The next four months are going to be the most important in Matthew's career,' said Brian Peters in December. 'He's ranked eight with the WBC, four with the WBO and five with the IBF.' Before undertaking a mandatory defence of his European title, Macklin had to deal with Uruguayan champion Rafael Sosa Pintos. 'He's looking for a shot at the middleweight title,' said Macklin. 'He's rough and he's tough. I'll have to nail him to the floor to stop him.'

Helping motivate Macklin was the fact that two other Irish middleweights, Andy Lee and John Duddy, had caught the attention of the public. When asked by pundit Mick Dowling how he rated himself by comparison, Macklin replied, 'I always had more experience than the two of them (but) I was probably in their shadows. In the last eighteen months some people are starting to say that I'm the best of the three.' The rivalry was a spur to his ambition.

Macklin was on the cusp of a lucrative period in his career. A sell-out crowd packed the National Stadium for a blistering scrap with the Uruguayan champion that went the full ten rounds. I wasn't at ringside for Macklin's triumphant return to Dublin. To paraphrase Ronnie Wood of the Rolling Stones, I had my own album to do. My band was playing a comeback concert thirty years after calling it a day in 1980. I'd rehearsed for a couple of weeks until everything was shipshape and then arranged for an understudy to deputize for me on tour while I'd confine myself to TV, radio gigs and admin duties. I'd secretly arranged for a set of framed platinum discs for record sales of over a million to surprise my bandmates with onstage at the O2 in Dublin. With the band rocking the house, I left my seat beside the mixing desk and headed backstage where there was a TV in the catering area. I grabbed a free beer and pulled up a seat.

I invited the man on security to join me, saying we could both keep an eye on the corridor. It soon became apparent that he knew his stuff. We watched approvingly as Macklin negated Pintos' high guard and spoiling tactics by landing a crashing right hook under his ribcage, sending him to the floor at the end of the second round. Knockdowns followed in the fifth (a pulverizing right hook to the ear) and ninth rounds (a body shot, which Pintos protested was low). As we discussed the action, I discovered that my companion was none other than Christy Rock, father of Jim, the four-weight Irish champion who'd retired after a win on the Bernard Dunne world-title card in March. When the fight ended, I rushed downstairs, donned a makeshift Santa outfit and surprised my bandmates as they came on stage to play an encore. In front of an audience that included Nobel Prize-winner Seamus Heaney and Def Leppard singer Joe Elliott, I made the presentation. 'TCB.' Taking Care of Business. Job done, Elvis-style. Everyone seemed pleased. Some were emotional.

Meanwhile, at the National Stadium, our old stomping ground in the 1970s, Macklin's 99-88 points win came at a cost. A cut on his left eyelid that required three stitches would delay his return to competitive action. He also ended the fight with swollen hands and badly bruised knuckles. 'You get bumps and bruises. It's not a tickling contest,' said Macklin. Coach Joe Gallagher said, 'I think he's ready to go for a world title.'

During the build-up, Gallagher had appeared thrilled to be involved in a headline show in Ireland. He'd known Macklin since he was twelve years old. Something the Mancunian shared with Macklin was being the son of Irish parents. 'My parents are from Sligo,' revealed Gallagher. 'Gurteen, to be exact.' Raised on the sprawling Benchill estate in Wythenshawe, Manchester, with four siblings, he persuaded his father to take him to the local boxing club. He began boxing competitively when he was eleven and fought in tournaments all over England. Much has been written about the contribution of people of Irish descent to culture in Britain. In his book *Irish Blood, English Heart*, Cambridge media studies lecturer Sean Campbell writes about second-generation Irish Mancunian musicians Morrissey and Johnny Marr (born Maher) and the Gallagher brothers, Noel and Liam. The connections to Ireland proved strong for many other musicians including Elvis Costello, Shane MacGowan and Kevin Rowland. I once drove through narrow Co. Cork roads with John Lydon. I thought he was joking, when we turned down an old boreen and parked outside an isolated cottage. But there was no mistaking the warmth of the exchange between the punk rocker and his elderly uncle in the countryside that sunny afternoon.

In 1984 I called unannounced to the O'Dowd family home in south London. Culture Club singer Boy George, whose breakthrough hit was 'Do You Really Want to Hurt Me?' had been insulted by the town council in Thurles, Co. Tipperary, and I wanted to discuss the matter with his father, Jeremiah, whose family came from the area. Jeremiah wasn't at home but I was greeted by George's brother Gerald, an amateur boxer whose one pro fight was on a card that featured George Foreman. Jeremiah was coaching in the club and Gerald would have him phone me later. To my surprise, Jeremiah (Jerry) rang and, to my even greater surprise, when we'd discussed the matter on hand, enthusiastically engaged me in a conversation about European champion Barry McGuigan, who had six KO wins in 1984, two of them title fights. Jerry was convinced that McGuigan would become world champion. His expert analysis of McGuigan concluded with the detail that convinced him most. "E 'as fast 'ands,' he declared excitedly. 'Fast 'ands.'

For two centuries, Ireland's biggest export was its people, creating an extensive global diaspora that prides itself in a carefully curated set of characteristics not least the concept of the Fighting Irish. More recently, the emergence of inward migration has begun to enrich Irish society in ways previously unimagined.

III

While working on building sites with his father, Joe Gallagher still found time to get involved in coaching. A diligent student, his application was forensic. In 2011 he was training Macklin in Billy Graham's old gym in Denton. Having staged two successful European title defences, Macklin was preparing for a WBA world super-middleweight title fight with holder Felix Sturm in Cologne in June. Macklin was totally switched on.

'A world-title shot is what I've dreamed about all my life,' he said. 'I'll be bringing a different intensity.'

With the central heating system simulating tropical conditions and a sound system blaring out a nerve-jangling techno soundtrack at maximum volume, conversation had to be shouted. As Macklin went through six high-tempo rounds with Quebecois super-middleweight Sébastien Demers, flown in to give Macklin a taste of the Sturm style, Joe studied the exchanges as if monitoring a chess match. Nothing escaped his eye as he barked instructions.

'Finish strong.'

'Don't let him recover.'

'Composure!'

'Don't complicate it. Hit what you can see.'

When Demers, bruised and bleeding, began to flag, Gallagher introduced super-middleweight Paul Smith. Just as in a theatre when the audience senses a unique drama unfolding, a hush fell over the gym. Fresh and energetic, Smith attempted to bully Macklin but, despite giving away weight advantage, the contender was having none of it. This was a ding-dong scrap that people would pay good money to watch. Afterwards, while a perspiring Macklin was set to work on a speed bag, I pressed Gallagher to assess Macklin's progress. 'He's more mature,' he said. 'His shot selection is much better.'

Having coached British and European champions, Gallagher was as keen to win the world title as his client. 'We're going out there to bust his jaw,' he vowed. 'This is Matthew's moment.' Having watched Paul McCloskey, Willie Casey and Brian Magee all come up short in recent world-title bids, the two-time European champion was confident that he could go one better in Cologne. 'The way to open up somebody who has a good defence is to punch in combinations and not be predictable with your attacks,' he explained. 'His jab is his main weapon. It's a sickening punch.'

Macklin was the underdog but as someone once pointed out, 'Nothing wins a fight like throwing punches.' Macklin impressed in the early rounds, turning on the pressure with body shots that controlled Sturm. The tide turned noticeably over the last few rounds, with Sturm imposing himself and landing some eye-watering uppercuts in the tenth. Macklin withstood the barrage. Sturm's late surge didn't seem enough to deprive Macklin of a famous victory. But, fighting his tenth title defence in his home city, Sturm had an unspoken advantage. Matthew celebrated at the final bell. One judge gave the fight to Macklin 113-115. The other two went with Sturm 116-112. Despite the German TV commentators having him winning by four rounds, Macklin was denied. Sturm looked relieved.

The fight had been broadcast live in the US, including on a big screen in Times Square. In New York, Lou DiBella signed Macklin to a promotions deal saying, 'He has a claim at being the second-best middleweight in the world. One thing is for sure – you'll never see Matthew Macklin in a bad fight. Ever.' DiBella envisaged a clash between Macklin and Andy Lee. As promoter of lineal middleweight world champion Sergio Martínez, he had other thrilling options.

Argentina's Martínez had been stripped of his WBC title when he opted to fight an unbeaten challenger rather than the mandatory contestant. Positioning himself for a title fight, Macklin agreed to fight the man regarded as the best of the lot for the newly created Diamond middleweight belt, a title obligingly devised by the business-savvy WBC. The fight was set for St Patrick's Day 2012.

At thirty-seven, Martínez was eight years older than Macklin. But he had a three-inch reach advantage and skills that helped him to forty-eight wins in fifty-two fights. 'This is it,' said Macklin. 'This is for the World No. 1 spot. I don't believe he'll be able to cope with the intensity I bring to the ring.'

When fighters build themselves up, physically and psychologically, for the biggest test of their career, where, after years of sacrifice and effort, victory is expected to ensure fame and financial independence, defeat can be devastating.

There was a lot for Macklin to unpack in the immediate aftermath of his eleventh-round subjugation in Madison Square Garden. He'd disrupted the veteran's composure with his aggression and had dominated rounds in the middle of the fight before throwing a powerful overhand right, which unbalanced Martínez and resulted in an eight count. From there, Martínez drew on reserves of gumption, guile and big-fight experience as he strove to take back control with a ramrod jab and explosive lefts. Overeager, Macklin took risks which the savvy Martínez exploited in the eleventh round. Macklin beat the count when floored by a heavy left towards the end of the round but Martínez set about him with a vengeance and put him down again. Macklin got up for a second time as the bell sounded. In his corner, Buddy McGirt had seen enough. He made the call to end it. Afterwards he explained, 'He was starting to get hit with clean shots. So why take a chance for three minutes? You live to fight another day. He fought a hell of a fight, better than anyone thought he would.' While those at ringside believed Macklin had been outclassed by the best middleweight in the world, Macklin felt he contributed to his own downfall. 'I could have played it safer,' he said. 'But I was here to win, not just to take part.'

Describing Martínez as 'a freak of nature', promoter Lou DiBella praised Macklin. 'He proved he's the second- or third-best middleweight in the world.' Such an endorsement looked set to translate into further big pay days. In September, when Martínez defeated Julio César Chávez Jr for the WBC world title in Las Vegas, Macklin appeared on the undercard, knocking out Joachim Alcine in the first round.

Macklin was a contender. He was box office. He was earning big bucks but he wanted a word title. In April DiBella and Tom Loeffler strode into Gallaghers Steakhouse in midtown Manhattan to publicly announce what insiders had been speculating on for weeks. Matthew Macklin would fight Gennady Golovkin at Foxwoods Resort Casino on 29 June for the WBA and IBO world middleweight titles. Everyone agreed this could be a classic. And by that they meant a blistering, bloody display of aggression and brutality. I asked Macklin how he rated 'Triple G' by comparison to Martínez. 'He's a good ring general,' he ventured. 'An all-round complete fighter really. He can box. He can punch. Golovkin is probably more of a scary proposition – a bit of a Mike Tyson-type guy – but he's hit-able and I can punch hard too. I'm very confident about this fight now.'

Triple G was boxing's hottest property. The Kazakh fighter had blazed an unbeaten trail through the ranks, knocking out twenty-two of his twenty-six opponents. But, Macklin's twenty KOs in twenty-nine wins wasn't too shabby either. While Golovkin was being avoided by many, the underdog was prepared to take his chances. 'I'm not going to turn down a world-title shot,' he explained. 'It's the bird in the hand,' mused manager Brian Peters, weighing the risk. 'With a win, Matthew could become one of the biggest stars in the sport.'

Having trained in his own gym in Marbella, where he could relax at night strolling by the harbour, Macklin was coming on strong. 'I want to go back to the era of Graziano and Zale,' he told me. 'I watched all those old-school fights. I fought Martínez. I fought Sturm. I'd love to fight Chávez. People think Golovkin is probably the best. So it's an honour to fight him.'

A lethal sniper with an explosive punch, Golovkin eased into round one, sneaking a damaging jab to Macklin's head and, as Macklin attempted to orchestrate an assault, landing a powerful right hand, which sent him toppling onto the ropes. The second round offered little respite for Macklin as GGG kept the pressure on, gliding around the ring as if operating on radar, dropping tactical missile strikes. One opened a cut over Macklin's left eye. In the third round, clearly frustrated, Macklin reverted to type. He fought back, unleashing an array of body shots and head shots. But Golovkin kept pushing forward.

Then came the moment of alchemy which dissolved Macklin's defences. As Matthew moved along the ropes, Golovkin threw three innocuous-looking punches. The first two, a left and a right, hit Macklin's high guard. The third punch, a left, curled sharply behind his right elbow, blasting his liver. It was as if someone had pulled the canvas from under Macklin's feet as he keeled over. Like the crippling spasm of sudden onset kidney stones, there's no escape from the pain of such a shot. Knotted in agony, Macklin curled into the foetal position, writhing and stretching painfully. The referee counted ten. 'It was a perfectly placed shot,' said McGirt. 'You get hit with a body shot, there's nothing you can do about it.'

'It sounded like something cracked,' ventured Lou DiBella. X-rays revealed a fractured rib.

IV

After eight years working together, Macklin had switched from promoter Brian Peters to a new adviser, New York-based Anthony Catanzaro. Fourteen months after the bitter Triple G encounter, Macklin was set to headline in Dublin in August 2014. His opponent Jorge Sebastian Heiland, a southpaw from Buenos Aires, held the WBC International middleweight title. Macklin's ambition was undimmed. 'I've proved I'm world class,' he said. 'I want to be fighting for world titles.'

Life is what happens to you while you're busy making other plans, sang John Lennon shortly before he was shot dead.

Ahead of the Heiland fight, Macklin was training in the MGM gym in Spain with coach Jamie Moore who had retired from fighting in 2010 when the BBBofC expressed concern over a series of brain scans. Three weeks out from the fight, when Moore called to the home of Daniel Kinahan, a gunman stepped out of the shadows and fired five shots. One bullet went through Moore's left thigh. Another lodged in his right hip. Another hit his shoulder and a fourth grazed his wrist. Not the intended target, the coach was the victim of a botched gangland hit.

As he lay bleeding by the gates of the mansion, Moore remain calm and phoned for assistance. 'It all relates back to boxing and staying calm under pressure,' he reflected later. 'I could have easily panicked and stood up and I would have bled even more then.'

The casual manner in which the horror unfolded had elements of a B-movie film script. When Moore saw a figure wearing a grotesque rubber mask suddenly appear, he assumed it was a friend playing a prank. Then shots rang out. 'I was thinking, "This is it. I'm not going to see my kids,"' Jamie said later. 'I felt helpless and lonely, lying on a driveway at night bleeding to death.' Moore dialled 999 but didn't know the name of the road he was on. 'If you don't trace my phone, I'll die,' he instructed. 'I'm bleeding really badly.' Twenty-five minutes later he was in an ambulance, losing consciousness and pleading, 'Please don't let me die.'

Neither Moore nor Macklin had ever been linked to organized crime, facts that newspaper reports regularly clarified. Speculation in the media suggested the coach was mistaken for Daniel Kinahan, a claim Moore refuted, telling a British journalist, 'I've known Daniel eight months and never seen any problems. I've just seen him in the gym working with the lads. He's a great bloke and I cannot see that being the case.'

Heiland v Macklin was postponed. Having originally sold out the National Stadium in ten minutes, promoter Eddie Hearn switched the rescheduled fight to the 3Arena (formerly the O2).

Having come up short in three world-title shots, Macklin knew the importance of the Heiland showdown. 'This is the acid test,' he said. 'I beat this guy and look good doing it, I know that's me on the way to becoming world champion.' Eddie Hearn left no room for doubt. 'This is a 50–50 fight,' he said. 'I believe Matthew has got world titles in him, certainly world-title shots. But he has to beat Heiland. If he loses, the dream is over.'

As he strode towards the ring, flanked by brother Seamus and MGM business partner Kinahan, Macklin had his game face on. The rows nearest ringside were occupied by friends and associates of the Kinahans, many of them known to the police. Macklin looked prepared to confront the Furies and find an answer to the question, 'Can dreams be trusted?' The fighter from Argentina seemed a callow youth compared to a malevolent 32-year-old all too familiar with the ravages of trench warfare.

The pair snapped into action with Macklin measuring distance with his jab. Counterpunching, he had the better of the first two high-tempo rounds. Heiland grew busier. Livelier, he began beating Macklin to the punch. After four, it was even. Looking the more impressive, Heiland continued to take the fight to Macklin who was starting to look sluggish. With a creeping sense of dread, Macklin's supporters sensed something was wrong. Had he overtrained? Was he attempting Ali's rope-a-dope ruse? Or had three gruelling world-title fights run down his engine? Macklin was punching through heavy air as Heiland pressed forward, piston-pumping hurtful strikes and winning rounds. The tenth round held the key. Trapping Macklin in his own corner, Heiland executed a right-right-left rat-a-tat. It had the desired effect. As Macklin attempted to offer resistance with his left, BOOM! A right hand connected with his jaw. Like a farmer hearing the first corncrake of the year on the Shannon Callows, a distracted look flitted across Macklin's eyes and his face tilted wistfully towards a distant horizon before he slumped in a heap at the base of the corner post. It was all over.

Macklin's Promised Land was cruelly revealed as a mirage. The Fates had condemned the revered warrior to be grievously punished in front of his army. In the immediate aftermath of the battle, bruised and battered, Matthew struggled to understand what had gone wrong. Joe Gallagher reckoned he 'couldn't pull the trigger quick enough'. With pundits and punters asking if we'd seen the last of Macklin in the ring, he cut a forlorn figure heading for the changing room, the consoling hand of his crestfallen friend and business partner Daniel on his shoulder.

Knowing when to quit is often a difficult decision for fighters to make. Whether Macklin noticed it or not, there was a sense of the circus leaving town. On another night, in another jurisdiction, he could easily have been crowned champion against Sturm. And he'd been cursed to meet Golovkin, one of the biggest hitters in the division and the man with the greatest ring IQ, at the height of his powers. Martínez had gone on to become the first fighter to beat Julio César Chávez Jr and reclaim his world title in the process. Macklin's loss to him was no disgrace. In Dublin, beyond mere disappointment, there was a sense of sorrow in the stale air. This time, Macklin had been beaten by a man no one believed was world-champion material.

After months of reflection, Macklin said, 'The LaMottas and all of them, they lost many times and still went on and won a world title.' Hope springs eternal. He resumed business in 2015, perhaps finding a modicum of personal redemption in picking up the WBC International super-welterweight belt, a mere bauble to someone with world-title aspirations. In 2016 he beat Brian Rose on a majority decision for the vacant IBF Inter-Continental middleweight belt. It was vintage blood and thunder from the 'Tipperary Tornado' who got the win but not the belt. Macklin had missed weight for IBF's second-day weigh-in so the title remained vacant. Macklin had come to the end of the road.

11
KT

'There's no such thing as the perfect boxer.'
Katie Taylor

I

IN 2009, SIX MONTHS before the IOC decided to include women's
boxing as an Olympic sport, Team USA visited Ireland for a tournament
with Irish boxers. Eleven of the twelve bouts featured men. Katie Taylor
fought Queen Underwood in the one that didn't.

A former pipe-fitter from Seattle, Quanitta 'Queen' Underwood had
overcome greater adversity in life than a bout at Dublin's National Stadium.
Following an abusive and traumatic early childhood, Underwood's life was
spiralling out of control when, at nineteen, she discovered boxing. By the
time she fought Taylor, Underwood had been US champion for two years.
But she'd never met anyone as talented as her Irish opponent. Taylor was
in full effect, punching with precision and gliding out of range. Underwood
found it difficult to land a single shot on Taylor. As she sat on her stool after
the second round, Underwood struggled to hold back tears of frustration.
She seemed demoralized by how elusive Taylor was. The score cards revealed

that, having trailed 9-1 after round one, she was 22-2 behind going into the third round.

'Hustle Queen. Get in and work,' urged her coach. Queen wasn't a nobody. She'd boxed a weight above Taylor at the World Championships in China a few months previously. Spurred on by pride, she displayed much more aggression in the final round. Both boxers stood their ground. Taylor wasn't intimidated. Light on her feet, she unleashed a series of fast combinations that were devastating in their speed and accuracy. The fight ended 30-3. Remarkably, Taylor had taken just one clear punch in each round.

Taylor was already a boxing marvel. But she wasn't in the public eye. With her father, Pete, scheduling her overseas itinerary, she operated successfully outside the system. Billy Walsh, director of the Irish Boxing High Performance Unit, was in awe of her talent. 'Katie's a phenomenal athlete,' he told me. 'We've never had a boxer who's been twice World Champion and three-times European Champion. She is the best pound-per-pound boxer Ireland has ever produced.' Despite her world-champion status, Taylor was working on a snag list. She'd already had her nose broken at least three times and insisted, 'Every other girl in the world is getting better and better as well. So I have to keep improving.'

When Taylor met Underwood again in the semi-finals of the 2010 AIBA World Women's Boxing Championship finals, the American showed she had learned from her earlier experience. Combining strength and determination, Underwood's impressive performance had her 16-15 ahead with just thirteen seconds left in the bout. Taylor responded defiantly, scored three vital points and clinched victory at 18-16. In the final, Taylor outboxed Cheng Dong of China and became world champion for the third time. She was also voted Boxer of the Tournament.

By now, Taylor was being tipped as Ireland's brightest hope for a gold medal at the 2012 Olympic Games in London.

II

Taylor's London Olympic odyssey began with a first-round bye before she met Natasha Jonas (GB) in the quarter-final. She remained unruffled as the decibel level soared when she entered the arena. 'I try to stay calm and composed,' she told me later. 'I prefer to save energy.' From Liverpool, Jonas came with a plan but Taylor systematically dismantled that strategy and secured bronze, 26-15. Observing as a spectator, coach Tony Davitt said, 'Katie didn't allow herself become distracted. I'd never seen her as totally focused on a bout before.'

Tajikistan's Mavzuna Chorieva tried a different approach. Determined to win the semi-final, she drew the referee's attention for holding and adopting roughhouse tactics. As Katie beat her to the punch, Chorieva dropped her hands and called Taylor forward hoping to hit her on the counter-attack. Taylor ended the round 3-1 in front. Deploying some lightning three-punch combinations, Taylor won round two 4-2. There are many ways to go about winning a fight. An attempt to smother an opponent's punches by clinching and hugging is one. In the third round the referee had a word with Chorieva who seemed as if she'd be happier grappling. Eventually Taylor replied with her own mini version of the Ali Shuffle. The round went to Taylor 6-3, but, at the break, coach Pete appeared animated by that flash of self-indulgence. There was no way back for a frustrated Chorieva. Taylor booked her place in the final, 17-9. 'I knew that she was going to be physical in close,' she said afterwards.

Before Taylor's Olympic final, Pete put things into perspective, saying, 'She's had over 150 fights at this stage. All senior fights. All international fights. It takes a lot out of you. You play football. You play tennis. You play other games. But you don't play boxing. If you go in there and play, you'll get hurt.'

In the final, Taylor met Sofya Ochigava, who she'd beaten twice already. However, in March the Russian had inflicted a first defeat in three years on Taylor when they fought in the Czech Republic. This was likely to be close. Genial IABA historian Joe Kirwan expressed concern. 'I'd be worried that Ochigava has been holding something back. She may have reserved something for this bout.'

On the afternoon of the final, I slipped out from the ExCeL Arena to a nearby hotel where I drank a whiskey with Ireland's 'Mr Boxing'. Gerry Callan had invested his life in boxing. Or at least those parts that didn't involve the heroic task of successfully rearing a family under tremendously difficult conditions. He is also author of a Barry McGuigan biography. We both knew the place this fight would have in Irish sporting history. Sitting in the sun, we talked about songwriting legend Kris Kristofferson, an acquaintance of Gerry's, who won a Blue for boxing when studying at

Oxford, and toasted John Jameson, who founded his distillery in Dublin in 1780, and his family motto *'sine metu'*. 'Without fear.' Heading back to the venue, I shared a lift to the next floor with veteran broadcaster Jimmy Magee. 'You look nervous,' he noted.

What I didn't explain to Jimmy was that, daft as it sounded, I felt I had skin in the game. This was the bout I'd imagined fighting when I was a small child. An Olympic gold-medal decider. I didn't tell Jimmy that I was feeling the same surge of excitement the pale youngster, with his cheap thin-soled runners, had felt on winter nights many decades earlier going to a 'boxing gym' that had been magicked up in a shabby Victorian-era school. Desks piled against the wall by community volunteer trainers. The dreams generated on the old wooden floorboards in this local classroom still vibrated in colour. Dreams sustain. Forgotten childhood aspirations can lie dormant and suddenly manifest themselves decades later. This was personal. When learning to read in the 1950s, I had precociously entertained my father's friends by giving halting utterance to accounts of title fights in Madison Square Garden from the pages of the *Irish Press*. Now I was filing reports from ringside in London.

The noise was spine-tingling as Katie Taylor arrived, her concentration suggesting the resolve of a neurosurgeon entering an operating theatre. Her more muscular Russian competitor appeared, skipping lightly, shoulders gleaming. Headguards strapped on, the women touched gloves. A chorus of 'Olé, olé, olé' rose from a predominantly Irish crowd.

Springing forward, Taylor took the fight to Ochigava. Against a former bantamweight champion, Taylor landed the first punch. She kept going forward. Suddenly, Taylor appeared to slip. These were going to be tense rounds. Both boxers were familiar with each other's styles. It would be close. An error or a flash of brilliance could decide this fight. A sharp counter-puncher, Ochigava boxed southpaw. She landed one. Taylor ducked another and countered with her own powerful right. The judges scored the first round 2-2.

Ochivaga kept her guard low as round two commenced. Bouncing forward and back, Taylor probed for an opening. Ochigava began showboating. Taylor got on the inside but the Russian tied her up. Back in the corner, Pete remained calm. 'No problem for ya,' he shouted above the din. 'Relax.' The judges gave the round to Ochigava 2-1, putting the Russian ahead 4-3.

Fifteen seconds into round three, Taylor, parrying with her left, landed a laser-guided right full flush on Ochigava's face. The response by the Russian was to clinch until the sting subsided. Taylor, alert to incoming fire, ducked underneath a haymaker swing. The Russian boxer attempted to dominate but the spite in Taylor's punching caused her problems. Ochigava eventually moved into range. Taylor slipped her shot and countered, not with the right but with a double left. Anticipating Ochigava's attacks, Taylor ducked out of trouble forcing her opponent to grapple and attempt to foul. Leaning on Taylor, Ochigava forced her head down and delivered a strong illegal right to her kidney. The referee reprimanded the Russian for holding. Taylor responded with a left and a right. Boxing beautifully, she appeared in command. The referee called a timeout while the Russian boxer was sent to her corner to have a bootlace tied. The break in concentration didn't hinder Taylor. This was a contest of fine margins.

Before the bell for the final round the scores came in for the third. A 4-1 round put Taylor two points ahead, 7-5. It was anybody's fight. Pete Taylor remained unflustered. The dynamic changed. Ochigava knew she had to score to win. Reading the danger signals, Taylor made herself difficult to hit. As Taylor slipped out of range of the southpaw jab, Ochigava's frustration increased. With a minute left, the Russian appeared to tag Taylor whose momentum saw her stumble past her opponent. Ochigava turned sharply, in pursuit. The headguard came low on Taylor's brow as the pair clinched. This was becoming a brawl. But Taylor landed a clean left. Another clinch. As Ochigava unleashed a bomb, Taylor nearly fell. Her gloves touched the canvas. It was a heart-stopping moment for her supporters. Would she lose a point? No. It had been a slip. Taylor's gloves dusted off, the fight went on. Taylor scored with a strong right. The clock ran down. The final bell rang. Both boxers knew it was close.

Having seen too many controversial decisions over the years when Irish boxers would come up short against opponents from Eastern bloc countries, I was apprehensive. Ochigava had her arm up but her head down. Taylor stared straight ahead. The announcer's voice cut across the noise of the crowd. 'The winner by a score of ten points to eight and Olympic champion, in the red corner, representing Ireland, KATIE TAYLOR!'

Looking heavenward, Katie fell to her knees. There were tears of joy as she embraced her coaches. Grabbing an Irish tricolour, she jogged a victory lap around the ring. From trailing by a point at the halfway stage (3-4), Katie performed a two-minute miracle with a stylish third-round performance to carve out a two-point lead. Having tenaciously drawn the final round (3-3), that lead clinched Olympic gold. Newly crowned Olympic champion, Taylor said, 'There was a bit of a delay and I thought it might have gone back to countback. Before the fight my dad said that if I went a couple of points down to stay calm and composed. And keep to the game plan. I had to stay relaxed.'

'Katie was magnificent,' declared Barry McGuigan. 'She's an incredible talent, the greatest representative of female boxing I can imagine.' Boxing pundit Steve Bunce waxed lyrical about what he called 'the Katie Enigma'. 'I'd heard the fans at the O2 in Dublin cheering her name when she was announced at Bernard Dunne's bouts but now I know she's the best female amateur boxer in history.'

Ireland went crazy. The general public, emotionally exhausted by the financial crisis, celebrated as if the gold-medal win was an omen that everything would be alright. News editors got to use their 'Million Dollar Baby' headline.

A few days later, I had a chat with Jimmy Magee. 'It's fair to say that Katie Taylor was the best known and least seen Irish sports person,' he said of the four-times world champion. 'People didn't even know what she looked like. She's unbelievable.' This was proving to be a particularly auspicious Olympic Games for Magee. While in London, Jimmy had been awarded a miniature replica of the 2012 Torch at an official event called Journalists on the Podium, honouring pundits who'd covered more than ten games. Between Summer and Winter Olympics, Magee had worked on an impressive fourteen. He'd been in his element at the awards ceremony. Especially when Dick Fosbury, the American who devised the high-jump back flip, approached him.

Magee said, 'In the whole history of sport you're the only man who flopped and won.'

The American, credited with 'the Fosbury Flop', was delighted with Magee's wit. 'I'll use that,' he said.

Smiling, Jimmy quipped, 'Don't forget the source.'

Overnight, Katie Taylor became a brand. Back in Ireland, she walked into a whirlwind of national celebration. Street parties, civic receptions, public appearances and book signings became part of her routine. Following a family holiday in Portugal, Taylor and her father spent a couple of weeks in Marbella, training at the MGM gym. She nurtured a new ambition, to emulate the three Olympic gold-medal wins of László Papp and Félix Savón. 'My dad has everything set in place,' she said. 'Nothing will ever interfere with training.'

The public demanded to see Taylor in action so, in time for the Christmas market, promoter Brian Peters announced a number of exhibition bouts for Katie around Ireland, beginning with a headline show at the Daniel Libeskind–designed Bord Gáis Energy Theatre in Dublin. More used to staging *The Lion King* and *The Nutcracker*, the venue became as intimate as the Bray boxer's gym when Taylor took on German champion Maike Klueners in front of an army of admirers. Peters' hi-tech production provided fans with a glorious opportunity to relive the thrills of Taylor's medal-winning exploits. This was boxing as channelled through U2's *Zoo TV* with giant screens beaming out a selection of Taylor's favourite psalms, including 'Give me your shield of victory'. The champion's entrance, with all the razzmatazz of a Las Vegas show, was greeted with cross-generational mania. This was a night of genuflection and reverential thanksgiving. A concelebration, with every punch cheered to the rafters. Acknowledging that the majority of the audience had come to see Taylor the iconic heroine, the 'overnight' sensation, a bemused Mick Dowling noted, 'There are people here tonight who've never been at a boxing event before.'

Katie told her fans, 'The best is yet to come. I'll be a better boxer in four years.' That's what they'd come to hear. Taylor was on the road to Rio.

III

Katie Taylor had dominated women's world and European championship boxing for a decade. But often in life there comes a time when the falcon cannot hear the falconer. Things fall apart.

'A sad day for Irish boxing,' was how Taylor greeted the news in October 2015 that Billy Walsh, Head Coach of the IABA's High Performance Unit, had resigned. With the public concentrating on Walsh's departure, the absence of Pete Taylor from his daughter's corner early in 2016 didn't ring alarm bells.

'I'm training with Zaur [Antia] the whole time,' Taylor told reporter Johnny Watterson. 'Zaur has been there from the get-go. You wouldn't want to be making too big of a change in such a big year.' It seemed to be a case of 'business as usual' just months ahead of the Olympic Games in Rio. But all wasn't well. While it wasn't widely reported, Taylor's parents had split up. Her father had a new partner.

Taylor's loss to Yana Alekseevna of Azerbaijan in an Olympic qualifying tournament in Turkey in April was a shock. She'd beaten her opponent ten months previously. Pete had been in her corner then. But not now. 'I don't know what went wrong today,' said Taylor, aware that a slip-up at the World Championships in Kazakhstan a month later could cost her Olympic qualification.

Taylor had remained unbeaten in major tournaments since 2006. In Astana, she dispatched three opponents before gloving off against French boxer Estelle Mossely in the semi-finals. The bout was declared a split decision. On countback, Mossely was declared the winner. Crucially, Taylor's bronze medal position ensured qualification for Rio. However, it was now clear that the breakdown of her parents' marriage was having a negative effect on her performances.

In Rio, having received a bye to the last eight, Taylor shrugged off pressure: 'Those losses haven't changed my mindset.' However, with her father absent and without the steadying hand of long-term head coach Billy Walsh, an aura of chaos surrounded the Irish team.

Taylor's first bout was a quarter-final duel with Mira Potkonen, a 35-year-old from Finland, who had failed to qualify for the London Olympics. Taylor had dominated Potkonen in competition previously. This time was different. Taylor seemed off-form. Her movement wasn't fluid nor were her shots assured. She was getting caught more easily and Potkonen's powerful right hand was leaving its mark. While not emphatic, Taylor looked to have done enough to win.

The scores from the three judges had it a draw. On the dreaded countback system, Potkonen got the victory. Taylor was shattered. Coach Zaur Antia was apoplectic.

As the implications of the decision sank in, Taylor struggled to contain her emotions. 'It's very disappointing,' she told the TV reporter. 'It's been a very, very tough year. I've suffered a lot of losses this year and it's very, very hard to take.' It was clear she was grieving.

On her return to Ireland, Taylor took a short holiday and reflected on events that had led to three high-profile defeats in five months. Without her father's guiding presence and with a power struggle raging between IABA officials and the Irish Sports Council, the body which effectively controlled funding, Katie took matters into her own hands. Quietly, she set about exploring the possibility of becoming a professional boxer.

IV

Taylor had a lot of questions, not least concerning the relevance of women's pro boxing, which didn't have much of a profile. Occasional women's fights, which had the air of carnival attractions, smacked of tokenism on the undercard of men's events.

Taylor was diligent. She discussed matters with promoter Brian Peters, who outlined the difficulties of attempting to launch a career in a business as fragmented and disorganized as women's professional boxing. He knew if Taylor was to have any chance of surviving, she'd need the support of a powerful international promoter. He arranged a meeting with Eddie Hearn of Matchroom Sport. Having joined his father's company, which had achieved global success promoting snooker, table tennis and boxing, Hearn became established as a high-profile operator.

'We don't need to sign more boxers,' he insisted. Yet when Hearn met Taylor, her passion for boxing burnt brightly and he promptly changed his mind. 'I need this girl in boxing,' he enthused later. 'She has an obsession.'

With no existing market for women's professional boxing in Britain, Hearn would have to create a credible competitive infrastructure. The likelihood was that most fans would snort at the idea of women fighting. Few could imagine two women providing the punishing, bloody, epic fights that paying customers craved. But Eddie committed to the challenge.

'If you're going to grow a sport, you need role models,' he explained to me. 'And you're never going to get someone better than Katie Taylor.' A master of the hard sell, Hearn knew he was embarking on uncharted waters. Weeks before Taylor's first pro fight, he said, 'I've no idea if it's going to work. But, if I've got the product, I can sell it. And I believe I've got the product.'

Taylor also had another crucial decision to make. She needed a new coach, someone she could put her faith in. Having established contact with Ross Enamait, the author of *Infinite Intensity: The Revolution Is Here* and other fitness manuals that littered the Taylor household, she flew to the US, hired a jeep and drove to Connecticut to meet the man who ran the ROC Gym. 'I knew I needed a change,' she told me. 'But I didn't know what I wanted to do.' A few weeks in the ROC Gym showed her a way forward. 'The more I was around him [Ross] and the pro boxers, the more I got an appetite for the professional game,' she revealed. 'I wanted to get straight back into things.'

Ahead of her pro debut in November, three months after Rio, Taylor spoke of 'a new chapter' as she unveiled the uniform of her new career: black trunks and a top trimmed with gold. Fighting *sans* headguard wasn't a problem as Taylor systematically destroyed her Polish opponent, winning by third-round stoppage. 'The tests are only going to get tougher from here,' said Taylor. With the promotional machine purring sweetly, she was back in action less than three weeks later. In the Manchester Arena, her fight was positioned before the bad-blood battle of the big beasts, heavyweights Dillian Whyte and Derek Chisora. Brazil's Viviane Obenauf was outclassed by Taylor's superior skills.

Like a man with a winning ante-post docket at Cheltenham, manager Brian Peters considered his latest project. 'It's got a lot of momentum,' he enthused. 'But we've got to keep the feet on the ground.' Two more bouts followed in March. Both wins. All four fights had been screened by Sky Sports. Taylor's talent was being appreciated by a wider audience.

With the Anthony Joshua–Wladimir Klitschko world-title decider due for Wembley Stadium in April, Hearn ensured that Taylor would perform on the bill. Nina Meinke, a German southpaw with a five-unbeaten record, was produced to challenge for the WBA International female lightweight belt. Taylor dominated and finished work in the seventh round leaving her opponent battered and bloodied. 'I think I'm ready right now to box for a world title,' she said.

Eddie Hearn was pleased with how his project was developing. When he originally signed Taylor, Hearn told me, 'Our plan is to have about eight fights before the world title. Ultimately the world-title shot should come in Ireland. That's the objective.' Despite Taylor's progress, an explosion in feuding gang violence in Ireland, ignited when gunmen stormed a boxing weigh-in in Dublin the previous year killing one and wounding others, ensured a big homecoming fight was looking less likely.

V

At the end of May, two months before Katie's first pro fight in America, I met her father, Pete, the man who guided her to amateur world titles and Olympic gold. He'd kept a low profile since his last appearance in Katie's corner, at the European Games in Azerbaijan in 2015 when Katie won gold.

I met Pete in KO Fit Food, a bright bijou café that he'd opened in Bray with his new partner. 'I was always working with boxers on making the weight,' he explained. 'I knew about nutrition. So I said, "I'll open a café." It's about eating healthy.'

Pete had fought tooth and nail for permission to have his daughter box in competitions. 'I had her boxing boys in competitions because she was the only girl boxing,' he recalled. 'I'd been on to the Stadium (IABA) every day of the week trying to get them on board. Eventually they succumbed and they put her on a show.'

That first show Katie boxed on at the National Stadium is legendary. Andy Lee was boxing. Katie boxed Alanna Audley-Murphy in an officially sanctioned bout refereed by Sadie Duffy from Buncrana. She was about five or six kilo lighter than Alanna but she and Pete still took the fight. She won and was voted Boxer of the Tournament. Katie was just fifteen at the time.

She wasn't the only star of the future in action that night. 'Nicola Adams [Olympic gold medallist in London and Rio] boxed Debbie Rodgers, another girl out of my club, who won an EU bronze medal,' added Pete. 'Nobody realizes that two gold medallists boxed that night. But they were still totally against it. It was a battle then just to keep Katie boxing. And keep the Association interested in women's boxing.'

Katie was invited to box in an Olympic trial for women's boxing at the World Championships in Chicago in 2007. She boxed a Canadian who was four kilos heavier. 'They were going mad because she stopped the girl in the first round,' recalled Pete.

Having coached his daughter since she was ten through to five world titles, six European titles and an Olympic gold medal, there was no underestimating the frustration and disappointment Pete felt at his daughter's defeat in Rio. 'It was a golden era of boxing,' said the man who'd also coached another member of the Ireland team at the London Olympics, Garda Adam Nolan. 'The mistake with the IABA, and the public, is that they took for granted the medals the boxers were winning. They thought, "This must be easy." But now we're not winning medals. It's not easy.'

Later in the afternoon, I joined Pete in the gym he'd set up in the picturesque cul-de-sac that is Bray Harbour. Sunlight was dancing on the water. It seemed idyllic. There were even a couple of swans relaxing on the slipway. The gym crackled with energy as his clients went through their paces. Between routines, we continued our chat.

When I said that Katie seemed to be throwing an impressive volume of punches as a pro, Pete stopped me. 'Katie's style hasn't changed that much,' he pointed out. 'She's a little bit more aggressive because now you don't have to worry about point-scoring. But the quality of her opponents is nothing compared to the quality she was boxing as an amateur. As an amateur, everyone you box is a champion of their country. The people they've been putting her in with, it's nearly disrespectful. Essentially, they're getting paid to get beaten up. Katie has been boxing elite boxers at the highest level.'

It was early day's in his daughter's pro career but Pete had obvious concerns. 'It's hard to judge it,' he shrugged. 'Even Katie's last opponent, at 5-0, hadn't boxed outside the gym. That's not boxing. Eventually they've got to be matched. Unless it's a title fight, it's not competitive.'

VI

Taylor made her American debut in Brooklyn in July on the Mikey Garcia–Adrien Broner WBC super-lightweight title fight. The fight was a mismatch. Taylor's opponent, Jasmine Clarkson, was stopped in the third round. Eddie Hearn reckoned it was time to step up. With her record at six unbeaten, Taylor was offered a shot at the WBA world female lightweight title. Her opponent in Cardiff would be Anahí Esther Sanchéz, the Argentinian who'd held two world belts at super-featherweight and had lost just two of nineteen pro fights. She'd fought a total of eighty-three rounds on the tough South American professional circuit. Taylor's pro experience amounted to thirty-two rounds.

In the ring, fighters are bathed in one equal light. Although five years younger than Taylor (31), Sanchéz had height and reach advantage. The Irish woman asserted herself in the opening round with a punishing left jab and a series of blistering combination punches. In the second round, Taylor smashed a vicious left hook up into the ribcage, which sent Sanchéz down on her knees. She recovered and fought back. As Taylor tried to finish early, she got sucked into a free-for-all, the type of fight that suited Sanchéz. Despite a cut which required stitches, Taylor was in control and showed she could both box and brawl. All three judges gave her the title 99-90. 'I got a bit wild and left myself wide open a few times,' she said later. 'I've a lot of bruises on my face but I'm coming home with the belt.' With the WBA title secured, she now aimed to unify the division. 'I want to take over the lightweight division,' she said. 'One step at a time.'

Following a successful defence against Jessica McCaskill in London, for her ninth fight, WBA belt holder Katie met Argentina's IBF world champion Victoria Bustos in Brooklyn in April 2018 hoping to unify the titles. Bustos had twenty-two pro fights, five of them successful defences of her title. While the IBF champion brought aggression and desire, Taylor skilfully outboxed her opponent. 'I needed to be sharp for ten rounds,' she said. 'She just kept coming. It was a tough contest.' Taylor was now a unified champion and planning to become the undisputed world champion by annexing the belts of the two remaining sanctioning bodies.

In June, Taylor's team debated possible opponents for her next big fight while, in Bray, Pete continued to run his boxing gym. Shortly before 7 am one morning, as his class prepared for their fitness workouts, Pete concentrated on setting up a suitable high-tempo soundtrack for the session. It was just then the door opened and a latecomer stepped into the gym.

Dressed in black and wearing a yellow hi-vis vest, a balaclava and sunglasses, the new arrival was clutching a semi-automatic handgun in two hands. Scanning the room, the gunman opened fire.

As people dived for cover, local man Bobby Messett (50) was shot in the head. The bullet entered through the face, rupturing blood vessels in the brain stem before exiting at the back of the skull cavity. Death followed rapidly as the victim slumped to the ground in a pool of blood. Ian Britton (35), from Greystones, was blasted in the leg. When the shooting started, the 57-year-old coach rushed the lone gunman. He was closing in on the killer when a bullet struck his arm and deflected into his upper body. The force of the impact spun him around and knocked him to the floor where he lay in excruciating agony, bleeding. The sudden explosions of gunfire in the confined space turned the air to sludge and caused panic, confusion and fear. The gunman escaped.

Taylor and Britton were rushed to hospital, their injuries described by Gardaí as 'very, very serious'. Pete was traumatized. 'Bobby was my close friend, training partner and sparring mate,' he said. 'I am utterly heartbroken that he is gone.' On release from hospital, he left the country to recuperate.

The violent attack threw Katie Taylor into an emotional spin. The trauma of her father's brush with death was compounded by the way media reports linked her name to the story. Extending condolences to the Messett family, and acknowledging that she had been 'somewhat estranged' from her dad for a few years, Taylor asked the media to leave her, her mother and her family out of their reportage of the horrific incident.

Meanwhile, manager Brian Peters was dealing with a business conundrum. It was proving difficult to find boxers who could match Taylor's status with fight fans. A clash with Taylor was a big pay day for opponents. Her name was selling seats but, to help generate widespread interest, her opponent needed to be an attraction. 'We are having some problems getting opponents lined up,' Peters complained when we next spoke. 'This is, by far, their biggest purse. They have to bring something to the table. They need to have a good ranking.'

Few doubted Taylor would prevail. 'There's two more belts to go and I'm very, very hungry for them,' she said. There would be even bigger fights ahead. On her campaign, she found good counsel, support and motivation in her Bible. One of the psalms she turned to most contains the lines, 'He trains my hands for war; my arms can bend a bow of bronze. You give me your shield of victory, and your right hand sustains me; you stoop down to make me great.'

Unstoppable and on a winning streak, the legend continued. Taylor beat Rose Volante and Delfine Persoon to become one of a select few to hold all four titles simultaneously. Having started fighting boys, Taylor went on to reshape both boxing and social norms. Someday we might get forensic detail of the petty indignities and downright misogyny endured by Taylor in pursuit of her goals in what had been an exclusively male world. What is undeniable is that, as she continued to smash glass ceilings, she further helped highlight gender inequality, the root cause of women's social, economic and political inequality.

12
THE MEXICAN

'To get between the ropes everyone has to have some sort of courage.'
Jamie Conlan

I

A SUSTAINED ARPEGGIO of punishment played by Jamie Conlan's fists on the head of Benjamin Smoes early in the seventh round clinched the WBO European super-flyweight title for the Belfast man. Having already been down in the sixth round, Smoes was deemed unfit to continue when Conlan resumed his assault after the interval. It was his eleventh fight as a pro, and Conlan was European champion.

An intriguing prospect, Conlan was emerging as a bona fide box-office attraction. Nicknamed 'the Mexican' for his gutsy style, he and his team came to the ring for a WBO Inter-Continental title fight wearing colourful Mexican sombreros. Looking like a stag party in Benidorm, the trio painted a surreal tableaux. Unimpressed, his opponent José Estrella, a hardman from Tijuana, encouraged Conlan to stand and fight but the Belfast man wasn't stupid. He preferred to use the skills he'd honed as an amateur.

Their bout went the distance. Conlan picked up a cut, which impaired his vision. He hit Estrella with some of his best shots, punches so hard they hurt his hands, but the visitor absorbed the punishment. 'He just nodded back at me and smiled,' recalled Conlan afterwards. It was to prove a useful experience ahead of his next meeting with a Mexican opponent. Ten months later, Conlan met Junior Granados in what would prove to be one of the most thrilling fights ever witnessed at the National Boxing Stadium in Dublin.

Setting his sights on a world-title push, Conlan (28) switched from Barry McGuigan's Cyclone Promotions to Matthew Macklin's Gym Marbella (MGM). Understanding the importance of television exposure, Macklin arranged a co-promotion with Frank Warren to ensure Conlan's title defence against Granados would be transmitted live on Warren's dedicated boxing channel BoxNation.

Brimming with confidence, Conlan declared, 'Granados is going to feel the pain.' His opponent was not amused to be fighting an Irishman with such a colourful nickname. 'I will show I'm the true Mexican by beating him,' he vowed.

With a strong selection of Irish talent on the bill, both Macklin and business partner Daniel Kinahan were planning a glorious future for MGM boxers. 'Hopefully this will be the first of many shows here that will continue television exposure of boxing in Ireland,' said Macklin. 'Television exposure is crucial to any young fighter's development. You can be the best in the world but if nobody knows who you are you're never going to become a household name and get the big fights that generate big money or bring titles.'

By now there were three main promoters working on the island: Brian Peters, Barry McGuigan and MGM. Other promoters such as Mark Dunlop, Leonard Gunning and Tony Davitt were also regularly staging shows with emerging talent.

Macklin liked what he'd seen of Conlan. 'I'm confident he'll win big world titles,' he said. And this was before Conlan painted him a blood-splattered portrait of bravery, stubbornness and sheer grit across ten rounds of agony and redemption at the Stadium.

For all his bellicose posturing, Conlan was a fighter who seemed to ease into the task. This encounter was no different. Granados walked through Conlan's jab and won the early rounds. It looked as if Conlan might pay for his profligacy when a ferocious right staggered him in the fourth round. But as we'd seen before, a punch in the mouth was catnip to Conlan, who fought back and won the fifth round with some authority.

Granados found his target again in the seventh. This time, a crippling body shot caused Conlan's diaphragm to spasm and expel the oxygen from his lungs. He sank to the floor, breathless and weakened. Struggling from a hands-and-knees position, he beat the count only to find himself trapped on the ropes as Granados unleashed an explosive repertoire of vicious hooks, uppercuts and body shots in a whirlwind attempt to finish the fight. Conlan tucked his elbows under his ribs and crouched low, creating a protective shell.

What strange alchemy is played out in such situations? What symbolic shamanistic-like trade is exacted? Confronted with violence and the terror of witnessing the hero vanquished, a psychic cocktail of sympathetic magic, a full-throttle spear-rattling din was generated by the spectators. Like a tribe of anxious villagers tapping into the deeper recesses of a buried mythic landscape, they willed their hunter-warrior home.

The wave of primal energy that reached into the square of light stoked Conlan's raw courage, fuelled his resolve and drove him onwards. But the bombardment didn't stop. On his knees again, it looked as if the champion was out. Until, like a mind-bending conjurer, he unexpectedly dragged himself upwards and made it to the bell. Battered, bruised and cut, he had soaked up everything the Mexican could throw and was still conscious, still standing, still in the game.

With three rounds left to save the day, and galvanized by the energy being generated by the raucous communal will, Conlan astonished Granados by taking the fight to him with unexpected reserves of determination. Attempting to pick his shots, the visitor was frequently ambushed and beaten to the punch. It was as if those two pulverizing knockdowns had never happened. Conlan showed himself to be the more experienced and stylish fighter. Each time he needed to, he commanded himself to come back stronger and make a statement. In doing so, he gave his opponent moments of doubt. More importantly, he landed shots that impressed the judges.

In microcosm, Conlan's performance captured the essence of boxing's appeal. Like a work by Sophocles, this was theogonic drama in the moment. When down for the second time, he rose and withstood the beating. He refused to fall a third time. He made it to the top of the hill and brought us with him in Holy Communion. All of us in the room. Thieves and sinners. The saintly and pure of heart. The rich, the poor, the struggling and the sick. Unbowed, he showed how we might endure. He lifted our spirits and gave us strength.

I scored it closer than each of the three international judges but we all agreed. Conlan, by unanimous decision, retained his WBO Inter-Continental belt. He was still champion. It had been an epic contest. 'You never want to be in a fight like that,' cautioned MGM boss Macklin.

Afterwards, Conlan was sanguine when addressing the brutality of the seventh-round onslaught. 'It was a very worrying round,' he conceded. 'He was gaining momentum and courage. I could see him pointing and laughing and shit. My head was clear. It was just the body shot. When he was throwing those punches I was trying to ride the storm, catch my wind and strike back. I knew that was his best. I knew I could beat him.'

His face may have looked like it had been hit by a bin lorry but, once again, the Irishman had proved himself the embodiment of the quality most prized by fight fans – Mexican machismo. Conlan downplayed his resilience. 'That's part of the game,' he shrugged. 'To get between the ropes everyone has to have some sort of courage. I knew, 'Right, c'mon, don't feel sorry for yourself.'

As he reclined exhausted, festooned with his European and Inter-Continental belts, hard-won symbols of his prowess, Conlan's misshapen face reminded me of the aggression and courage that I'd just witnessed. Ugly swellings above and below his right eye were forcing its closure. There was a cut along his right cheekbone. Despite a quick clean up by his medical staff, blood was beginning to seep from a nasty-looking slit above an eyelid. Swollen lips distorted his mouth. His shoulders were streaked with rope burns. Taking in the scene, I considered how the privilege of a ringside seat facilitated me in rewilding, however temporarily, that self I'd devoted years to cultivating with art, recitals and tender relationships.

A year later, Conlan went on to win the Commonwealth belt. It was a big deal. When he was twelve, he'd seen Eamonn Magee win the Commonwealth super-lightweight title and became hooked. Before he fought super-flyweight title holder Anthony Nelson in March 2016, he told me from his base in Spain, 'I've always had my sights set on this title since I was a kid.' A further twelve months on, he took his unbeaten record to 19-0 when he won against Yader Cardoza, a tough Nicaraguan fighter who had twenty-two wins in thirty-three fights, and claimed the WBC International Silver super-flyweight title. I'd seen less blood in an abattoir. Slumped in a chair in his dressing room afterwards, a patchwork of ecchymoses and haematomas, the result of Cardoza's handiwork, making a mockery of his normally puckish features, Conlan, relaxed in victory, laughed, 'To quote *Lethal Weapon*, "I'm getting too old for this shit."' Unbeaten, it was expected he'd fight for a world title within the year.

II

Jamie Conlan's professional career had begun with a unique twist. In 2009, when he'd found himself on course to meet his brother Michael in the Ulster final, Jamie quit the tournament and turned pro.

As the older brother, he'd been expected to win. 'He let me win,' Michael acknowledged. That sacrifice provided a kick-start to Michael's career. Jamie was in the ExCeL Arena in London with parents, Theresa and John, a coach on Team Ireland, and the rest of the family, supporting Michael when he represented Ireland at the 2012 Olympic Games.

'I hate sparring with him,' Jamie confided as we left the arena. 'If he hit me five times, I'd want to hit him six back. But then he'd hit me nine times in reply. He never lets up. You could see those traits in him tonight. He never wants to be second.'

'Jamie is Michael's hero,' said Theresa. The Conlans are a boxing dynasty. Their father, John, a Dubliner, was coach at the St John Bosco ABC in West Belfast. Jamie was a three-times Irish amateur champion. Another brother, Brendan, won an Irish title before quitting the sport. Michael began boxing when he was seven. 'My da was in the club and that's why I didn't get involved in anything else,' Michael told me. 'You see kids with great potential coming up and just getting dragged into drink, drugs and stealing cars and stuff like that.'

While Jamie was punching his way to professional titles, younger brother Michael became the stylish poster boy for amateur boxing. Both men credited John with their success. 'He made us what we are,' Jamie insisted. After his WBC title win against Yader Cardoza, a fight that saw Conlan repeat a pattern by being down in the eighth and picking up a bad cut in the tenth, he jokingly blamed John for his never-say-die attitude. 'That's my dad's fault,' he said. 'He instilled in me and Michael since we were kids that, no matter what, I'm going to win.'

In Michael's Olympic quarter-final against an aggressive French boxer, the score was 12-12 going into the final round. There was no quarter given. Michael displayed neat footwork, effective upper-body movement and an ability to switch from orthodox to southpaw and score with both fists. Looking on, veteran Irish coach Tony Davitt was impressed. 'I've seen boxers who think they can switch and get knocked out,' he noted. 'But Michael can box brilliantly either way. He's special.' Michael Conlan clinched the result.

Teammates Katie Taylor and John Joe Nevin had made it through to the 2012 Olympic finals. Michael Conlan hoped to join them. Unfortunately, in Robeisy Ramírez Carrazana, it was Michael's bad luck to come up against a freakishly talented Cuban fighter. Conlan switched from southpaw to orthodox in the second round but the precocious Cuban met and mastered that too. He saved most of his aggression for the last round as if to chastise his Irish opponent for being too persistent. It looked too much like one-way traffic to the judges who scored it 20-10.

His Olympic final dream shattered, Michael was visibly upset. In the moment, a bronze medal was as nothing to him. Wiping a bloody nose, he said, 'I have amazing support. I'm sorry I let them down.' Still sweating, he attempted to analyse his performance: 'I got a bit eager tonight. You always want to be the best. I'm devastated.'

III

Of the many boxers who make it to the High Performance Unit, it's those boxers who become Olympians that gain the most publicity. The country got behind the five young men who represented Ireland in Beijing. Two of those five, Paddy Barnes and John Joe Nevin, also qualified for London in 2012.

Discovery is always a thrill.

Seeing John Joe Nevin in action for the first time, I experienced a similar rush of excitement as when first encountering an unknown young New York band called Talking Heads playing in a café. In both cases, I was unprepared for performances that were breathtaking in their poise, ingenuity and originality.

Nevin had an eye-catching style. Slippery, with quick feet, a confident counter-puncher, he was difficult to hit. His jabs were fast and accurate. He seemed tailor-made for the amateur game. He was eighteen when he qualified for the Beijing Olympics. He won his opening bout but met the eventual gold-medal winner in the round of sixteen.

Nevin arrived in London as a career fighting man. He'd been Irish national senior champion five times, had two world bronze medals and silver and gold from the European Union Championships. He'd boxed on the Paris United team in the World Series of Boxing (WSB) league and was used to fighting five rounds without headguards and vests. A clash of heads in a WSB bout in March had left him nursing a broken jaw. Before he left for London, the injury was already a distant memory. What if his opponents were familiar with his style? It didn't matter to Nevin. 'If they are going to beat me, they're going to have to change tactics,' he said. 'I'll let them mess up their own game.'

In the London Olympics, Nevin had five bouts. To get near the podium he would have to battle some of the best in the world. In the quarter-final, Mexico's Óscar Valdez stood in his way. Nevin edged ahead on points but Valdez connected with a ferocious body shot, which dropped the Irishman like a rag doll in the last round. Taking a long count, Nevin recovered to outbox Valdez down the home stretch and go through (19-13) to the semi-final. Afterwards, Nevin admitted, 'That's the hardest I've ever been hit.'

The day after Katie Taylor won her Olympic gold medal, light flyweight Paddy Barnes fought his nemesis from Beijing, China's Shiming Zou. Their electrifying fight was scored a draw at 15-15. Barnes lost, 45-44 on countback. About thirty minutes after Paddy's barnstorming performance, John Joe Nevin met the 21-year-old Cuban world champion Lázaro Álvarez in a men's bantamweight semi-finals. 'I came for gold,' Nevin told me. Turning on the style, he sailed through the rounds like a will-o'-the-wisp, winning all three rounds. 'John Joe gave a masterful display of boxing,' said Billy Walsh. 'The Cuban is world champion and John Joe made him look ordinary.'

Nevin was familiar with Luke Campbell, the man he had to beat to win gold. 'We had two fights in the past and one of them was tight,' said Nevin. He'd beaten Campbell 13-2 in a European semi-final in 2009. When they met in a world championship semi-final in 2011 the fight was a tie, 12-12. Campbell won on countback. From Hull, Campbell revealed, 'I've got Irish family and they know his family.'

One of a number of professional promoters assessing the talent in the tournament, Barry McGuigan said:

> John Joe Nevin's semi-final performance against the Cuban was extraordinary. If he's going to turn over, I'd like to talk to him. I took Carl Frampton on board because I thought he had a tremendously efficient pro style that suited and, I thought, would make the transition easily. The others will not find it so easy. John Joe's got serious ability.

What decided the final was strategy.

The British boxer cleverly dictated the pace and style of the action, picking off Nevin with his fast jab. An assured point-scoring counter-puncher, Nevin was sucked into pursuing Campbell. It was an approach that didn't suit him. By round two, his efforts began to display a hint of desperation. Campbell kept an effective high guard when necessary and countered with the sort of combinations that had been Nevin's trademark. In the third round, like an angry man wanting to scrap, Nevin was powering up his punches. It was a dangerous gamble that didn't pay off. Midway through the round a swift combination from Campbell caught Nevin off balance and put him down briefly for a count.

Campbell later explained how he'd set a trap that won him the fight 14-11. 'He's a very clever fighter and the plan was to draw him because if he'd have got on his back foot, that's what suits him best. I needed to take that away from him.' Nevin knew he'd been outfoxed. 'He got his tactics right on the day,' he admitted. 'I'm heartbroken.'

Nevin came to appreciate that Olympic silver is a rare accolade. By the time he won gold at the 2013 European Championships in Minsk, he'd been inundated with offers to join the professional ranks.

In October, his plans were revealed to a gathering in the plush Grafton Suite of Dublin's Westbury Hotel. 'The buzz of winning medals is gone now because I've won everything,' declared Nevin. 'I need something new to go after and this is it.'

Involving a company in Philadelphia called GreenBlood Boxing and Berkeley Sports & Media from London, Nevin's management deal seemed complex. Also involved was his amateur coach Brian McKeown of Cavan BC. Genial Tom Moran of GreenBlood, a former manager of

Tim Witherspoon, explained, 'This is the beginning of a golden age of Irish boxing. The Irish boxing marketplace in America is untapped. We believe John Joe is perhaps the best fighter in Irish history. Our vision is to develop a team of Irish talent in an innovative way.'

Brian McKeown agreed. 'John Joe is the most decorated male boxer in Irish history,' he said. 'He's done it from very humble beginnings and has made a lot of sacrifices. He's an exceptional athlete.' Importantly, McKeown believed Nevin would make a successful transition. 'The professional game is more based on endurance and physical strength,' he explained. 'Everyone thinks John Joe is the Dancing Master. But he can hit as hard as than anyone I've ever held pads for.'

Nevin was switched on. 'It's time to move on and hopefully bring back a world title to Ireland,' he said. Moran was aiming for the top. 'One of John Joe's dreams is to win a world title and defend that title in Croke Park,' he said. 'It's our responsibility to bring that dream alive.' Nevin knew that Luke Campbell had already successfully embarked on his pro career. His new ambition was for a fourth meeting with the Hull fighter. This time for a world title.

Nevin's pro debut was in Boston on St Patrick's Day 2014 on a show at the House of Blues that also featured a win for super-lightweight Jamie Kavanagh. Fighting at super-featherweight, Nevin had a convincing win over six rounds against a rugged Puerto Rican.

Less than three weeks after Nevin's debut, disaster struck.

He was rushed to Regional Hospital Mullingar for emergency treatment after being on the receiving end of a savage beating during in a row between members of his extended family, which resulted in his right leg being broken in two places. He also sustained a fracture above the ankle on his left leg. Doctors transferred him to the Midland Regional Hospital Tullamore where surgeons in the specialized orthopaedic unit worked to repair the damage. His injuries were described as 'severe but not life-threatening'.

Coach McKeown was deeply concerned. 'The bone was sticking out of his leg,' he said. 'He was in a state of shock.' When asked if the weapons used to inflict the damage had included a golf club and a cudgel with nails protruding, McKeown didn't comment on the specifics but noted, 'they obviously weren't there for ornaments'.

'It has been a shocking experience,' said the coach. 'Especially after such an impressive performance in his professional debut. His promoter, Tom

Moran of GreenBlood Boxing, had a terrific itinerary planned for him over the summer, including a major headlining event in Mullingar.'

While there had been a number of mass brawls involving feuding Traveller gangs in the area in recent years, details of the incident remained sketchy with an official statement claiming Nevin had been acting as a peacemaker at the time.

As he recuperated in a wheelchair, Nevin said he forgave his assailant. 'We have shook hands, enjoyed a drink and just put what happened behind us,' he told journalist Claire Healy. 'I'm back on speaking terms with him and I know the incident never should have happened.' Released from the disciplined routine of the National Elite squad, Nevin had begun to explore a sociable lifestyle that involved drinking and later admitted ruefully, 'I went off the rails a bit.'

Remarkably, seven months later, Nevin returned to competitive action, meeting a guy in North Carolina who'd never fought before. Following a round one KO, Calvin Stifford never boxed again. His record remains 0-1-0.

Two years and three months after his Olympic silver-medal bout in London, John Joe Nevin got to perform in Ireland as a pro for the first time. Bigging up his appearance on the undercard of Matthew Macklin's WBC title fight with Jorge Sebastian Heiland, Eddie Hearn said, 'John Joe Nevin could go on to be a true world champion.' On the night, Nevin illustrated the gulf in class between him and hapless journeyman Jack Heath, taking just eighty-eight seconds to end the proceedings. His radiated confidence and ambition. 'When the time comes, I'll be ready to win that world title,' he told Mark Gallagher. 'And take it back to Croke Park to defend it.'

IV

Teammates on the international stage, boxers have to navigate their own careers. While Sutherland and Nevin turned pro, captain of the Irish team in Beijing, Kenneth Egan, became a psychotherapist. John Joe Joyce became a respected coach and set up his own club. Captain in London, Darren O'Neill, was a qualified teacher. Adam Nolan remained a member of An Garda Síochána. Paddy Barnes became a three-time Olympian before turning pro with MGM, 'the ideal team to guide me to world-title opportunities'.

Having been forced to settle for bronze in London, Michael Conlan was determined to bring home Olympic gold from Rio. In the build-up to the tournament, when he wasn't training with the Elite squad, he was sparring brother Jamie in Belfast. 'He's great sparring because he's physically stronger,' Michael explained. 'Sometimes he's mentally stronger because he's my big brother.'

Conlan went to Brazil having won gold at the Commonwealth Games, the European Championships and the World Championships. He was the first Irishman to achieve such distinction. A world champion, his confidence was understandably high. Displaying an almost messianic sense of conviction in his own ability, he declared, 'Nothing is going to stop me getting that gold medal.' Michael had considered his mother's belief in the life lessons gleaned from reading *The Secret* an eccentricity. That is until he saw MMA star Conor McGregor reading the self-help book (which had become a bestseller after it featured on *The Oprah Winfrey Show*). Michael soon bought into the book's message of maintaining a positive mental attitude. 'I've lived by what it says and it's working for me,' he told me before flying to Rio.

Wary of the capricious nature of competition judging, he noted, 'Anything can happen in boxing. But I know what I have to do. I just can't wait to get it on and come out the best in the world.'

Unfortunately the Fates must have skipped a chapter or two of *The Secret* because Michael Conlan was about to find himself at the centre of the most controversial scoring decision in Olympic boxing since Roy Jones Jr was deprived of a gold medal in Seoul in 1988. Jones had been in imperious form as he landed eighty-six punches to his opponent's thirty-six; an opponent who'd received two public warnings and had been down twice in the bout. But Roy Jones Jr lost. That fight will live forever in infamy as a murky mercurial magic trick that combined blatant robbery and an odious whiff of corruption.

In Rio, Conlan faced Russian Vladimir Nikitin in a quarter-final bout. Commentators wondered why the referee warned Conlan to keep his head up *before* the first bell had sounded. Displaying masterful footwork, a keen ring intelligence, superior speed and punching accuracy, Conlan dominated each round, yet according to the computer-scoring system he was second best. When his arm was raised in victory, a battered and exhausted Nikitin sank to his knees. He'd been so badly damaged by Conlan that he was unable to compete in the semi-final.

Denied justice, Conlan's despair drove him to speak in tongues. Possessed of a powerful sense of righteousness that came from having his years of toil ridiculed and his dreams hijacked by incompetence or corruption, he tore off his amateur vest, delivered a pronounced middle-finger gesture to the sports authorities and thundered, 'Amateur boxing stinks, from the core to the top. AIBA are cheats. Fucking cheats. Simple as that.' The result reverberated through the Irish camp. 'Michael didn't get beaten,' said teammate David Oliver Joyce. 'He got robbed. After Michael's fight none of the boxers went back to watch any more fights. We were disgusted. We just wanted to go home.'

Viewed by millions around the world, Conlan's defiant scorched-earth condemnation of the amateur boxing system threw a harsh spotlight on the machinations of the mandarins who controlled the sport. Embarrassed in the court of public opinion, the IOC eventually became involved. Officials were sacked and reform demanded. But for Michael Conlan there was no turning back.

A month later, a tweet from Bob Arum, Top Rank CEO, proclaimed 'amateur hour is over' with a photo of himself and Conlan grinning cheekily while mugging the camera with middle-finger salutes. Accompanied by his new manager and adviser, Matthew Macklin, Michael was in LA to sign a record-breaking deal with the company that promoted stars such as Oscar De La Hoya, Floyd Mayweather Jr and Vasiliy Lomachenko. Announcing plans for Michael's pro career, Top Rank president Todd DuBoef declared, 'There's a saying in America, "Go big or go home." So we went big. We believed in the product.'

'He has the ability, which is what counts,' pronounced Arum, with Conlan and Macklin standing by. Collaborating with one of the most powerful forces in boxing illustrated the growing reach of Macklin's MGM brand.

'A golden age of Irish boxing,' the glittering phrase so casually bandied about by promoters, hints at a time of plenty, when opulence and virtue were gifts bestowed by a celestial harmony wrought through a fortuitous alignment of planets. In reality, the hackneyed expression conveniently camouflages the often treacherous odds stacked against hard-pressed boxers. As Conlan, Nevin and Taylor, teammates at the London Olympics, would discover, success and glory in boxing can come with a harsh price tag, one pitched much higher than they could have ever imagined when first committing in youthful innocence to the sport they loved.

On St Patrick's Day 2017, a week after brother Jamie beat Yader Cardoza for the WBC International Silver super-flyweight belt, Michael made his pro debut in Madison Square Garden.

For his first fight with the smaller pro gloves on, Michael had Conor McGregor and Niall Horan visit his dressing room beforehand. Conlan predicted a win by knockout in round three of a six-round fight. Tim Ibarra was an experienced pro but he couldn't contain his opponent, whose repertoire of damage and affliction persuaded the referee to intervene in round three. Conlan was back in the prediction business.

It proved to be a momentous year for the Belfast blood brothers. In November Jamie lost his IBF world super-flyweight title fight on a sixth round TKO to Jerwin Ancajas from the Philippines. The following month, Jamie retired and was announced as MTK Global's Professional Development Coordinator, a role which would help shape the careers of over 130 fighters signed to the company.

Although Michael fought and won in Chicago, Brisbane, Tucson and New York that year, he didn't foresee how the murderous gangland feud that began with an attempt on the life of Daniel Kinahan would take the gloss off his victories and eventually lead to him denying association with MTK as the company attracted the attention of police and immigration officials across a global law-enforcement network.

From amateur to professional, commitment to improvement is key to a boxer's success. Yet, all the painful hours of developing strength and endurance, perfecting skills and absorbing punishment, are no guarantee against the cruelty of fate. While over the decades, showbusiness has learned to disguise its shady corrupt roots, the business of boxing remains Machiavellian and hermetic. You could say the Conlan brothers were among the lucky ones. Too often, brave and talented fighters, dazzled by a fast-talking, spell-weaving confluence of promise, prestige and fame, and oblivious to the forces of greed and sleaze lurking in the shadows, are denied by the murky alchemy of the deal.

13
THE JACKAL

'There are no easy fights now. Each one is harder than the last ...'
Carl Frampton

I

'HE CAN REALLY FIGHT!' An excited Barry McGuigan is struggling to maintain his composure. 'He's a phenomenal puncher.'

We're backstage at the cavernous Belfast Odyssey Arena just minutes after Carl Frampton has dramatically forced a fourth-round stoppage in a Commonwealth super-bantamweight title fight. McGuigan seems powered by a mix of electricity and adrenaline as he enthuses about the boxer he plucked from the amateur ranks two years earlier and moulded into a compact fighting machine, one now unbeaten in eleven professional fights.

This is what boxing's alpha-male environment looks like. A tidal wave of testosterone is coursing through McGuigan. We know who the top dog is around here. 'People say, "McGuigan's talking through his backside saying Frampton's the best Irish prospect in the last thirty years,"' he snorts. 'He's got incredible ability.'

McGuigan should know. He'd fought professionally thirty-five times and won twenty-eight of those encounters by knockout. An Irish icon since he was crowned WBA world featherweight champion in 1985, he also understands how fickle fate can be. Having had to defend that title under the blazing Nevada sun, a folly in any language, he'd been taken from the pop-up arena in the carpark of Caesars Palace Casino in an ambulance, battered, bruised, demoralized and dehydrated, pleading in a slurred whisper with a priest, 'Don't let me go to sleep. I don't want to be like young Ali.' Then, as now, McGuigan knew how close boxers could come to death, his punches having once ended the life of a young Nigerian boxer.

In Belfast now, these are happier times. Frampton has just won the most important fight of his short career. With a local hero as manager, he's becoming a great news story. Famous for his battles inside and outside the ring, McGuigan had been enjoying a high-profile career as a respected boxing pundit. His successful Boxing Academy (BMBA) had worked to integrate boxing with education and create careers in sport. The Clones Cyclone's most ambitious venture had been to become a boxing manager. His fight now is to convince the world that the young super-bantamweight from Tiger's Bay is destined for greatness.

II

The next time Frampton, dubbed 'the Jackal', fought in the Odyssey, he headlined with two belts on display, the Commonwealth strap and also the IBF Inter-Continental super-bantamweight title. It was September 2012 and 'Judgement Day' saw Frampton defending his titles against Canadian two-time world champion Steve Molitor.

With a conviction normally reserved for articles of faith, McGuigan, a Catholic, believed fully in Frampton, a Protestant. 'This fight is the first step on a run-in towards a world title,' he told me. 'He's got a magnetism I haven't seen in other fighters for years.' Promoter Eddie Hearn was pleased to be involved with a rising star. 'Carl has everything to be a world star in the fight game,' he wrote in his programme notes. 'Great technical ability, superb work ethic and great guidance from Barry, and Shane McGuigan and Gerry Storey. And tonight we find out whether he can mix it at world level.'

Molitor had lost just two of his thirty-six fights and he wasn't shy. 'I'm world level,' he announced. 'This is too soon for Frampton.'

Unable to cope with the home fighter's ingenuity, speed and power, the flinty Canadian southpaw discovered he'd misjudged Frampton. Referee John Keane stopped the fight in the sixth round. 'My apprenticeship is over,' announced Frampton.

The Jackal was building towards something extraordinary. He'd won his Judgement Day fight, yet his manager's judgement was also under scrutiny. Was he expecting too much, too soon, from Frampton?

With world titles as the end goal, McGuigan was determined to have the Jackal fight for the European title next. His opponent would be title holder Kiko Martínez. La Sensación was a formidable champion. At twenty-six, just a year older than Frampton, his record was twenty-seven wins in thirty fights. Explosive and durable, he'd stopped nineteen of his opponents and had gone the distance in his three losses. The rugged Spaniard would be the most dangerous opponent Frampton had yet encountered.

Kiko Martínez arrives in Belfast in February 2013 confident of retaining his European title. 'Frampton will try to run,' he predicts. 'I'm a lot stronger than him. I'll beat him by knockout.'

As if to underline his confidence, the visitor makes throat-cutting gestures towards Frampton at the weigh-in. The Jackal remains unruffled. 'He's going to come forward throwing big bombs,' he says. 'I can outbox this guy.' McGuigan cautions, 'Kiko is danger from first bell to last. This one will be a barnstormer.'

When fight night arrives, there's a shock change in Frampton's corner. Absent is veteran trainer Gerry Storey, whom McGuigan called 'a sage'. Overnight, Shane, McGuigan's son, has stepped into the role of head coach. Days earlier the manager had outlined the vital role the experienced Storey played in the campaign, describing him as 'a very clever coach and tactician'. The last-minute switch raises the stakes on an already critical night.

With a European title on the line, the packed Odyssey is a churning vortex of psychic epinephrine. Warming up with the Spanish flag loosely knotted around his shoulders, Martínez is scowling. Frampton has Barry McGuigan bouncing alongside him like someone ready to get involved in the action. There's a quiet ferocity to the aggression Martínez unleashes in the second round in retaliation for what has been a stylish opening round by Frampton, who's working behind his jab and scoring with body shots.

Now Martínez accelerates from the bell and throws a deluge of shots, many potential fight-finishers. By the fourth, Frampton is tempting fate, keeping a low guard, fists poised by his belt. Martínez is cut first, under the left eye, over an ugly swelling. From the fifth, the Spanish fighter begins to slow down. Frampton appears more clinical, picking his shots. They square up violently in the seventh, with Frampton looking the more assured. Despite the bullying intent being shown by Martínez, Frampton is landing important punches. In the eighth, they resemble two young bulls, with Martínez upping his level of aggression, intent on doing damage. No one's taking a breather. Frampton's low slung fists invite crafty counterpunches from Martínez. The Belfast man absorbs them without flinching and appears content to trade with the Spanish master of the knockout art. It looks as if it's going to take a superhuman effort by both men to survive the pace and the punishment. The local boy is heading into unknown territory.

In the ninth, Frampton engages on Martínez's terms, head to head. As Martínez pursues him, Frampton shows his skills, sliding along the ropes and out of danger. Martínez takes some heavy hits. But he's relentless. As he pursues Frampton, the Belfast challenger opens up some space between them. His jab is frustrating Martínez. With about thirty seconds left in the round, Frampton has his back to me and I can clearly see the malice in the approaching Spaniard's eyes as he computes a way to finish the fight. Frampton looks as if he's about to use his footwork to get out of trouble. Martínez throws a right hook, the momentum of which carries him forward towards the challenger. In that instant, Frampton's left fist is also in play. Crucially, with Martínez's guard down momentarily, Frampton adjusts his stance and unleashes a whip-smart short-range right. The Jackal's torso swivels, adding the force of his body weight to a punch that lands, max strength, flush on the exposed face of the oncoming Martínez and sends him, arms and legs akimbo, to the canvas. In desperation, Martínez struggles to his feet but can't stand unaided. He topples onto the ropes – they hold him up long enough for the referee to wave off the fight. It's the first time Martínez has been stopped.

The packed Odyssey Arena erupts in a frenzy of celebration. The guy sitting in front of me at ringside turns and wails, 'I missed it. What happened?'

'A short right head shot.'

He has the best seat in the house but blinked at the wrong moment.

Splitting with a veteran cornerman on the eve of a major title fight had been seismic. But, in an intensely pressurised situation, Shane McGuigan stepped up and shouldered the responsibility. The fight had been brutal and merciless. Martínez's punches burst Frampton's eardrum. First time in the driving seat, Shane McGuigan remained calm and focused. Urgent voices around the ringside, including Barry's, were advising Frampton to move and keep out of danger but in the corner eagle-eyed Shane disagreed. Going into the ninth round, he had instructed Frampton to stand his ground and trade punches. It was a calculated risk. On a night when he too had been under the microscope, Shane McGuigan called it right tactically.

European champion, Frampton (25) is now moving towards a world-title shot. Everyone in Camp Jackal is overjoyed. Manager Barry lauds the punch that finished the fight as 'a dynamite shot'.

Frampton says, 'I want to be a world champion. I'm sort of halfway there.' Promoter Eddie Hearn, whose company Matchroom had a TV deal with Sky Sports, enthuses, 'The aim is for Carl to become world champion. We'll provide the best route for that to happen ... Sky have said they'd like a show on 11 May. That date's available in the Odyssey so we'll discuss it. Carl is blessed with a huge following.' Frampton is now a hot property.

McGuigan has another trick upon his managerial sleeve. Within a few months, it's announced that he has taken Frampton away from Hearn's Matchroom Promotions and signed a new arrangement with rival promoter Frank Warren whose television arm is BoxNation, a boxing subscription channel. Barry explains, 'BoxNation offered us a substantially better deal.'

Stung, Hearn meets the challenge head on. He claims the real reason for the switch is that McGuigan wants to co-promote Frampton's fights. 'Whilst we had no problem in agreeing purses for Carl Frampton, we felt such a relationship represented a potential conflict of interest with Barry's role as Carl's manager and we could not agree to be involved on this basis,' he states.

Ever alert, Hearn then signs the interim WBA champion Scott Quigg (25-0). While McGuigan's switch seems like a bold and potentially lucrative business initiative, the pressure is on him to deliver for Frampton. Hearn's 'potential conflict of interest' remark indicates an area of possible contention and dispute. Later in the year, Frank Warren offers Quigg £200,000 to fight Frampton but Joe Gallagher shrugs off the offer saying, 'Scott Quigg is in the frame to fight for the vacant WBA title. He became a professional boxer with a view to being a world champion – not beating Carl Frampton.'

The seeds of a sharp rivalry are beginning to sprout.

III

With a world-title fight in his sights, McGuigan announced an IBF world-title eliminator for Frampton in Belfast in October. Facing Frampton would be experienced Frenchman Jeremy Parodi. The 26-year-old Toulon fighter, ranked fourth with IBF, had lost just once in thirty-seven fights. 'Once I beat him I'll be in pole position for the world title,' said Frampton.

No sooner was the Parodi fight announced than events took an unexpected turn. The IBF world super-bantamweight champion was Jonatan Romero, a 26-year-old Colombian who'd boxed in the 2008 Olympics. He came from a tough neighbourhood in Cali and had lost four brothers to violence. He had an unblemished record of twenty-three wins and looked set for a series of big money-making fights. A decision to fight Kiko Martínez in Atlantic City proved costly. Despite his experience, Romero couldn't cope with the Spanish challenger's relentless aggression. Martínez won by TKO in the sixth. Despite having lost his European belt to Frampton, Kiko Martínez was now IBF world champion.

'I beat a world champion,' reasoned the Jackal. 'And I'll be the number one after this fight.' Ranked just one place below Frampton by the IBF, Parodi predicted, 'I will outbox Frampton.'

Frampton's fights in Belfast had become landmark events of noisy, joyous celebration for a community enjoying the benefits of what was termed 'the peace dividend'. Thanks to the mix-tape skills of fight night MC Mike Goodall, 9000 fight fans from across both loyalist and nationalist traditions were united in woozy pre-fight choruses of 'Sweet Caroline' and 'American Pie'. The mood was akin to a beer fest: Frampton had never failed to deliver serious action. With his wedding just eight days away, the Jackal wasn't taking any chances against Parodi. A blur of fast footwork and brutish punches saw the Frenchman last until midway through the sixth round at which point he wound up on his knees bleeding, demoralized and struggling for breath. After the fight, Frampton declared, 'I'm ready for anyone.'

Newly crowned world champion Kiko Martínez was in no rush to accept a challenge from Carl Frampton, the only fighter ever to have knocked him out. In December 2013 he fought a first successful defence in Spain and three months later flew to Japan for a second, this time winning by knockout.

'He never wanted to fight us again,' complained Barry McGuigan, who was finding it difficult to arrange a title-fight opportunity for Frampton. Switching his attention to the WBC belt held by Leo Santa Cruz, described by McGuigan as 'the one everybody wants', he said the Santa Cruz camp were keen for the test but already had an opponent lined up for March.

Frampton kept busy, meeting former two-time world champion Hugo Cazáres in April. For his fight against 'El Incredible', Frampton surprised his fans by entering the ring to the heavenly sound of Jackie Wilson singing '(Your Love Keeps Lifting Me) Higher and Higher'. The deafening din of full-throated fight fans became the new definition of Northern Soul. Inspired, Frampton conclusively floored the Mexican with a lethal left hook in the second round.

Would Santa Cruz be next? 'Me against him would be huge,' said a satisfied Frampton. A few weeks later, McGuigan Snr flew to the US for talks, saying, 'If Santa Cruz isn't available to fight Frampton, we might take a big showcase bout in the States for Carl earlier. That's where the money is.'

Many's the slip twixt cup and gumshield. While fans were expecting a WBC title fight with Santa Cruz, the Mexican they called 'The Earthquake' had other plans. Behind the scenes, McGuigan was shrewdly embellishing an alternative proposal. In June we learned that IBF champion Kiko Martínez had grasped the opportunity to prove he was a better fighter than Carl Frampton. Their rematch was set for 6 September at an outdoor venue in Belfast that was yet to be announced. 'Kiko is a much tougher fight than Leo Santa Cruz,' said the Jackal. 'He's looking for redemption.'

IV

Two giants, Samson and Goliath, dominate the Belfast landscape. These are the hulking steel cranes that testify to the city's shipbuilding history. It was in the shadow of the skeletal towers, on the slipways of the historic *Titanic* dockyards, that Barry McGuigan built a boxing amphitheatre to host Frampton's world-title challenge against Kiko Martínez. Familiar with the exploits of both Samson and Goliath in their respective Bible stories, the punters in Belfast anticipated something truly epic.

La Sensación agreed. I caught up with him again when he paid a fleeting visit to inspect the proposed dockyard site. 'It's going to be an historic fight,' he predicted. Courteous as ever, he still relied on an interpreter to navigate conversation in English. Was his only loss by KO the toughest of his career? 'Maybe it was the hardest in my life,' he replied, adding, 'It was a bad time in my personal life and the fight, and all the things around it, made it the hardest. But this time will be different. I'm a more complete person. I've my family and my daughter and now I'm mentally stronger. Knowing I'm the champion is everything for me. I'm ready now.'

Both the Northern Ireland Executive and Belfast City Council contributed financially to the staging of the fight, which was set to be screened in ninety countries, including China and Brazil. The Northern Ireland Tourist Board and all official bodies were full-square behind the local boxer and the business he was generating. With an attendance of 16,000 expected, this world-title fight was set to be the biggest sporting event to hit Northern Ireland since the 2014 edition of the Giro d'Italia powered off in Belfast. Now billed as CEO of Cyclone Promotions, Barry McGuigan thanked First Minister Peter Robinson and deputy First Minister Martin McGuinness, for 'their vision and support'. Given such a global platform, the spectre of unscheduled violence between rival breakaway loyalist and republican paramilitaries hung like a ghost of times past in the consciousness of most. If such concerns reached Martínez, they didn't faze him. His focus was on the threat posed by Frampton. 'The fight will be in the ring rather than outside it,' he insisted.

Since losing his European title to Frampton, the man from Alicante had put himself through a sensational finishing school. First, he went to Argentina and claimed the WBC Latino belt with a knockout. Next he knocked out the reigning IBF world champion Jonatan Romero in New Jersey. Then he demolished an experienced challenger in Spain before defeating the former WBC champion Hozumi Hasegawa in Japan. Now, the man who'd knocked out twenty-three of his thirty-five opponents was determined to make up for the only KO blemish on his record by defeating Frampton.

The promoters called their pop-up arena 'the Jackal's Den'. Local wags had already dubbed it the 'Carl-osseum'. The venue would be within earshot of Frampton's old family home in Tiger's Bay. 'It's the stuff of fairy tales,' he said. Everything about the fight was unprecedented. If the pressure of expectation was proving a distraction, the Jackal wasn't showing it. On fight night, a photo of Frampton's grandfather, his 'biggest fan', who had a died a couple of weeks earlier, hung in his dressing room, an ornate trailer borrowed from the production crew of *Game of Thrones*.

At ringside during one of the undercard fights, a journalist who'd been delayed by traffic sent a whispered bulletin down the ranks of the press corps. 'Hatchet's been shot in Spain.' A shockwave rippled through those from Dublin. The last time we'd have seen Gerard Kavanagh, he was working the corner for his son Jamie. How bad were his injuries? 'Fatal. It was a planned hit in a bar. An execution.'

This didn't bode well. Gerard, an associate of Daniel Kinahan, was based in Marbella, home of the MGM Gym. The shooting happened just a month after Matthew Macklin's coach Jamie Moore had been shot outside Daniel Kinahan's mansion in Marbella. Given the aura of paranoia and suspicion that lay behind the ritzy exterior of the criminal underworld lifestyle, such acts would most likely result in a wave of bloody recriminations. Given the web of connections that saw extravagantly wealthy criminals training and socializing with a cohort of starry-eyed fighters, the fallout was likely to infect boxing. Things could get ugly.

Frampton arrived in the ring first, amid a fervent fanfare from a crowd who, until relatively recently, had lived through their own hellish war. With the Belfast man a study in concentration, a hostile chorus greeted the entry of Martínez, whose body language signalled a ferocious intent. Frampton had taken his European title but now Martínez had a world title to defend and an old score to settle. He'd knocked out four opponents since last meeting Frampton. As Referee Steve Grey gave the fighters their final instructions, behind Frampton, a baleful Jimmy Tibbs, legendary East End hard man, moved into Kiko's eyeline. Coach Shane McGuigan now had an astute, cold-eyed big-fight operator alongside him. The first Frampton–Martínez fight had been a see-saw of mutual punishment. This time the needle was already veering close to the red zone.

The opening round was a cagey affair as both men, Frampton in white trunks, Martínez wearing black, tentatively explored their options. Martínez exerted pressure in the second, unleashing punches designed to concuss. Displaying fast footwork, Frampton slipped out of range and retaliated with an accurate jab and counterpunches. The fight's dominant choreography was set.

Martínez stalked his prey with frightening conviction, but slipping away from danger, Frampton was landing clean, crisp punches. Towards the end of the fourth, a slight cut appeared on the side of the Spaniard's left eye. In the fifth, Martínez seemed convinced his power shots would finish the fight. As he moved Frampton towards a corner, he crouched and lunged in with a right to Frampton's body. The Jackal parried the shot and swung a left hook. Anticipating the move, Martínez ducked and the glove sailed harmlessly through the air but, as he came out of his crouching position, he was caught by the force of an unseen right hook from Frampton that knocked him to the floor. Martínez beat the count.

Over the next few rounds, Martínez continued to roll forward, a menacing wrecking ball, bursting with animosity. Alert to the danger, Frampton maintained his concentration. Both men appeared animalistic, ready to pounce on any perceived weakness. By the eighth round, as Frampton's accuracy and eye-catching punches gave him a clear edge on most observers' score cards, Martínez became more determined to end it with his explosive power. Finding his target, he began to win some rounds. But this was a two-way street. Frampton, whose shoulder rolls helped him avoid major hits, unleashed high-speed combinations that stated his claim to the IBF belt.

As he pulverized his opponent's cut eye, the spray released by Frampton stained his white trunks red. The killer Martínez punch never came. The final bell rang. In an instant, a jubilant Shane McGuigan lifted Frampton aloft without waiting for the official scores. The result from the judges was unanimous. Frampton was world champion.

Climbing between the ropes, his father handed the new champion a bundle. Swaddled in a blanket and wearing pink earmuffs, his daughter Carla, who on the previous Monday had experienced her first day at 'big school', slept contentedly.

Afterwards, Frampton announced, 'The only one I want to fight is Scott Quigg. Eddie Hearn needs to remember that I'm the one with the legitimate belt.'

Evidence of the brutal war of attrition we'd just witnessed was carved out all over Frampton's bruised face and swollen lips. 'My head is sore,' he admitted. 'My hands are sore. But I intend to hold on to this belt for a long time. Although I have lumps all over my head, I think I was more clever. He gave me some good shots but I proved I've a good chin.'

The sense of giddy delirium that enveloped Frampton's followers was nowhere more evident than at the post-fight press conference when the normally diplomatic Barry McGuigan addressed the room. 'I said a long time ago that this guy was going to be world champion and people laughed at me ... so ...' he paused, 'fuck you.'

McGuigan's *faux pas* was greeted with laughter. Almost immediately, like a man waking from a dream, the out-of-character nature of his barb dawned on him and he apologized. No one took offence. Everyone in the room knew that, from a standing start, McGuigan had astutely charted the roadmap that took Frampton to the elevated heights of world-championship boxing. Perched on the table in front of Carl Frampton, visible for all to see, was proof of the fighter's courage and skill and his manager's unshakable belief – the red leather IBF super-bantamweight championship belt, embellished with glittering double hemisphere maps swathed by the wings of a gilded mythological aquila-style bird and replica swags of the Corona Civica once bestowed on Romans who had displayed great acts of valour. No trinket this.

V

Zealous as a heretic visionary, McGuigan had unerringly guided his protégé to the top. At twenty-seven, with a record of nineteen unbeaten with thirteen knockouts, Frampton looked set to become boxing's new poster boy.

When McGuigan fought Eusebio Pedroza in 1985, eighteen million television viewers watched. For Frampton's first title defence, Barry arranged for it to become the first live fight on terrestrial TV since 2008. It was a major promotional coup.

Ahead of the Jackal's defence against Chris Avalos, McGuigan reminded the media, 'Carl is the real deal. Armchair fans are going to love him.' More experienced than Frampton, Avalos insisted, 'He's not special.' The Californian planned to spoil the party. Mandatory challenger for the WBO title, the self-styled 'Hitman' said, 'This fight was a no brainer ... I will shock the world.'

Nine of the Jackal's fights had been in Belfast. The challenger's manager, Mike Criscio, was businesslike in his assessment. 'With Chris's punching power, it doesn't matter where the fight is.' Unburdened by modesty, Avalos, who'd lost just twice in twenty-seven fights, declared, 'I sparred with Kiko and beat his ass. When I hit Frampton, he's getting knocked out.' He taunted Frampton directly, 'You're weak, dude.' Every fight brings unique pressures. When Frampton learned that his former promoter Matchroom had teamed up with Avalos, he teased, 'Eddie Hearn is like an old girlfriend who won't go away.' With his title defence reaching a bigger audience on terrestrial television and his opponent promising to scupper Frampton's US ambitions, everything was on the line in February 2015.

Avalos quickly posed problems but foolishly abandoned his six-inch reach advantage and got sucked into close-range combat where the swagger was systematically knocked out of him. Mike Tyson's much quoted assessment came once again to mind: 'Everybody has a plan until they get punched in the mouth.' Blood was soon trickling from the Californian's mouth. Crisp body punching knocked the oxygen out of his burning lungs. Head shots left him dazed. He had opportunities to go down, but fought on, aimlessly throwing punches at thin air. What amounted to vicious target practice by Frampton was interrupted by the referee midway through the fifth. Another win for the champ.

Frampton was in demand. Eddie Hearn, Scott Quigg's promoter, suggested a pay-per-view fight but was rejected by McGuigan. The most attractive possibility for the Frampton camp was a fight with Leo Santa Cruz. But the WBO champion seemed reluctant. Team Frampton had a problem to solve.

VI

To make a major breakthrough in America, be it in sport, the arts or business, you've got to have promotional muscle. In US boxing there have always been a number of major gatekeepers. In May 2015, when Barry McGuigan announced that he had formed a partnership with Al Haymon, some people asked 'Who?' Others bowed to McGuigan's business acumen and chutzpah.

Haymon, a discreet powerhouse in American boxing, was adviser to Floyd 'Money' Mayweather. During the 1980s and 90s, Haymon, a Harvard graduate from Cleveland, was a hugely successful concert promoter who worked with many of the top names in R&B including Whitney Houston, Janet Jackson and MC Hammer. In 1999 he sold his concert promotions company and began concentrating on the business of boxing. Over the years he set up a network of promotions and managerial companies and was equally comfortable dealing with hedge-fund bosses as he was with gym spivs and hustlers.

With his IBF world title intact and with Haymon on board, Frampton was ready to take a major step towards the big-time in the US. A title defence against rising Mexican star Alejandro González Jr was scheduled in El Paso on 18 July.

Not everyone was impressed by Cyclone's US push. In April, Eddie Hearn attempted to embarrass Frampton into taking a unification fight with WBA champion Scott Quigg by publicly waving a cheque for £1.5 million (€2.1 million) at him. The offer was declined. Jilted at the altar of a major payday, Quigg complained, 'No disrespect to the guy Frampton is fighting, but we'd never heard of him.'

With Frampton's El Paso fight screened live coast-to-coast on CBS, and with Haymon on his team, a convincing win could see him on the way to super-fights stateside. But the scorching border town had proved a tough place for an Irish fighter to get a win. John Duddy failed there. Andy Lee too. The 22-year-old Mexican, son of former world featherweight champion Alejandro Martín González, was coming to add to his twenty-five wins. 'Corbita' had knocked out fifteen opponents, many of them fellow Mexicans, and as Jamie Conlan noted, 'If you've been stiffing Mexicans, you have to have a powerful punch.'

Speaking to me from El Paso, Barry McGuigan nixed negative thinking. 'It doesn't matter where the fight is because it's going into every household in America for free. Our overall objective is to capture the Irish-American audience but we want to woo the Mexican audience as well, just like GGG has done. I want them to admire Carl.' The golden ticket was within touching distance.

Fight Night began as Fright Night. González, with a five-inch reach advantage, dropped Frampton with a left to the body after just thirty-six seconds. Unhurt, Frampton shrugged off his embarrassment. This certainly wasn't how he'd envisaged his US debut. Frampton's jab was a lethal weapon but he'd been made look inept by an innocuous-looking straight left. Worse was to come.

Frampton landed some clean shots. Then, just before the end of the round, a right cross from González forced his knee down on the floor. Another knockdown and a second standing count. Both in the first round.

'It's important to create a legacy,' Frampton had said before the fight. In his first three minutes, he'd been floored twice and was three points down. With eleven rounds remaining, he had an opportunity to rectify the situation but his opponent, ranked thirteen by the IBF, had been revealed as extremely dangerous.

The Jackal began to box clever. He varied his tactics, picked his shots and absorbed those hits he couldn't avoid. Slowing the pace, the Belfast man looked the more menacing despite being subjected to occasional manic bursts of aggression from the rangy Mexican. Low punches from González resulted in a point being deducted in the third round, and again in the eleventh. Frampton's composure in adversity, subtle ring skills and ability to punch, were eye-catching features of an exciting fight he clearly bossed. The judges agreed. Two scored it 118-108 and the third had it 115-109. The stats showed Frampton had connected meaningfully with 36 per cent of his 692 punches, as opposed to González Jr's 24 per cent of 593. Despite the win, Frampton said he was 'disappointed' with his display.

Later, González revealed, to John Dennen of *Boxing News*, that Frampton advised him to drop four pounds and fight at bantamweight (118 lbs). 'He told me I'm strong and a hard hitter and that I'll smash everybody there,' he said. 'I'll just carry on and keep learning.'

Sadly, Alejandro González Jr had just two more fights. Seventeen months after delivering what Frampton described as 'the biggest fright of my professional career', he was found dead with two others in a jeep near his home in Guadalajara, Mexico. Two were wearing just underpants. One was naked. All had their hands and feet tied and they had clearly been subjected to violence before being killed. The murders were described as 'execution style'.

VII

Having promoted Frampton, Eddie Hearn was incensed when McGuigan created Cyclone Promotions and shut him out. The Matchroom boss artfully manoeuvred Scott Quigg into the top WBA slot.

The animosity between Quigg and Frampton had grown since Hearn's stunt with the £1.5 million cheque. A feud sells seats. Deal done, the unification fight was tipped as one of Britain's great super-fights of 2016.

Intriguing though it looked on paper, the showdown in Manchester wasn't the high-octane cocktail that had been expected. Frampton won on a majority decision. 'I knew it was going to be a boring fight,' he said dismissively. Quigg's only complaint was that he'd fought most of the fight at a disadvantage. 'At the end of the fourth round he caught me with a peach of an uppercut that done my jaw,' he revealed. When Quigg's friend Wayne Rooney encouraged him to 'keep his chin up', the Bury fighter replied he couldn't even keep it straight. His jaw required extensive surgery.

Having grossed at least €2 million for the fight, Frampton turned his attention back towards America and 'a blockbuster' title fight with Leo Santa Cruz.

Floyd Mayweather's favourite fighter, Santa Cruz believed he'd beat Frampton. 'He drops his hands too much,' he said. 'I could finish him.' On the night that Frampton took his record to twenty-two undefeated against Quigg, Santa Cruz stopped Kiko Martínez. He was now unbeaten in thirty-three fights. A WBA world super-featherweight fight between the two was arranged for July.

The Mexican, taller, two years younger and with a longer reach, was a three-weight world champion at bantamweight, super-bantamweight and featherweight. An experienced operator from a tough school, he displayed exceptional punch selection and physical strength and frequently averaged over a hundred punches per round. Not for nothing had he been nicknamed 'El Terremoto' (the Earthquake).

Santa Cruz *v* Frampton was likely to be seismic.

VIII

The concept of an 'acid test' became popular during the years of the California Gold Rush, which began in 1848. For the Forty-Niners, prospectors of all sorts, diggers, panhandlers, claim-jumpers and grafters, a simple test involving nitric and hydrochloric acid was employed to verify whether a sample was indeed a noble metal or just a base metal.

In boxing, small-hall shows are a means to an end. World titles and TV pay-per-view receipts are the real goldmine. At that level, while there's plenty of money to go round, fees and percentages have a way of eating into the financial pie. Sanctioning bodies, managers, agents, promoters, coaches, cut men, matchmakers, PR agencies and others, quite apart from the undercard fighters and their teams, all have to be paid. Some get a bigger slice than others. If the boxer has a good accountant, he or she can still be handsomely remunerated. Apart from the purse, there's the possibility of sponsorship and advertising, maybe even merchandise, to consider. At stake in a world-title fight is the motherlode.

It was said that the corrosive punching of Santa Cruz would provide Frampton's acid test. The Jackal was the underdog for the fight in Brooklyn on 30 July. Notwithstanding McGuigan's assertion that the Santa Cruz challenge would 'bring the best out of Frampton', the question remained as to whether this expedition, instead of confirming a route to a series of lucrative mega-fights, would result in nothing but fool's gold.

When I spoke to Frampton, ahead of a promotional photo session with Santa Cruz on the observation deck of the Empire State Building, he revealed how he'd factored in the experience of being stunned by González in El Paso. 'My punch resistance will be up at featherweight and I've dealt with bigger punchers than Santa Cruz,' he said. Another factor of concern, I ventured, were the 'uncontrollables', the random disadvantages, like, for example, an overly spongy ring surface, that featured in Texas. 'There were issues we weren't happy with in El Paso, and we've learned from our mistakes,' Frampton replied. 'Obviously we have more control when I'm boxing in Belfast. But the team has worked very hard to make sure everything is right and in place.'

Hydration in the Texan heat had been problematic. Frampton had admitted that he hadn't had enough time to acclimatize properly. 'Things were wrong,' he'd admitted. But preparation for this fight had been meticulous. Fighters who'd sparred with Santa Cruz in previous camps were brought in. Having studied the champion in depth, McGuigan said, 'Carl's punch selection and timing is going to pay off.' McGuigan had also brought Carl on a tour of busy Irish bars in the New York area to help drum up support. The ploy paid off. Enthusiastic Irish New Yorkers joined the young migrant Irish and planeloads of Frampton fans from Northern Ireland in creating a hothouse football international atmosphere. With the Irish contingent bellowing along to Northern Ireland's favourite chant, 'Will Grigg's on Fire', Frampton felt at home as he entered the Barclays Center arena on Atlantic Avenue.

From the opening bell, against an experienced volume puncher with a reach advantage, Frampton became like a Spitfire in a dog fight, rolling and wheeling. 'Turning and turning in the widening gyre,' as Yeats might put it. He remained elusive, landing clean shots. In the second round, Santa Cruz felt the impact of a Frampton left hook to the head and staggered backwards until embraced by the ropes. Frampton wasted no time in following through with a rapid-fire fusillade. The assault gave Santa Cruz plenty to think about and afforded Frampton an element of influence.

The fight became a dizzying assault course as both men exploited openings with varying degrees of success. There was power in the punches but Frampton seemed more compact, more in control. His ability to sidestep trouble and strike effectively on the counter was eye-catching. Santa Cruz's father urged his son to get closer. In the sixth round, Santa Cruz began to stamp the authority of a champion on matters. The action became trench warfare which, given the number of rapid punches he was firing off, swung the balance back towards the Mexican. Just when it looked as if Santa Cruz was back in the driving seat, Frampton became the aggressor in the eighth. No quarter was given. Both men fought as though their lives depended on it.

Bobbing and weaving, Frampton continued to make Santa Cruz miss. But, given the quantity of punches he threw, the Mexican was still tagging his man. Despite having been shaken by a turbocharged right from Santa Cruz in the tenth, the Jackal wasn't going away. The last two rounds were frantic, with both men landing punches at a furious rate. This was going to be close.

Both men raised their arms at the final bell. The two champions knew they could do no more. Shane McGuigan lifted Frampton aloft. Santa Cruz's corner followed suit. Both teams laid claim to the title. The judges double-checked their tallies. The score cards were collected. The gloves were removed. Head bowed and hands clenched in supplication, Barry McGuigan prayed. After what must have seemed like an eternity for both teams the announcer declared, 'We go to the scorecards …'

Each judge scored the fight differently. Two gave the opening round to Santa Cruz. And two gave the last round to Frampton. In general, they deemed Frampton to have bossed the early rounds, Santa Cruz to have been on top in the middle of the fight and Frampton to have regained control late on: 114-114, 116-112, 117-111.

By majority decision, Frampton was declared the new world champion.

Barry McGuigan burst into tears. It was a historic result, making Frampton the second Irish fighter, after Steve Collins, to become world champion in two weight divisions. When the stats were crunched it was discovered that Frampton had landed more punches than Santa Cruz who hit with 225 of 1002 punches thrown. Frampton threw 668, but 242 found their target. Afterwards, the Jackal provided his own cogent analysis. 'I won the fight because I didn't lose control,' he explained. 'I earned his respect early in the fight with my distance control and hard punching.' His tactics had been correct but Frampton had to walk through fire to achieve his goal. When perseverance was called for, the Jackal tapped into a deeper reservoir of courage. He wasn't going to disagree. 'I won it with my heart, not with my head,' he conceded.

Santa Cruz left Barclays Center vowing, 'We'll get the rematch and we'll win.' The fight had earned Frampton half a million dollars. His opponent took away a million. An era of big-money fights appeared to have dawned. 'That's the fight of the year,' declared promoter Lou DiBella, already computing how to maximize the gross for a rematch. 'That was sensational. That was rock-em, sock-em robots. The work rate was unbelievable.'

IX

Victory in Brooklyn handed Carl Frampton the key to unlock a string of lucrative headline fights. His time had come. The prospect of million-dollar-plus purses lay ahead. He considered possible options. There was IBF champion Lee Selby as well as Abner Mares, Óscar Valdez (WBO champion) and Gary Russell Jr (WBC champ). 'I'll fight anyone,' said Frampton.

A title defence in Belfast would prove a gilt-edged earner. But, desperate to reclaim his belt, defeated champion Leo Santa Cruz insisted on putting the rematch clause in his contract into effect.

With Las Vegas selected as a 'neutral' venue, the fight was set for 28 January. 'Unfortunately for Leo he's going to be left crying again,' said Frampton. 'If I nail him a little bit cleaner, I could knock him out.' Santa Cruz had other ideas. 'When I get the win, we can make a third fight and we can come here to fight in Belfast,' he said at a press conference in Frampton's home town.

First published in 1922, *The Ring* magazine is regarded as the Bible of boxing. For over ninety years it has been selecting a Fighter of the Year. As 2016 ended, the *Ring* editorial team named Frampton Fighter of the Year and featured him on the front cover. Having been nominated ahead of Vasiyil Lomachenko, Terence Crawford, Manny Pacquiao and Román González, it was a big deal. Frampton was just the fifth European to be decorated. He was king of the hill, top of the heap.

Leo Santa Cruz didn't think so. With his father, José, in remission from a cancer diagnosis, back in his corner, Santa Cruz was a happier fighter. 'I want people to remember our fights,' he said. 'I want a trilogy.' He predicted a win by knockout.

From the opening bell, both fighters were a study in concentration. Caution was their watchword. Soon, Santa Cruz was making his four-inch reach advantage count, doubling up on the jab and bruising Frampton, who struggled to get up close. The second round showed Santa Cruz had learned from the first fight. The stars of the show were the same but somebody had hired a new choreographer.

Not as busy as in the first fight, Santa Cruz used his piercing jab to fend off Frampton. His technique underlined the old adage, 'A right hand can take you around the block but the jab will take you around the world.' A multipurpose straight-arm shot, a jab acts both as a defensive measure and a scoring shot which, when used effectively, can do sustained damage and demoralize an opponent. Here was evidence of how it helps a fighter measure distance. When a jab snaps the head back, it can create a split-second opportunity to key up more damaging punches.

More methodical, less eager to rush in, Santa Cruz kept Frampton at bay. His whip-smart jab continued to score points and upset the Jackal's game plan. He made his counterpunching work while his upper-body movement had Frampton's dangerous hooks flashing through empty airspace. In the fourth, Frampton raised the tempo when he got inside. As the Jackal continued to search for an opening in the fifth, he was kept at bay by the piston-like jab. He eventually landed a telling right hook, but Santa Cruz responded waspishly, unleashing a series of fast lefts. The sixth was marked by frenzied action as both men backed themselves to land a knockout punch.

Going into the second half, things were poised on a knife-edge. The champion upped his aggression and appeared eager to dominate. Into the eighth, he looked the sharper and more menacing in the clinches. Santa Cruz's reach made a difference in the ninth. But neither fighter had a firm grasp of the belt. With some rounds too close to call, the last three seemed set to confirm the destination of the spoils. 'Come into my parlour,' was Santa Cruz's invitation as he positioned himself to offload a spidery web of counterpunching. While Frampton tried to drop big bombs in the eleventh, Santa Cruz showed his skills in avoiding the shots and responding in triplicate.

This had been a punishing fight. Santa Cruz employed the old trick of finishing each round with an eye-catching burst of action, which might just sway a wavering judge. The twelfth round saw Frampton unsparing in his effort as he waded in with clubbing rights and lefts against a man displaying mercurial evasive techniques.

While Frampton had been energetic and bullish, the Mexican, a champion at three weights, hadn't looked like a challenger. The close rounds would decide the result. That intuition was confirmed by the judges, one of whom scored the fight a draw, 114-114. His colleagues both scored it 115-113 and handed Santa Cruz the title by majority decision.

Frampton greeted the announcement with a nod of wry bemusement that failed to disguise his disappointment. Santa Cruz had won the tactical battle. 'My head was telling me, "Go forward. Pressure. Pressure," he said. 'But my dad and my corner were telling me, "Box him. Box him."' Frampton, his face disfigured and swollen, was graceful in acknowledging his first defeat. 'The best man won on the night,' he said. A rematch seemed an inevitability.

The stats were unforgiving. Santa Cruz unloaded 884 punches to Frampton's 592. The Mexican fired off eighty-one jabs. Frampton managed just twenty-eight. The Jackal's manager offered no excuse. 'He was outboxed … It was just a sluggish performance.' The defeat scuppered Frampton's dream of a spectacular outdoor unification fight with IBF featherweight champ Lee Selby at Windsor Park in summer 2017. But McGuigan remained positive, saying, 'Carl can bounce back.'

In Frampton's camp, talk was of a third decider with Santa Cruz, this time in Belfast. McGuigan explained how he'd spoken with fight broker Al Haymon who had said there would be another fight. 'They have given us their word,' said McGuigan. Ominously, the Cyclone boss added, 'He mentioned other options which does concern me slightly.'

Meanwhile, Haymon had joined the celebrations in the Santa Cruz dressing room.

X

An unexpected heatwave lifted the public mood in Ireland in June 2017, but Windsor Park wasn't going to be the venue for Frampton's first fight in his home town in over two years. Neither would it be against Santa Cruz or IBF champion Lee Selby. At the Europa Hotel, we were introduced to Andres Gutierrez (23) and Frampton (30) who would fight in the SSE Arena (formerly the Odyssey).

A busy Mexican fighter who'd lost just one of his thirty-seven fights, Gutierrez announced, 'I'm looking for a war with Frampton so that people can see what I'm made of.' The Belfast fighter revealed that he'd been close to fighting Gutierrez for his American debut in El Paso. 'With the performance I had that night, who knows what would have happened,' he mused. That Santa Cruz appeared to be avoiding a third Frampton fight was playing on his mind. 'Before our last fight, Santa Cruz was definitely coming to Belfast,' he said. 'But, after that fight, he quickly changed his mind. I understand. The money he gets in the States would mean that this would need to be a PPV fight and there were no dates available here.'

From Mexico's mining area Querétaro, Gutierrez had to be tough to survive. 'I started fighting when I was five years old so I could defend myself,' he said. 'The people I've fought before have never been able to punch me on the face.' A win for either man would ensure a fight for the WBC world featherweight title held by Gary Russell who had ended Dubliner Patrick Hyland's challenge in the second round in the US the previous year. A third fight with Santa Cruz was now on the long finger.

It had been an astonishing four years since Frampton received the Irish Boxing Writers' Association award for Boxer of the Year 2012 at a ceremony in Belfast. Of the various gongs being handed out that day, it was my duty to present the award for Manager of the Year to Barry McGuigan. Since then, Frampton's odyssey had taken him to a European title and world titles at two weights. The Frampton-McGuigan dream team had proved it was world class. What made the epic quest all the more satisfying was that both men were cordial, humorous and immensely likeable. While I maintained a professional distance, our relationship felt like friendship and I derived huge personal satisfaction from Carl's spectacular development and success. His career was the stuff of storybooks.

Frampton's coach, Shane McGuigan, was a less-visible presence in the public eye. The media tended to focus on Barry, his father. Yet Shane was adding to his list of accomplishments. A few weeks before the Gutierrez presser, he'd guided George Groves to a WBA world super-middleweight title win. In Belfast, we met for coffee away from the media scrum. Because he could sometimes look like an overgrown schoolboy, it felt like Shane could be the youngest coach to guide fighters to three world titles. He was twenty-five when Frampton took the IBF belt from Kiko Martínez. Nineteen months before that fight, he'd worked the corner for Frampton in his European title win against Martínez. It was the night Shane suddenly took over as Frampton's chief coach. It was then that he realized he and Frampton could go all the way to the top.

A short sharp right from the Jackal finished the contest that night. Afterwards, Shane's tactics were criticized. Some insisted the coach had got lucky. McGuigan admitted, 'People gave me stick saying, "He hasn't got a clue."'

A great coach proves he's officer material in the white heat of battle. In the bear-pit excitement of big pro-box nights, how difficult is it to avoid getting distracted? 'It's about controlling that stressful environment,' said Shane. 'And making sure you tick off all the boxes. If you've done everything that you set out to do in camp correctly, then you've got nothing to worry about. It's down to the fighter to prove it. It is fine margins. Winning a round. Losing a round. You've got that sixty seconds [between rounds] but ten seconds of that is getting up and down from the stool, so you've got fifty seconds to get the gum shield out and settle him down and give him two or three points that he can trust and believe in.'

'We got it wrong in Vegas,' he admitted, referring to Frampton's defence of his world title against Leo Santa Cruz in January. 'His dad got a good strategy down. He took Carl out of his rhythm early on and we were playing catch-up. At the top level, it's fine margins.'

Although mannerly, analytical and unflustered, Shane didn't shirk getting involved in psychological warfare. 'I don't want to be the trainer that's going out there having to shut people down,' he began. 'But these guys are my family, my friends. I consider them my family. They're my fighters, but if anything happened to them I'd be soul-destroyed and devastated. When someone like Eddie [Hearn] or others try to get a rise out of you, you've got to stick up for yourself and your team.'

Alex Ferguson, who built a succession of great title-winning teams at Manchester United, was asked by John Carlin what he looked for in promising young talent. 'Ability is the first attraction of any player,' he replied. 'But just as important in the long run is to try and assess what kind of character he's got. Has he got the enthusiasm all the time? Character, enthusiasm and ability are the three important factors.' Given that most young boxers are enthusiastic, what did Shane look for in a fighter before committing to working with him or her? 'Athleticism,' he began. 'Whether they can take a good shot. Whether they can learn and adapt.' Discreetly lowering his voice for fear of being overheard, he continued, 'And that they're not arrogant. Arrogance is one of the worst traits you can have.'

XI

'This is my city,' Frampton had declared ahead of the Gutierrez fight. 'I'm the boss.' Ahead of his first fight since defeat by Santa Cruz, he was acquisitive; determined to land another world-title fight.

However, as he stepped on the scales at the weigh-in, he looked distracted. With good reason. While his Mexican opponent made weight at 126 lbs, Frampton hit 9 st 1 lb, a pound over the limit. It was a major setback. Even if he won the fight, overweight Frampton wouldn't qualify for the world-title fight with Gary Russell Jr. Only Guterriez could benefit from a win. This wasn't a good look. It suggested ill-discipline and unprofessionalism. Almost immediately the miscalculation began to draw flak from respected observers. Worse, following on from a spiky reaction to the loss in Las Vegas, it hinted at something hitherto unimaginable – underlying tensions between fighter, coach and manager.

Frampton apologized to his supporters via Twitter. 'I tried everything I could to cut down, but unfortunately, my body just wouldn't allow it ... I'm gutted, but at the same time I acknowledge that I am responsible.' Former IBF champion Dave McAuley criticized Cyclone. 'It's not only Carl's fault, it's the trainer's fault and manager's fault,' he told BBC. 'How they misjudged it is beyond me. Your weight's monitored about four months previous to a fight and then you weigh twice a day, seven days a week. They would have known last week or the week before that Carl was having problems.'

The weigh-in took place in front of a crowd of fight fans on Friday afternoon. Their enthusiasm was undimmed ahead of Saturday night's clash. But later that evening they received word of something truly 'grotesque, unbelievable, bizarre and unprecedented'. It was revealed that, back in his hotel room, Gutierrez had slipped in the shower and sustained head and facial injuries. He broke his teeth, received a gash on his chin, an injury to his nose and had been concussed.

The fight was off.

Within a couple of weeks, stories began circulating in Belfast of a rift between Frampton and Cyclone. Those rumours gained traction when it was learned that the boxer had resigned as a director of Cyclone Promotions. On Monday, 21 August 2017 Frampton issued a statement that carried seismic news for Irish boxing:

> I can confirm I have parted company with Barry McGuigan and Cyclone Promotions.
>
> I would like to thank Barry, the McGuigan family, and Cyclone Promotions for our time together.
>
> Having taken time to consider my future and discussed it with those closest to me, I am confident that now is the right time to move forward and take my career into my own hands.
>
> I still believe that I'm the best featherweight in the world and I promise my fans that I am continuing with my efforts to get my homecoming fight rescheduled in the very near future.

Rival promoters, including Eddie Hearn (Matchroom), Frank Warren (BoxNation) and Matthew Macklin (MTK) were already expressing an interest in working with the Jackal. 'He's a top fighter,' said Macklin. 'They don't get much bigger than Frampton and we're in the business of managing fighters, so we'd love to be involved in his career.'

Within a couple of weeks, Frampton had signed with MTK Global, who were now extending their reach into the upper echelons of boxing. 'I want to be involved in super-fights from here on in,' he said. 'To fight Leo [Santa Cruz] at Windsor Park and beat him, that would be pretty perfect and ideal.'

Arranging a fight with Santa Cruz wasn't the only thing Frampton had to worry about as Cyclone Promotions sought to mediate a settlement for loss of earnings. In November, soon after Frampton's first fight with MTK, Cyclone lodged a claim at the High Court in London relating to his breach of their promotional contract. Some weeks later, Frampton responded with a counterclaim in Belfast over disputed withheld earnings. With Cyclone seeking £4 million and Frampton demanding £6 million, and with both sides denying any wrongdoing, the acrimonious public legal wrangle took three years to settle. The split carried uncomfortable echoes of the bitter falling-out between McGuigan and his manager Barney Eastwood following the fighter's world-title loss to Steve Cruz in Las Vegas. Hugh McIlvanney had noted then 'how an almost filial bond between McGuigan and Eastwood gave way to mutual and litigious hostility'.

XII

Five months after Frampton had teamed up with MTK Global, the company's CEO, Sandra Vaughan, made a decision with far-reaching consequences for Irish boxing.

'With immediate effect, MTK Global will be boycotting all media in the Republic of Ireland,' she announced. 'Despite announcing MTK Global cutting all ties with Mr [Daniel] Kinahan in February 2017, and announcing the complete management buy-out by myself in October 2017, the Irish media have continued to sensationalize and slander MTK Global and its boxers and I cannot and will not allow this to continue.'

Wife of MTK coach Danny Vaughan and the driving force behind the Fake Bake tanning brand, Vaughan, a self-confessed workaholic, outlined her initiative in further detail:

This witch-hunt by the Irish media has left me with no choice but for MTK Global to pull out of the Republic of Ireland for the immediate future. We will not host fight nights in Dublin nor will any MTK Global athletes fight on a Dublin card ... We will no longer issue press releases. Our team and athletes will no longer participate in interviews. Media from the Republic of Ireland will no longer be welcome at any MTK Global hosted events.

MTK had twenty-nine Irish fighters on its books when the ban was introduced. Most of them, some more enthusiastically than others, adopted an MTK-endorsed logo – 'no comment for Irish media #fairnews' – on their social media platforms. Having written features on almost all of these fighters, most of whom myself and other boxing writers had a positive working relationship with, this was counterproductive and disappointing. There were other Irish boxers to write about so it was no great hardship to comply with Vaughan's directive. But, having been invested in Frampton's ambition and career since his amateur days, I was intrigued at how his training was progressing with new coach, Jamie Moore, while the legal machinery was grinding away in the background ahead of his court hearing.

Having beaten Hector Garcia in Belfast in November and with Santa Cruz avoiding a rematch, Frampton was set to face a tougher prospect in Nonito Donaire (38-4), a former four-weight world champion, in a WBO interim world featherweight fight in April in Windsor Park. Intrigued that I'd received an invitation from a UK PR company to join an international press conference call, I accepted.

The first interviewer's opening gambit, a reference to those who doubted Frampton, seemed designed to unsettle the Belfast fighter. Frampton took the obstacle course in his stride. 'People like to moan,' he opined. 'I lost a close fight to Leo Santa Cruz and suddenly it was, "Frampton's done. He's over the hill." I'm using this as motivation to prove that I still have a lot left. It's almost like sticking two fingers up to people who think I'm done. I'm far from done.' This was the self-confident, pragmatic Frampton I'd known on the way up. His tone made it clear that he wasn't just whistling past the graveyard. 'I believe I can beat any featherweight in the world,' he said. I was pleased to hear him sound as ambitious and passionate as ever.

Most of the important ground had been covered by the time I was introduced. I felt I detected a subtle change of dynamic. Frampton knew that, unlike the august journalists from the UK broadsheets and red-tops, I'd been there in draughty conditions on winter nights back when he wore a vest and headguard.

'It feels like a big fight,' he enthused:

I love fight week. I love staying in the Europa Hotel and walking around the city centre and soaking up the atmosphere. I get a right buzz off it. Nonito Donaire may be the best fighter I've come up against but I believe I'm in the best place, physically and mentally. I see the end goal. Win this fight and the dream comes true.

Endearingly, he displayed the self-awareness that had separated him from so many wannabes, adding, 'I know boxers say things automatically but I'm really up for this fight. I'm in a very good place.'

Faster and stronger, the Jackal dominated the fight and got a decisive 117-111 win on all three judges' cards against the 35-year-old Filipino. He still wanted to fight Santa Cruz again but the champion had no appetite for meeting the only fighter who'd beaten him. Three days before Christmas, Frampton suffered a second loss when he failed to relieve Josh Warrington of his IBF world featherweight belt in Manchester in a fight that was so torrid and so blistering it earned a standing ovation from the crowd.

Almost two years, and two fights, later, Frampton's legal battle with Cyclone Promotions was played out in court. The £6 million he was seeking was in alleged withheld earnings in relation to purse fees, broadcasting rights, ticket sales and merchandising.

In November 2020, after nineteen days of evidence, a surprise confidential resolution to the bitter dispute was reached without the need for a judicial determination when thousands of emails, believed to have been lost, were discovered in a back-up archive. Afterwards, Frampton announced himself 'very, very happy with the terms of the settlement'. Barry McGuigan issued a statement saying his family was 'pleased to see this lawsuit come to an end'.

Frampton fought again five months later. By then he'd given up on ever fighting Santa Cruz a third time. He put the blame squarely on his opponent. 'Leo has to take sole responsibility,' he said. 'He didn't expect me to beat him the first time. I don't think he wanted to lose again.'

When he became the third contender to fail to relieve James Herring of his WBO world super-featherweight title, Carl quickly reviewed the situation. His bid to become a three-weight champion ended in a sixth round TKO in 2021 in Dubai, where his management company, MTK Global, had been based since abandoning Marbella in the wake of the Regency Hotel shooting. It was the first time Frampton hadn't finished a fight. 'I'm deeply upset,' Frampton announced. 'I said I'd retire if I lost this fight and that is what I'll do ... Boxing has been good to me. It's also been bad to me.'

It had been a remarkable twelve years. Frampton's thirty-one fight career had delivered many truly memorable nights. Historically, despite the Troubles, boxing and boxing gyms in Northern Ireland were neutral territory. Ironically, the most violent sport had the capacity to create an impartial middle ground. The Irish rugby team represents all of the island of Ireland. But the appeal of the sport doesn't reach across all social strata. Boxing appealed to a working class whose other sporting affiliations could be divided along cultural or political lines. Frampton's flag had been one that both staunch loyalists and ardent nationalists could rally behind. Frampton's victories had brought joy to communities emerging from the trauma of decades of terror and mutual destruction. He had presided over events at which his lively supporters from both sides of the sectarian divide stood shoulder to shoulder, singing and cheering. For a moment in time, under Frampton's flag, everything seemed possible.

14
ANDY LEE

'This is a tough profession. Everyone's coming to win.'
Andy Lee

I

THE NIGHT WIND that blew in across Belfast Lough was unforgiving. Unseasonably sharp for September, it mocked the pretensions of those who were inappropriately dressed for the occasion – urging on local boy Carl Frampton in his quest to become world champion. It had been a unique gala outing for the majority of the 16,000 who turned a pop-up, open-air dockside amphitheatre into a noisy showcase of tribal pride and primitive demand.

Frampton, the newly crowned super-bantamweight champ, was back in the warmth of his changing room as the riggers set about dismantling the canopy of lights that dominated a boxing ring in the lee of the Titanic Quarter on the port city's old slipways.

As the officials, organizers and VIPs headed for the reception halls of the imposing architectural marvel, Andy Lee hesitated. Despite the knifing breeze, Lee, wearing a light finely tailored suit, had been assured as a ringside TV analyst. But now he was momentarily indecisive. Should he swing in the direction of the sponsors' soirée with its corporate bonhomie or head towards the fighters' changing rooms?

Friends from their amateur days, Frampton had been in the junior ranks when Lee represented Ireland at the Athens Olympics in 2004. Almost three years younger, Frampton was now, in 2014, world super-bantamweight champion at twenty-seven with a record of nineteen unbeaten fights. At thirty, Lee had two defeats in thirty-five fights. One of those defeats had come in El Paso two years earlier when his world middleweight title shot ended disastrously at the fists of Julio César Chávez Jr.

If Lee sensed that some felt he'd missed his chance of ever becoming world champion, he didn't show it. As his media colleagues headed towards the sound of clinking glasses and gregarious chatter, Lee turned and walked towards the cabins that housed the fighters. The world he knew best. He was a fighter. A fighter who still believed a world-title opportunity was, as he told me, 'one or two fights away'. With time running out, this mantra had become a reassuring act of faith for Andy Lee.

II

Ten years before, while people were enjoying the summer, I found Andy Lee in a place where the sun didn't shine; the gym at the National Stadium just weeks before the Athens Olympics. Frequency, intensity and specificity were the day's watchwords as trainer Zaur Antia, whose expertise would prove to be pivotal in helping waves of Irish boxers win medals at Olympic and world tournaments, put him through his paces.

Qualification for the 2004 Olympics had been the hardest ever. Andy Lee would be Ireland's only boxer in Athens. 'The standard is so high in eastern Europe where there are twenty-five different countries,' he shrugged. 'They're the real powers in boxing.'

The twenty-year-old Limerickman was surprisingly soft-spoken. His measured, calm assurance carried its own aura of menace. Lee was a silent, and deadly, point-scorer. 'I don't have to get violent,' he explained. 'My style of boxing is more technical. I stay calm and relaxed.'

Two years earlier, Andy Lee had won a silver medal at the World Junior Championships in Cuba. Tony Dunlop, who had been Ireland's head coach in Cuba in 2002, would tell me later, 'I trained the Irish

Youths and when I saw Andy spar I couldn't believe it. He never got hit. He had great defence and he had a powerful punch. I saw him knock out a European champion in training. And break the nose of another. He was phenomenal.'

His silver-medal-winning performance caught Emanuel Steward's attention. Earlier in the year, Lee had received an invitation to visit the legendary Kronk Gym in Detroit. The gym's driving force, Steward, had guided Thomas 'Hitman' Hearns, Lennox Lewis and countless others to world-title greatness. After that, Andy's progress was monitored from Detroit. Although flattered, Lee had other things on his mind. 'It's a good sign to be acknowledged by him,' he said. 'But if I don't do a job at the Olympics he's not going to be looking for me.'

He'd notched up two Irish senior titles since then. 'At junior level you're fighting guys your own age, teenagers,' he said. 'Then you're fighting 33-year-old men. I'm still maturing.'

In Athens, he went through to the last sixteen, and met Hassan N'Dam N'Jikam (Cameroon). The fight ended 27-27 but, on a countback, Lee came up short; his Olympic dream was over. Despite the defeat, he became the centre of a tug of love between the Irish Sports Council, which remained eager to hold onto his talent ahead of the 2008 Beijing Olympics, and Emanuel Steward, whose interest hadn't been shaken.

Steward was boxing's equivalent of a horse whisperer. People in the business knew that when he spoke, it paid to listen. Thomas Hearns did. He was a skinny underprivileged ten-year-old from Detroit's toughest neighbourhood when he first came in contact with Steward, under whose watchful eye he grew to become a boxing legend. The Hitman was just the first of over twenty world champions who benefited from Steward's intuitive ring savvy.

One of the go-to guys in pro boxing, Steward, as he hit sixty, was dreaming of going back to basics and moulding the pro careers of some promising young boxers. Andy Lee was top of his list.

As a teenager Emanuel had won the national Golden Gloves bantamweight title and then given up boxing. Later, when he began coaching youngsters at the local Kronk Recreation Centre in the early 1970s, his achievements became one of the foundation myths of contemporary American boxing.

Named after a local councilman of Polish extraction, the gym was in the basement under a municipal swimming pool. Thomas Hearns was just nineteen when he turned pro in 1977 and went on to win world titles in five different weight divisions before he retired in 2006. Even before his young charges began to turn professional, Steward had built an enviable reputation. At one stage, Kronk notched up a record-breaking twelve consecutive wins in the Golden Gloves. In 1984 Emanuel temporarily put aside his work in the pro game to concentrate on his role as assistant coach for the US team at the Los Angeles Olympics. The team won a record nine medals that year.

At the end of 2005 Andy Lee went to live in Steward's Detroit house. He fought his first pro bout in March 2006. By the time he arrived back in Dublin to announce his first headline event, a fight with seasoned Jason McKay for the vacant Irish super-middleweight title, Lee's record stood at ten unbeaten. He'd fought in Detroit, Memphis, Las Vegas and New York in the US and in Mannheim and Cologne in Germany. Now he was coming home.

Jake LaMotta, who'd been in Madison Square Garden when Lee knocked out Carl Daniels in the third round, declared, 'This Irish kid's got class.' Lee had developed into a mature young adult who carried himself with the quiet confidence of a successful business executive. I joined him for breakfast in Dublin. His transition to the pro game may have seemed assured but Lee pointed out, 'I still had to go over and show that I was meant to be there.' How steep was the learning curve? 'I was learning a different style of boxing,' said Lee. 'The European style is more upright, rigid boxing. Over there, it's much more loose and fluid. The emphasis is on power. People look for shots.'

When doing commentary work for the networks, Steward brought Lee along to acquaint him with life behind the scenes. Lee had even been Steward's assistant cornerman for some of heavyweight champion Wladimir Klitschko's title defences. Emanuel had also been fine-tuning Lee's techniques. 'You've got to learn the craft in the ring,' revealed Lee. 'You've got to know that when a fella is tiring you've got to press him. And know when you've got to take a rest, without letting anybody else know that you're taking a rest. There are a lot of things you can pick up.'

Former world champion and ring legend Joey Gamache did coaching work for Steward. Charismatic, with a grasp of the vernacular suitable to a Scorsese scriptwriter, he'd been through the wars and spoke a truth born of fire. He would later put Lee's move into perspective. 'You've got to have total respect for Andy Lee,' he told me at ringside. 'He left his country and moved to Detroit with nothing. He wanted to become a champion. When he came in Kronk Gym, he faced a crowd of tough experienced guys who lined up to be the one to take his head off. But Andy proved he's an intelligent fighter. He's courageous. He's strong. He's fast and he's skilful.'

In his three years with Steward, Lee had also become more streetwise. 'People are clapping you on the back,' he noted. 'Respectable people invite you to their house. Eventually, you see their angle. "I don't think you should be doing this with your money." There are plenty of slick conmen hanging around the gyms in America. Every service is a self-service.'

In the lead-up to his Irish title fight, affable Andy was replaced by a man struggling to contain his anger. This was a version of Andy Lee I hadn't seen before. He'd been ambushed at a pre-fight press conference in Belfast by his opponent Jason McKay and coach John Breen, who'd attempted to unnerve him.

'His heart is very suspect,' declared McKay in Dublin, reworking a riff Breen had thrown into the mix in Belfast. 'We'll see that when we get into the later rounds. Can he stick the pressure? I don't think so.'

Believing he'd located Lee's Achilles' heel, Breen addressed him directly. 'Andy, I think you've taken a gamble that's going to backfire in your face. All this talk about fighting for a world title is going to go out the window tomorrow night. Jason has more heart than Andy.'

Lee remained calm. 'He's made it personal,' he told the assembled media. 'We handle ourselves with class and we respect everybody. But he's like a fella who's never ate at a nice restaurant before. He just walks in, insults everybody and embarrasses himself.'

While important ranking points come with a national title, Lee downplayed the test, saying 'This is just another fight on my resumé.'

The returning emigrant had won six national titles, from junior to senior, in the draughty old National Stadium. He cut a confident figure entering the arena. From the opening bell, the ferocity of the exchanges suggested an early finish. There was malicious intent in the Limerickman's punches. As McKay attempted to figure out how to cope with Lee's explosive southpaw style, his rangy opponent set him up with a right jab before unleashing a series of crushing lefts that stunned and unnerved the Banbridge fighter. McKay's eyes soon began to mark up from the repeated battering. In the second round, as both fighters became entangled, it was McKay who came off worse. When referee Emile Tiedt separated the two men, the blood streaming down McKay's face came from a nasty gash high on his forehead above his left eye. A clash of heads. Accidental maybe, but Lee banged his heart and taunted his rival, inviting him to take a shot.

Brave and tough, McKay didn't run. But, as he rode a big left from Lee, a disguised right hook sent him toppling to the canvas for an eight count. Both men stepped up a gear in the third round. As McKay connected, Lee knew he was in a fight. He greeted this impertinence with a display of the speed and skill that had helped him survive in one of the toughest gyms in the world. Calmly picking his shots in a cameo of brute hostility, he delivered a pulverizing left that snapped McKay's head back and broke his nose.

McKay appeared to be getting some purchase when he opened a cut below Lee's left eyebrow. The inconvenience merely spurred on Lee who, fighting with a robust poetic intensity, decorated McKay's bloodied face with a tattoo of bruising in the fourth. Lee was in control. Like a big cat, he toyed with his prey. He urged McKay to come forward, before unleashing bombs with left and right. Calculated and brutal, this had become a punishment beating. In the sixth, a jolting left from Lee sent McKay's gumshield careering through the air like a shotgun-blasted pheasant. For the more squeamish in the room, it was a relief when, demoralized and in pain, McKay failed to come out for the seventh.

No more Mister Nice Guy, the new Irish champion had been ruthless. After he'd had three stitches inserted in a cut, I grabbed a private moment with him. Behind us, the paternal figure of Emanuel Steward supervised his Kronk crew as they packed up the bloodied towels and accoutrements of the trade. The circus was moving on. 'I wanted to break him apart, physically, emotionally and mentally,' said Lee. 'I wanted to break his heart because he questioned mine.'

At the post-fight press conference, Thomas Myler asked if it was too soon to be discussing world-title fights. With decades of balanced reporting in newspapers and international boxing magazines to his credit, bespectacled Myler spoke with quiet authority. Steward defended his predictions. 'Jason fought the best middleweight in the world tonight. I saw Andy with Jermaine Taylor and all the other middleweight and light heavyweight champions and Andy has beaten everybody there. Great punchers like Tyson and Tommy Hearns, they knock people out early. Andy Lee knocks guys out. Most of our fighters win championships at sixteen to twenty fights. He will have about twenty fights.'

Myler, a noted boxing historian who was also familiar with the inside of the ring, looked directly at Lee and popped a follow-up jab.

'Might John Duddy get a [title] shot before you?'

Steward cut in. 'Me and Andy watched John's fight with (Howard) Eastman. Eastman was a very tricky guy. I think John has a much better chance than he believes himself.' As the press pack fired off questions, it was Gerry Callan who struck the evening's high note when he flagged the possibility of a world first. An all-Irish world-title fight. One that would feature John Duddy and Andy Lee. Steward nodded. It wasn't something he'd rule out. For Irish boxing fans, this was the stuff of dreams. A world-title fight that an Irishman was certain to win.

The McKay threat disposed of, Lee shared a personal dream. 'Every now and then, I think about getting off the plane at Shannon and having the WBC belt around my waist and walking home along O'Connell Street [in Limerick] and meeting the people,' he said. With Emanuel Steward insisting, 'By the end of 2008 he will be the champion of the world,' Andy Lee could dare to dream.

III

In February as he surveyed the poster for a homecoming fight in in the University of Limerick Sports Arena, Andy Lee felt a degree of job satisfaction. The undercard was studded with Irish talent. Paul McCloskey, heading towards a European super-lightweight title, Matthew Macklin, the popular middleweight, and Jason McKay. 'I've only fought fourteen fights as a pro and I'm the headline,' said Lee. 'The hard work is paying off.'

Promoter Brian Peters was happy. In Ireland, pro boxing was shedding its scruffy backstreet image and was being seen as an elite sport. The conveyor belt of local pro talent that Peters encouraged through his high-profile, celebrity-attended televised events was showing no signs of slowing down. Plans to move Irish fighters up through the world rankings by winning national and European titles was on course. At the end of this particular bloodstained rainbow were pots of gold. 'There were thirteen pro shows in Ireland last year and we were involved in ten of them,' Peters noted with pride. Pro boxing was now a growth industry in Ireland. An outlier on the edge of the entertainment industry, which was once described by a music business colleague as 'the industry of human happiness'.

The fight was a frustrating contest. Not stopped in his nineteen appearances, Alejandro Gustavo Falliga, from Buenos Aires, was a rugged customer with ambition. At twenty-five he viewed Lee as the perfect scalp to accelerate his career. On the receiving end of Lee's punishing jab, Falliga decided there was no future in fighting on the Limerickman's terms. So he changed tactics. In the second round, he threw himself theatrically on the canvas protesting he'd been poleaxed by an invisible illegal punch. In the third round, blood was smeared across Lee's face from a cut from a clash of heads. For his first fight in front of old neighbours and friends, Lee wasn't being afforded a chance to shine. 'Take your time and cut him off,' instructed Steward in the corner.

Stung by a right to the head in the fourth round, Lee upped the tempo. An unmerciful left found Falliga. There would be no recovery. In the fifth round, referee Emile Tiedt stopped the fight. The home-town crowd was jubilant. 'He caught me three or four times with his head,' complained Lee afterwards. 'I had to be careful. I got three stitches for a cut.'

'Professional boxing is also a show,' explained Lee. 'You have to impress people. I could have bored them to death and won every round and just boxed safe. But I had to take a risk. He was stinking the place out.'

As the celebrations continued around him, Lee reflected on what had been a historic marker in his personal odyssey. 'I'll remember this for the rest of my life,' he said. 'When I'm an old man, I'll tell my children, "The whole city turned out to watch me."'

IV

Like a first responder helping the victim of a motorway pileup, referee Tony Chiarantano ushered a bloody and bruised Andy Lee back to his corner and the dreams of Irish boxing fans spun into freefall. This wasn't how it was meant to pan out.

Back in the States, a month after his Limerick homecoming fight, Lee was making his debut on ESPN's Friday Night Fights, the gateway to the big league for aspiring title contenders. Unbeaten in fifteen pro fights, twelve won by stoppage, Andy was clearly on his way towards a world middleweight title challenge. His televised fight against Brian Vera would provide millions of armchair fight fans across America with an exciting introduction to 23-year-old-Irishman's talents.

Expected to be a perfect career-boosting showcase, the fight in the Mohegan Sun Casino in Connecticut turned into a disaster.

For those who might occasionally watch an amateur bout on TV, a professional fight is a different proposition. Primarily it's a fight in which the toughest or fittest or most skilful or most ruthless survives.

In this fight, Lee was unnecessarily three pounds lighter than Brian Vera. By the time the contest was stopped in the seventh round, he had punched Vera 212 times. He had put his opponent down in round one. But Vera responded in round two by opening a cut above Lee's right eye.

Lee was ahead on points when he was lured into a slugging match with the tough Texas Mexican in the seventh round. As Vera's crushing right hand did repeated damage, the Irishman was staggered, yet his warrior spirit remained intact as he shuddered under heavy bombardment. Lee clung on, punching through a fog. He was gamely attempting to throw a left hook when the referee decided he was no longer sufficiently in control of his faculties to continue. The fight was stopped. The fans wanted more. They had faith in Lee's ability to throw a fight-winning punch. Defeat wasn't in the script. While they complained, Lee didn't. He was exhausted. He'd been beaten up.

Pro boxing is probably unique among sports in that the athlete not only faces the possibility of death but also risks the humiliation of being knocked unconscious, faculties scrambled, in front of a large audience who've paid for the privilege of witnessing the spectacle. That can be spirit-crushing but the painful consequences of defeat don't end there. Like in the board game Snakes and Ladders, an unlucky shake of the dice can see a boxer slide back down to the bottom in an instant. Defeat means a drop in the rankings and boxers need to be high in the rankings to get a world-championship fight. Lee had been just a few bouts away from a world-title shot when the wheels came off the wagon. It was a serious setback.

Given the short span of a boxer's career, this was more than an inconvenience.

But, made of stern stuff, Lee got back to winning ways four months later when he stopped Willie Gibbs in the tenth round in Limerick. Then he took time out to have surgeons remove troublesome scar tissue from around his eye. He said, 'It can be a long and lonely road but my target is a world title.'

V

By its nature, a fist fighter's career is precarious. But the timing of some defeats can be more psychologically wounding than others. Andy Lee's career prospects had seemed assured ahead of the Vera fight. In defeat, he faced a period of personal recrimination and soul-searching.

When he arrived in Dublin to fight Alex Sipos on the Bernard Dunne–Ricardo Cordoba WBA world-title undercard in 2009, Lee admitted he remained tormented by the Vera defeat.

'It's still hard even now,' he said. 'Every day you think about it. I know exactly what I did wrong. I was a little naive and punched myself out. He had energy in the tank because he had that extra weight on me. It's simple, boxing. You either let it defeat you or you can grow from it and become stronger.'

Asked how had the defeat affected his approach, Andy replied: 'You do things harder, longer and stronger. You push yourself more because you beat yourself up over it.'

Days before the fight with Sipos, I watched as Lee was put through his paces in a light training session by Emanuel Steward's nephew Javan 'Sugar' Hill, under the watchful eye of former three-times world champion Joey Gamache. Joey was sanguine about Lee's unforeseen calamity against Vera. 'You got to go through the experiences,' he stressed. 'Years ago, your best fighters came from that background. Losing was learning. Learning to become better. Andy's that kind of fighter. He gets the education and gets the job done.'

Some of the best boxers are notable for having acquired a zen-like wisdom. Others simply spout cod self-care aphorisms. Gamache drew from a deep personal well of understanding regarding success and failure, ecstasy and despair. He evaluated Lee's achievements dispassionately and rationalized his one defeat. 'You've seen how courageous Andy was,' he said. 'He was dominating that night. He'll come back. He'll be a champion. Sometimes people get too caught up in being undefeated. Look at Barry McGuigan. He lost early on. So did endless fighters. Henry Armstrong, a three-times world champion. It's more common than not.'

'You're going to make mistakes,' he explained. 'It's part of what we do. But you see Andy's work ethic, his determination, his discipline. People want more of him because they like the way he fights. He's got nothing but time.'

There was a curious irony in Lee finding himself in rehabilitation mode on Bernard Dunne's world-title fight. A shock defeat was something Lee and Dunne had in common. 'At this stage there are no easy fights,' said Andy. 'Fellas are turning pro just to be called boxers. Sooner or later they'll realize it's not a game. Everyone's coming to win.'

Speaking with the weight of bitter experience, Andy cautioned, 'This is a tough profession. That's what I realize. Bernard does too. It will stand to the both of us.' Alex Sipos had the potential to cause another upset. He knew Lee's style from having sparred him in Wladimir Klitschko's training camp the previous year. 'I know how tough he is,' said Lee. 'I'll never make the mistake of looking past a guy again.'

Out of the ring for eight months, Lee wasn't as sharp or decisive as previously. But he outboxed Munich export Sipos and was judged a comfortable winner over the distance. He had three more wins that year, the last of which, in Limerick in November, was against Affif Belghecham, the reigning European Union and French middleweight champion who, at eight, ranked one place ahead of Lee in the European ratings.

Promoter Brian Peters had tried to arrange a Lee fight with John Duddy but the Derryman was targeting a title fight with Julio César Chávez Jr. The idea of a possible Lee–Macklin European title fight was proposed again, a prospect that had promoter Brian Peters dreaming of Munster rugby ground Thomond Park as a venue. Macklin was now European middleweight champion with world-title aspirations. Lee's loss to Vera had resulted in him slipping down the pecking order. Insisting his focus was on his French opponent, Lee refused to be drawn on the possibility of a big domestic clash. 'It's a crowded weight division for Irish middleweights,' he noted.

By then Lee had implemented changes to his preparations. While Emanuel Steward would be in Las Vegas commentating on the Manny Pacquiao–Miguel Cotto fight for HBO, Lee was working directly with Joey Gamache in New York. As Gamache put it, 'Affif is champion and we respect that. He's a tough, dangerous fighter. He goes upstairs. He goes downstairs. He fights through adversity. He's a guy who's going to be coming to you.'

For a professional fighter, every match-up carries an important significance. In Lee's case, yet again, everything was at stake. 'This guy's ahead of me in the rankings,' Lee told me. 'If I beat him, I could move up.' The expensive lesson that came with the Vera loss – expect the unexpected – had been punched into Lee's DNA. And there was no better teacher than Joey Gamache to remind him of the capriciousness of life in the ring.

The people's favourite, Gamache had been sucker-punched in a fight in Madison Square Garden in 2000 when he met all-action hard man Arturo Gatti. The injuries he'd received that night left him with permanent neurological damage that ended his career as a professional boxer. Years later, Joey and his wife took both Gatti and the New York State Athletic Commission to court alleging a breach of contract in relation to the fight. Gamache, who was fighting at 141 lbs, alleged that Gatti, who'd weighed in days before and not eight hours before the bout, was boxing at 160 lbs, affording him a monstrously unfair advantage.

No one could have foreseen the difficulties Joey had in getting his case heard. First, one the attorneys committed suicide and then, a few months before we spoke, when the case was finally going to court, Arturo Gatti was found dead with head wounds in a hotel room in Brazil. Days before the Lee fight, a still-shocked Gamache was generous in his response to the tragic news. 'I feel sad,' he admitted. 'People always thought that I should be mad at him for what he did, but I wasn't. He was a fighter and he did what he was supposed to do.'

Gamache had prepared Lee for every eventuality in his fight with the French champion. 'This guy is a step up,' he cautioned. 'Andy should be closing in on a title fight. But we're not in a rush.'

Despite dominating the fight and setting the pace, Lee found himself under pressure in the last two rounds when the French champion, a smaller man, stunned him with a powerful left hook and followed up with a brawling fury inspired in equal measure by hope and desperation. Lee survived to win 99-92, but the last two rounds posed many awkward questions.

The win moved him up the rankings to eleven but a world-title challenge didn't look imminent. Marooned in the sport's deadly doldrums, Lee was in danger of spending his career boxing in the boondocks. In 2010 he fought four fights. In each case he finished work early, fighting just nineteen rounds out of a potential thirty-eight. In May, when Mamadou Thiam refused to come out for the third round in Limerick, Lee dismissed suggestions of taking a European title fight. 'My goal has always been to be world champion,' he said. 'It's still my dream.'

VI

In March 2011, after a big-money showdown with John Duddy disappeared with the Derryman's sudden retirement, Lee battled on. He'd added another six fights to his CV by the time Matthew Macklin landed a St Patrick's Day headliner with WBC Diamond champion Sergio Martínez at Madison Square Garden. Lee was stung. He'd been with Lou DiBella before Macklin signed in August 2011. Scheduled to fight on the undercard, he refused. There was further disappointment when a proposed meeting with WBA super champion Felix Sturm came to nothing.

Then, out of the blue, he received an offer he couldn't refuse. Contender Martin Murray had encountered problems getting an American visa, and Lee was presented with the opportunity to fight reigning WBC world middleweight champion Julio César Chávez Jr. Lee took the fight. This was his chance to become king of the hill.

A Top Rank asset, 28-year-old Chávez Jr had turned pro when he was seventeen and came with a formidable record of forty-five wins and one draw. He'd notched up thirty-one KOs and had claimed the world title the previous year. He'd already staged two successful defences of his belt. Lee would be the third Irish fighter he'd face. Chávez Jr had already dismissed John Duddy (San Antonio, 2010) and Oisín Fagan (Las Vegas, 2004). The fight was set for in El Paso in June 2012. Emanuel Steward presented a confident front, declaring, 'Andy Lee is ready to fulfil his destiny.'

Straight away there were distractions. A war over the choice of venue rumbled on. Fixed for the Sun Bowl, the college football stadium, the fight was banned by the University of Texas chancellor who cited a 'higher than normal' security risk from warring Mexican drug cartels. The concern stemmed largely from reports that Chávez Jr was in a relationship with the widow of the dead son of a drug cartel boss. El Paso community leaders warned a cancellation could damage the city's image and, with plans in train to move the fight from the border city, a new State and federal security plan was put in place and the decision was reversed. While Chávez Jr prepared with coach Freddie Roach, a nervous mayor began promoting his city as 'El Paso – America's safest city'.

Assessing the threat posed by Chávez Jr, Steward lined up some formidable sparring partners including Adonis Stevenson. 'There have been some brutal exchanges,' revealed Steward, promising that Lee would be the 'most accomplished fighter and probably the hardest puncher' Chávez Jr had ever faced. The Mexican was already excelling in the family business. When Junior was born in 1986, his father had won fifty pro fights and had three successful defences of his WBC world super-featherweight title. 'Julito' went on to fight and win on the undercard of his father's 'Farewell to Mexico' scrap with Frankie Randall in Mexico City in 2004, a year before he retired with a record of 86 knockouts in his 107 wins.

'I'm not going to El Paso to make the numbers,' insisted Lee. 'I'm going to win the title.' There was a whiff of controversy at the weigh-in the day before the fight when the Chávez Jr camp refused to allow their gloves be weighed. Lee's team manager called for 'full disclosure' but Robert Tapia, the Texas Commission Sports inspector, refused to compel the Chávez camp to weigh their gloves, declaring, 'I'm the boss here.'

The gloves issue was just one of a catalogue of dubious admin uncertainties, not least Chávez's refusal to take a urine test before the fight, which bothered Lee in the build-up to the big night and pointed to an orchestrated dark arts campaign.

Taller than Chávez was expecting and boxing behind his accurate jab, Lee proved difficult for the Mexican and landed some troublesome punches. Chávez soaked up the punishment and replied with powerful body shots. While most of the partisan home support disagreed, Lee was ahead on the cards of all three judges, 58-56, going into the seventh. Chávez upped the aggression. A sharp-right uppercut followed by a vicious left hook to the body took an immediate toll and, when he piled in, referee Laurence Cole ended the fight. A deflated Lee admitted that his punches appeared to have had 'no effect' on Chávez Jr, adding ruefully, 'I've no excuses. I couldn't hurt him.'

Excluding sponsorship and municipal funding, the fight grossed $1.84 million in ticket and TV revenue for the promoters Top Rank Inc. It was the highest-rated boxing event on HBO in the United States in the previous three years. After the champion's next fight, a loss to Sergio Martínez in which the Argentinian fought eight rounds with a broken left hand, Chávez Jr tested positive for cannabis and was fined $900,000 and suspended for nine months.

VII

The soul-searching that followed the defeat by Chávez Jr had a sobering effect on Lee, who still harboured dreams of becoming a world champion. He'd been with coach Emanuel Steward for seven years. He was family. But, in the manner of his loss in El Paso, all the old certainties evaporated in the unforgiving desert heat.

In September 2012, while in Europe, Lee learned that Steward wasn't well. He contacted Steward who said he was going for some tests. A few days later his co-manager Perry Mandera phoned with the news that his mentor was seriously ill. It was an emotional sucker punch for Lee who rushed to Detroit and spent time sleeping in the ward at Beaumont Hospital. When Steward was flown to Chicago by private jet, Lee was on the flight. It was their last journey together. On 25 October, boxing's great tactician and guidance counsellor died.

Death invariably announces its imminent presence with a macabre flourish. My own great mentor, my father, earned his ten-bell salute a decade earlier on a November evening when fireworks lit up the sky. Making light of his symptoms and treatment, the man who introduced me to boxing hung in there gamely as long as possible before succumbing to the inevitable. Although he missed the great Irish resurgence that was spearheaded by Bernard Dunne, I take comfort from knowing that he lived to witness his eldest son win a lengthy eighteen-year legal battle to prove ownership of his disputed music copyrights. His advice and support had been crucial during the long fight.

That victory resulted in a reawakened interest in the old band, which led to me teaming up with my bandmates to record tracks for a radio session in 2012 to mark the rerelease of the entire album catalogue in digipak format. In June, I got to revisit my old sparring partner 'Dearg Doom' when we performed the song live on *The Late Late Show* with the RTÉ Concert

Orchestra. Driving the beat behind a band and an orchestra in full flight, and with Shane MacGowan and Liam Neeson in the wings, the old rock 'n' roll title-fight buzz was in full effect.

Choosing from my roster of deputy drummers, the band ploughed on with some further engagements while I headed to London to cover that summer's Olympic Games boxing tournament. When I met Andy Lee at the ExCeL Arena, it was just six weeks after his showdown in El Paso. No longer haunted by the spectre of defeat, he was relaxed, positive and calmly taking stock.

Unflinching self-examination led inexorably to an undeniable truth. Lee needed to expand his boxing knowledge. And for that he needed a new coach.

After Steward's death, Lee switched from the Kronk to Adam Booth's gym in London. Would the new partnership work? In February he had his first fight with his new coach. On paper, his appearance in Belfast on the undercard of Carl Frampton's tilt for the European title seemed straightforward enough, although Andy cautioned, 'It's still early days with Adam and we are learning and figuring each other out.'

Training with canny Crumlin coach Phil Sutcliffe, his opponent, Anthony Fitzgerald, from Dublin's north inner city was determined to make the most of this opportunity. 'The underdog will be the top dog,' he told me. Having worked with both fighters, Sutcliffe predicted a war. Believing he'd identified telling gaps in Lee's overall style, Sutcliffe sent Fitzgerald out to do a job. It was roughhouse. Fitzgerald was a blur of aggressive intent and Lee took shots as he attempted to create openings. Although he seldom looked comfortable over ten torrid rounds, Lee won 98-94.

Fitzgerald got the plaudits: concern was expressed at Lee's apparent difficulty in dealing effectively with a busy, aggressive fighter. No one thought Fitzgerald was anywhere near the calibre of Chávez Jr or Sergio Martínez, so where did the performance leave Lee? Some insisted he was in decline. The considered answer was that Lee was a fighter in transition. After his years with Emanuel Steward, he was making adjustments to his style and technique.

Adam Booth had taken some persuading to team up with Lee. 'I didn't know how I'd work with him because I've very limited experience of working with tall southpaws,' he explained later. But, having studied Lee's style and impressed by his character, he devised a plan to address those areas he felt could be improved. His view of Lee's win over Fitzgerald was positive. 'We knew he'd get criticized because it was the first fight where he allowed someone to get close to him,' he said. 'But he used that as a real practice session while winning the fight.'

With two more stoppage wins to his credit, news that the one-time Irish super-middleweight champion was dropping from 168 pounds to light-middleweight (154 pounds) for a fight in April 2014 with Frank Haroche Horta was greeted with disbelief. The French fighter, who had a patchy record, posed some very difficult questions. Lee scraped a narrow majority win over the eight rounds in Denmark. Having taken the fight when a proposed title bout with unbeaten Gennady Golovkin had been cancelled due to the death of the Kazakhstani boxer's father, there was a sense that Lee had dodged a bullet.

When Lee met John 'Dah Rock' Jackson in Madison Square Garden in June 2014, the NABF light-middleweight title was the prize.

Possessing a similar knockout menace to his father, former three-times world champion Julian 'The Hawk' Jackson, Lee's opponent had stiffed fifteen of the eighteen men he'd beaten. Casual ringside wisdom had it that Lee would need to move so much he'd run of steam and eventually succumb to Jackson's power. Andy was aware of the danger ahead. 'If I lose this fight any plans of going to the highest level are out of the picture,' he said. 'This is make or break.'

Jackson, ranked four by the WBC, had little difficulty in picking off his opponent. Being deposited on the canvas in the opening round was a disconcerting experience for Lee who had never wound up on the floor in a fight, either as an amateur or a pro. Convinced he could finish work early, Jackson rushed to capitalize. Lee received a battering in the first four rounds.

On the ropes in the fifth, Lee back-pedalled into a corner to escape the unmerciful onslaught. Jackson was humming the executioner's song. He'd beaten Lee around the ring and was treating the Irishman like a slab of beef hanging in Rocky Balboa's meat locker. At one stage, while twisting like a fish in a net, most of Lee's crouching body extended far outside the ropes. Just when it looked like Jackson had his man trapped, the blink of an eye could have caused a spectator to miss the fight's most spectacular moment.

Under pressure, Lee dipped his hip and, pivoting his upper body, unleashed a crippling short-range right hook that rendered Jackson unconscious on his feet. As his faculties took an unplanned trip on the Mystery Train, 'Dah Rock' collapsed, starched, zonked, out cold. From perpendicular to horizontal in an instant. For the first time in his career, he was knocked out. Hitting the floor like a lifeless puppet, Jackson's prone figure was mute testimony to the ferocity of Lee's power. The profundity of the punch remains etched on the subconscious of all who witnessed its wrath.

In the face of extreme adversity, with an act of impudent conjuror-as-pickpocket improvisation, Lee's right fist had staged a dramatic intervention and saved his career. Almost immediately the 'lucky punch' debate began. It hadn't been totally impromptu, Lee protested. It was part of the plan. 'It's something Adam and me worked on every day in the gym,' he said. 'We worked on squatting down, bending low and then throwing the hook.' The punch did the job. Jackson later described it as 'a real bad one'. But those who saw Lee's win as a 'one punch from hell' shot remained unconvinced he was world-champion material. The jury of boxing public opinion was still out.

VIII

Although he'd reminded boxing's powerbrokers of his credentials by knocking out Jackson, a world-title shot remained a mirage. Most matchmakers considered Lee too dangerous. But he stubbornly clung to the belief that a world-title opportunity was 'maybe one or two fights away.'

Nothing had changed when, a few months later, we met in the Peacock Theatre at the opening night of *The Well Rested Terrorist*, a concert play by his wife Maud Ní Riordain's group Maud in Cahoots. A couple of inches over six foot, Lee cut an impressive figure among the thespians in the subterranean space that's part of Ireland's national institution, the Abbey Theatre. His diplomatic response to questions about a world-title fight were readily understood by all associated with the acting fraternity, many of whom were also 'resting' between productions.

It's at times like these that a fighter's faith is tested. The tantalizing possibility of a fight with WBC champion Miguel Cotto had just been dashed. We'd heard that Cotto's coach Freddie Roach swerved Lee, saying 'He's too big and he hits too hard.' Given the risk-reward ratio and the danger he posed, it was proving difficult to see how Andy might get himself into contention for a title fight. However, nowhere can the art of the deal prove to be as mercurial and extravagantly baroque as in professional boxing.

Late in October, the WBO officially sanctioned a world middleweight title fight between Matt Korobov and Andy Lee. How could this happen, when Lee wasn't top of the list of contenders?

When a convoluted squabble involving managers and promoters ruled out a Peter Quillin *v* Korobov fight, WBO champion Quillin had to vacate the title. As mandatory challenger, Korobov was offered a fight with light-middleweight champion Demetrius Andrade, who was expected to move up a weight. Andrade declined and the spotlight fell on the WBO's first-choice middleweight, Billy Joe Saunders. But Saunders was set to fight Chris Eubank Jr for the EBU European middleweight title. At this stage, ever alert Adam Booth spoke to Frank Warren who was promoting Saunders and suggested that Lee fight Korobov on the understanding that the winner would then fight either Saunders or Eubank Jr. Warren consulted Bob Arum and a deal was arranged that set up a series of potentially lucrative fights. 'It's a nice little situation,' said the satisfied promoter.

The fight was announced for Las Vegas. Two and a half years on from his defeat in El Paso, Lee had one hand on the WBO belt.

Boxing for Russia, Korobov (31) had been world amateur champion twice. After the Beijing Olympics, he moved to America and turned pro. Unbeaten, he'd stopped fourteen of his twenty-four opponents. Given how Lee had received a ritual hammering from Chávez Jr and how he'd laboured against Jackson before redeeming himself with his thunderous right fist, it was widely believed that this was his last shot at a world title. Nothing shook Lee's confidence. 'He's beatable,' he said. 'This is my time.'

Allied with skills, experience and intelligence, the former St Francis Boxing Club amateur had the one requirement every wannabe world champion needs. A big punch. In all, twenty-three of his thirty-three wins had come via stoppage. But no one was overlooking Korobov.

IX

It's fight night in Sin City. The eyes of both fighters display nothing but malice aforethought. Referee Kenny Bayless delivers his final instructions.

It's time for action. One man unbeaten, with the promise of a glittering career ahead of him. The other keen to make good the promise that has driven his career thus far. Only one can become world champion. For both, there is danger ahead. 'Protect yourself at all times ...'

Fighting southpaw, both figures create a balanced kinetic motif in a tentative round one. Through round two, Korobov's snappy jab and fluid body movement make him difficult to tag. It isn't until the third that Andy Lee finds an opening with a smashing left hook. Again, the Russian shows his strength and skills by comfortably taking evasive action. The fourth round sees Korobov display the quicksilver movement that marked his amateur career, beating Lee to the punch and varying his lines of attack.

Don Quixote had more luck tilting at windmills than Lee has of landing a glove on Korobov in the fifth. How can you gauge the frustration of a fighter who, measuring his target, fires off a potentially winning punch only to see it sail through thin air, his opponent disbursing like smoke? Time and again, Korobov effortlessly evades Lee's power shots. This is tiring for the Irishman. Looking svelte, Korobov is landing the cleaner punches. Going into the sixth round, Lee has the appearance of a man who's in a torrid fight while Korobov's calm stance suggests he's the one controlling the exchanges. The judges at ringside have Korobov comfortably in front.

A fight can turn on the slightest misstep. Kept at bay by the Russian's jab, the Limerickman comes out of a clinch, eyes his opponent and swings a hopeful right, which again sails harmlessly through the air as Korobov ducks underneath and repays Lee's insolence by connecting with a left to his jaw. It's a punch that could have felled a lesser man. But in this instant, perhaps expecting Lee to go down, Korobov momentarily leaves himself open to the unexpected right hook the crouching Lee unleashes. It's an explosive punch. On impact, Korobov wobbles dramatically and staggers backwards.

Before the Russian can recover, Lee springs forward like a greyhound at a coursing meeting. Already shaken, Korobov can only attempt to cover up as a torrent of vicious punches rain in – fifteen, sixteen, seventeen, eighteen – in ten seconds of fury. With hooks, jabs, uppercuts, Lee hammers home his advantage. Compressed into these ten seconds of gloved savagery is every slight, every hurt, every sacrifice, every wish that have marked Lee's life. In these ten seconds he spares his soul from being condemned forever to a charnel house of regret and remorse. In these ten seconds he smashes his way to the world title he so desperately craves.

In Lee's thirty-sixth pro fight, Emanuel Steward's prediction has come to pass. Lee pays emotional credit to his departed mentor, 'the man who made me'. Barely controlling a surge of euphoria, he reveals, 'His wife Marie came here today to watch me fight, flew all the way from Detroit.' His litany of gratitude extends from Adam Booth to Sugar Hill to Joey Gamache. 'Matt Korobov was giving me a nightmare,' he says, acknowledging his supporters. 'I found it really hard in there and I heard the cheers from the people who came to see me.'

Weeks pass before I next speak to Andy. By then he's passed another marker in the dreamscape that had fuelled his vision. He'd brought the WBO belt home to Limerick. 'I was originally booked to fly into Dublin …' he reveals, 'but I said we had to change it and fly to Shannon. Then the word got around and there was a great homecoming. It's a fantastic honour.'

I catch the champ off guard by reminding him of how, many years before, he'd shared that dream with me. A dream of bringing a world title belt through Shannon airport to his home town. A dream that sustained him during many dark nights of the soul on a long, hard and often lonely road. A dream that over time had assumed the comforting power of prayer. He pauses and tries to sound casual but nothing can disguise the competing counterweights of loss and redemption in his tone. His voice lowers and, as if peering into a rattle bag of fractured memories and healing stones, Andy Lee replies softly, 'Yeah, I did it.'

15
NOTORIOUS

'I've been strangled live on TV and I've come back.'
Conor McGregor

I

THE SUCCESS OF IRISH boxers in the 2008 Beijing Olympics brought boxing back into the mainstream. The sport became front-page news again. The public had pride in the Ireland team.

The previous year, while the boxers were still working to qualify for the Olympics, I sat in a cramped store room on an industrial estate on Dublin's Northside. Overhead, the young patrons of an Irish dancing school kept up an incessant thudding tattoo on the floor as I chatted to an eager mixed martial arts (MMA) coach who'd taken a break from working with fighters in the ground-floor gym. When karate enthusiast John Kavanagh, an engineering graduate from UCD, discovered MMA in the mid-1990s it was like an epiphany. 'Combat sports excite people,' he explained. 'You're allowed to punch, kick, knee, throw, fight on the ground. For me, personally, it was a great test. It was the original Olympic sport, boxing and grappling. All the current Olympic sports were bred out of that.'

At a time when many were sceptical about a spectacle that had been described as 'human cock-fighting', Kavanagh responded patiently saying, 'If no one had heard of boxing and you tried to explain it to someone they might think it sounds bizarre. "What? They stand in a ring and hit each other in the head until someone falls down?"'

Kavanagh was evangelical about MMA. He'd set up a gym and was staging tournaments. He saw the future. 'Irish guys are getting good fast because many of them have a background in boxing or kick-boxing,' he told me. Among the novices exploring the many disciplines of MMA was a young plumber, Conor McGregor.

A year later, McGregor made his debut as a MMA fighter in an event billed as 'the Cage of Truth'. On a thirteen-fight card, his early-stoppage win went largely unnoticed. It would be some time before Kavanagh would realize he was watching a future world champion.

McGregor was a product of the Crumlin Boxing Club, a room where sentiment is in short supply. You came to train, spar, get hit and improve. Not everyone stays the course. But McGregor enjoyed training. He'd spend hours perfecting the techniques he'd been shown. Head coach Phil Sutcliffe, who watched McGregor for seven years from the age of ten, knew the youngster had a unique attribute. 'He could read his opponent brilliantly,' he recalls. 'He was slick. He'd move around setting up an opponent until he fell into his web. That ability is a gift in itself.'

Another boxer who Sutcliffe felt had a similar talent was Kenny Egan, who came within a questionable scorecard of winning an Olympic gold medal in Beijing. 'Kenny didn't like getting hit,' says Phil. 'He would make them miss and then make them pay. He had such quality, I called him Rolls Royce. Conor was similar. As he progressed through the MMA, he retained his boxing skills and his mental approach got stronger. He went from strength to strength.'

With Kavanagh, McGregor added to his arsenal of skills. As his reputation grew, he was signed to the Ultimate Fighting Championship franchise. Appearing dapper and boyishly starry-eyed on RTÉ's *The Late Late Show*, he revealed he'd promised his father that he'd be a millionaire by the time he was twenty-five. Asked his age, he sheepishly admitted he was twenty-four, before quickly adding, 'I already feel like a millionaire. I feel like a superstar.' His quick-witted personality, commitment and self-belief radiated from the screen. McGregor had our attention.

On a winning streak, McGregor's performances and colourful character elevated him to superstar status even before he became world champion with a left-hook knockout after just thirteen seconds in a featherweight title fight. He knew his left fist could be a decider. 'It's a whole other ball game when they get hit by me,' he said, before going on to become a two weight champion. It was then that he put himself in the frame for what would be the biggest money-making professional boxing fight in history, a clash with Floyd 'Money' Mayweather.

Not since Oscar Wilde had an Irishman recreated himself to such dramatic and profitable effect as the plumber from Crumlin. In 1882 Wilde landed in the US and announced to customs officers, 'I have nothing to declare, except my genius.' From there he crossed America, lecturing in 150 cities. Presenting himself as the Apostle of Aestheticism, he became an object of fascination – in satin knee breeches, silk hose, patent-leather court shoes with buckles, a velvet coat with lace trim, billowy shirts and colourful cravat – as he lectured on the decorative arts. His colourful pronouncements entertained reporters whose acres of newsprint made him a celebrity years before he got around to writing *The Picture of Dorian Gray* and *The Importance of Being Earnest*. Wilde knew he was winding people up. He didn't fear notoriety. He encouraged it.

Every bit as flamboyant, Conor McGregor was presenting himself as 'the Notorious' long before he made his American debut in 2013. The Dubliner set himself up to be knocked off his perch but rose convincingly to every challenge. His coach, John Kavanagh, liked the fact that with each fight McGregor posed a question that would engage both his critics and his fans. In calling out Mayweather (40), the Notorious was setting the most fascinating riddle of his career.

It was an outrageous ploy. Unbeaten in forty-nine fights, Mayweather had seen off such formidable talent as Manny Pacquaio, Saul Álvarez, Ricky Hatton and Oscar De La Hoya. Although he hadn't fought for two years, a win against the Irishman would ensure a record-breaking unbeaten fifty, one win more than the legendary Rocky Marciano. Had McGregor, who hadn't boxed since he left Crumlin Boxing Club and had never boxed professionally, let alone gone twelve rounds against the best in the world, a hope in hell against such an exacting talent as Mayweather? Five-time Irish national amateur champion Eric Donovan, a respected TV analyst, put it in simple terms. 'McGregor has a 1 per cent chance against Mayweather, because one punch can decide a fight,' he said. 'If he beats the greatest pound-per-pound boxer of his generation, it could be the end of boxing.' Ricky Hatton, who had won forty-three fights before losing to Mayweather, was perplexed: 'How can somebody who has not had one pro fight to his name fight the best of all time?'

One area McGregor excelled in was creating a pre-fight buzz. The outsider not only talked himself into the fight, his attention-grabbing hype sent the odds on an upset tumbling from 10-1 to 5-1. The bookies were having second thoughts. The match-up put bums on seats. Ringside at the T-Mobile Arena in Las Vegas was awash with A-list celebrities. Pay-per-view subscriptions reached astronomical levels globally. Every MMA fan and every boxing fan wanted to see how this would play out. A noted MMA coach put it, 'Neither one belongs in the other's arena. It's like, "Who wins? A lion or a shark?"' The world wanted to see the lion versus the shark. Vincent van Gogh once explained, 'I paint my dream.' Having dared to dream, the former Dublin tradesman had a chance to show he could paint his masterpiece.

In the changing room Conor appeared lost in a private reverie of patriotic fervour as, in the ring, Imelda May delivered the Irish national anthem, '*Amhrán na bhFiann*', a cappella *as Gaeilge*. The significance of every word of 'The Soldier's Song' would have resonated deeply with McGregor, whose formative years had been spent attending an Irish-language school in Harold's Cross. As he strutted into the arena with arms aloft, the ethereal voice of Sinéad O'Connor singing 'The Foggy Dew', a song commemorating the Irish who fought in the Easter Rising, further enflamed visceral passions of a nation's war against injustice. McGregor was here to fight.

Far from appearing overawed, the Notorious glided about the ring in round one with his hands behind his back, taunting his opponent. Mayweather didn't fall into the trap but McGregor landed enough punches to win the opening stanza. His next gambit was to get inside in round two and rough up Mayweather. In round three the McGregor contingent was chorusing 'Olé olé olé' but the tide was turning. By round four McGregor's power was beginning to ebb away. Having assimilated what he needed to know about the McGregor threat, Mayweather began to impose himself.

In a marathon, not a sprint, McGregor was finding the rounds, and Mayweather's body shots, energy-sapping. The Dubliner's sting drawn, Money went to work. Increasingly, his punches impacted with ease and accuracy. By round six there was blood around McGregor's mouth. In comparison to the hunched mass of menace that rolled towards him, McGregor appeared to be flapping. Gulping air, his legs seemed weak and his weary eyes betrayed the look of a labourer who'd had his hot cocoa and was ready for bed. Mayweather kept coming forward, an aggressive fighter with the strategic nous and decision-making skills of a chess grandmaster.

Looking like an excavating machine ripping into a building riddled with pyrite, Mayweather set about demolishing a ragged McGregor in round nine. The referee had seen enough when, in round ten, he spared McGregor further punishment and brought the fight to an early close.

McGregor shrugged off the defeat. 'I've been strangled live on TV and I've come back,' he said, complaining, but not too forcibly, that he should have been allowed 'to wobble back' to his corner.

Despite McGregor's painful defeat, the event had been a huge financial success. The Nevada State Athletic Commission revealed ticket sales alone grossed $55,414,865.79. Even with a temporary blip, when the servers in California and Florida crashed on the night, domestic PPV figures amounted to 4.3 million buys. Total revenue generated was $600 million. Mayweather is said to have earned $275 million from the fight with McGregor taking home $85 million. While the parties signed non-disclosure agreements, McGregor would later claim to have earned $120 million.

In the business of prize-fighting, where pro boxers strive to earn enough to provide a decent lifestyle and security for their families, the Notorious had blasted his way to the mother lode. His years of commitment to MMA, his talent and his business acumen paid off handsomely with a financial chunk of one of the biggest boxing matches of the decade. Phil Sutcliffe viewed his career with a mixture of awe and admiration: 'Everything he touches turns to gold.'

Mike Tyson was impressed by McGregor's performance. 'He did great,' he said. 'He never fought before and he went ten rounds. He's got a big set of balls to just go in the ring. He was better than I thought he'd be.'

II

Tyson knew plenty about courage and fear. He also knew how opponents could be intimidated before a fight. He later admitted that it hadn't simply been gamesmanship when he threatened to kill an opponent. After some fights, he was bitterly disappointed he hadn't.

Young Mike Tyson began collecting world titles when he was twenty. In his second year as a pro he met WBC champion Trevor Berbick, a taller man with a seven-inch reach advantage. In Las Vegas, the champion attempted to unsettle the challenger by opting to wear black, Tyson's usual colour choice, saying 'This is Judgment Day. The judge always wears black.' Tyson refused to change from his distinctive black trunks and was fined $5000 for breaching the dress etiquette. Having knocked out twenty-five of the twenty-seven professional opponents he'd met to date, Tyson went to work with ruthless efficiency. Berbick had retired Muhammad Ali in the Bahamas a few years earlier and was upbeat going into the fight. At the end of the first round, he stuck his tongue out at Tyson. Bad mistake. He didn't make it to the end of the second round. When Tyson connected with a pulverizing right to the kidney and then a left hook to the temple in the second round, Berbick went over backwards. Twice he struggled to get up but each time his legs buckled. Concussed, he collapsed calamitously. Mike Tyson, world champion, was now officially the most dangerous heavyweight on the planet. After the fight, he told interviewer Larry Merchant, 'I want to live forever.'

He was thirty-eight in 2005 when he met Kevin McBride from Clones in what was Tyson's fifty-sixth fight. By then he'd had five losses, but forty-four of his opponents had been knocked out. Although he'd lost his last confrontation and had been out of competitive action for eleven months, 'Iron' Mike was still a viable threat. Conventional pundit wisdom had it that McBride was set for a severe beating. McBride's $150k pay cheque seemed chicken feed by comparison to Tyson's $5 million. Denied the opportunity to fight Tyson on two previous occasions, he was fully motivated, telling 'Big Dog' Benny Henderson, 'My father has been dead six years now and he always dreamed that I would win the heavyweight world title. I am going to shock the world. Once I hit Mike Tyson, he's going to go "Damn, this is a real Irishman."'

With the crowd on Tyson's side, McBride swarmed all over the sluggish former champion, arcing in heavy shots and swamping the smaller man. Frustrated, Tyson reverted to his repertoire of illicit back-alley tactics. Low blows, rabbit punches, elbow slams, head butts – one of which opened a cut on McBride's left eye – and, alarmingly, a blatant attempt to break McBride's arm. All to no avail. McBride replied with a series of uppercuts. It was a dirty fight. At the end of the sixth, McBride pressed down on Tyson and shoved him to the ground. When he made it back to his corner at the bell, Tyson sat on his stool like he was waiting in the electric chair. He didn't come out for round seven. The switch had been thrown and Mike Tyson's career was fried.

In the opposite corner, McBride's crop-haired coach Paschal Collins sprang onto his colleague's back in jubilation.

Tyson's reign of terror between the ropes had finally ended. He cut a disconsolate figure as he lamented afterwards, 'I don't have the stomach for this no more … I'm not that animal anymore. I don't love this no more.'

III

Tyson came to Dublin for a dinner engagement in 2006. Eight of his forty-four knockouts had been delivered as world champion. As a fighter, Iron Mike was merciless and brutal. He left a trail of destruction behind him. And not just in the ring. In a glittering constellation of talent, Tyson was the unforgiving dark star that devoured everything in its orbit. Naturally I accepted an invitation to join the gathering in Dublin.

I've been at the high altar of many worshipful religious events, high-powered political rallies and ecstatic music concerts, and witnessed unabashed fervour and devotion. What I experience in the Burlington Hotel as the world's most formidable fighting machine walks among four hundred admirers, many of them champions, former champions or aspiring champions, is a testosterone-fuelled love-in. The pungent aromas wafting through the hotel lobby suggests an after-shave sales convention. A posse of newshounds descend on Tyson's chauffeur, Gerry 'the Monk' Hutch, a man regarded as a powerful and influential 'reformed' criminal mastermind and credited with some of the biggest, most spectacular robberies in the country. A boxing aficionado who set up a club, Corinthians, in Dublin's inner city, Hutch is owner of a taxi and limousine company called CAB (Carry Any

Body), cheekily referencing the Criminal Assets Bureau, the statutory body that tracks and seizes the proceeds of crime.

Security is tight. The visit is supervised by Tom Patti, who grew up with Tyson in the Catskill Mountains. Suave, diplomatic and efficient, Patti has half a dozen Golden Glove titles to his credit. Shortly before Tyson is due to enter the banqueting room, Tom surprises me by suggesting I should meet Mike. Quickly ushered into an anteroom, I'm confronted by the man who had terrorized a succession of the biggest and most dangerous fighters on the planet. The hand clasping mine is soft. So soft as to shock me. Inappropriately, a vintage TV jingle swims into my consciousness: '*Hands that do dishes can feel as soft as your face with mild green Fairy Liquid.*' Yet the gentle hand gripping mine belongs to the fighter they dubbed 'the Baddest Man on the Planet'. This hand, when clenched as a fist, had viciously concussed opponents in forty-four prize fights. This is Mike Tyson's hand, a lethal weapon. And its owner is staring directly at me.

It has happened so quickly. I'm unprepared, but realize I should say something. The gentleness of the touch has thrown me. I'm not engaging with the monster who had bitten chunks out of Evander Holyfield's ears, the house devil who'd been accused of domestic violence or the brute who'd served time in prison for the rape of eighteen-year-old Desiree Washington. What do you say when suddenly introduced to the man whose extraordinary physical power and natural propensity for raw, unadorned violence had been wielded in the ring with the sole intention of destroying people? In that moment, I choose to ignore his transgressions, seeing instead the abandoned child who endured a horrific life of poverty and bullying abuse below the lowest rung of the social ladder in the ghettos of Brooklyn and had gone on overcome insurmountable odds and perfect the art of winning.

As I shake the hand that menaced the world, I say, 'Respect.'

Tyson is taken aback. 'Thank you. Thank you,' he says softly, his voice lisping, his eyes no longer as cold as a reptile's. Is it my imagination that he appears almost vulnerable? Convinced he's being facetious, I blurt, 'No. Seriously, man. Respect.' In that moment, I feel like St Jerome removing a thorn from the lion's paw. 'Thank you,' repeats Iron Mike, holding my gaze as anxious minders attempt to usher him away in the direction of the banqueting room. Whatever I might have been expecting, this wasn't it. An individual displaying the serenity of a Bodhisattva. I remind myself that a fleeting introduction doesn't offer sufficient time to gain an insight into a man Frank Warren once described as 'very intelligent and very manipulative'.

'Everyone thinks he's baring his soul,' said Frank. 'But he hasn't got a soul.'

After dinner, Tyson engages in public conversation with Jimmy Magee. Much of what he says is fascinating. Asked to give some advice to former National Senior and World Military champion Henry Coyle who is turning pro, he replies, 'If you want to get involved, this is a serious career. Nobody is putting a gun to your head. This is not a tough man's sport. This is a thinking man's sport. If you want to be in this sport you've got to live a certain lifestyle.'

On a roll, he describes the dedication and long hours of training that are required. 'To win you've got to refuse to lose, regardless,' he says, adding:

> Sometimes trying to become the best in the world at anything has its setbacks and disappointments. But you learn from your mistakes and never get discouraged in life. Somebody could knock you cold but you still get to win that championship of the world tomorrow. You might get humiliated in front of millions of people but never lose sight of your dream. Never.

The crowd cheers. Everyone in the room, whether law-abiding citizens, members of the legal profession or hardened criminals, appreciates the sacrifices Tyson made to become champion. 'Everyone can become a fighter,' he tells them. 'We're all fighters in life. Cus D'Amato taught us discipline and co-ordination. Not necessarily in your physical aspect but in your thinking manner. Your belief and confidence. Things that you do in the ring, sometimes you have to do every day of your life. Basically, structures to live your life, the way you're going to fight. That was to be very determined, very hungry and to have a great deal of confidence. Because confidence breeds success. And success breeds confidence.'

Acknowledging the Irish talent at the top table, Steve Collins, Bernard Dunne, Joe Egan and Jim Rock, he appears relaxed as he offers a confessional glimpse of his life. 'These guys make me out to be a nicer guy than … er … I've been on the wagon for eighteen days but I'm just a mess sometimes.'

Far from being a nasty thug, Tyson reveals a different side to his personality, admitting:

> I was a street guy. I didn't care. I fought for glory. Glory meant more to me than money. When you're a street kid and you don't have family, glory could do you. Most fighters are very insecure. That's why they become champion fighters. They don't like the life that they live. People talk down to you. People don't show you respect. It's a cruel world we live in. But there are also beautiful people in this cruel world. In order to make people beautiful you have to make them respect you.

'Respect,' he says, glancing in my direction, 'is more powerful than love.'

16
NUISANCE

'I'm going to kill you.'
Anthony Fitzgerald

I

VIOLENCE IS PRO boxing's *raison d'être*.

When Kevin McBride withstood the persistent headbutting of Mike Tyson, he didn't just club his way into the annals of boxing history, he also cleared a pathway to a new coaching career for Paschal Collins.

Establishing a good working relationship with Murphy's Boxing in Boston, Collins opened up a successful trade route to North America for his Irish fighters including Steve Ormond, Niall Kennedy and Ray Moylette. The man who capitalized most on the arrangement was Gary 'Spike' O'Sullivan, who'd won the Irish middleweight and WBO International middleweight titles.

Adopting a distinctive sartorial image, Spike O'Sullivan introduced geometrically perfected whiskers to the sport. One man who wasn't impressed was Anthony Fitzgerald, a rugged inner-city fighter known as 'the Pride of Dublin', who'd held the Irish super-middleweight title. When

Fitzgerald won the WBF Inter-Continental middleweight title against Kevin 'Hammer' Hammond, his coach at the time, Phil Sutcliffe, noted, 'Anto got hit with a few hard ones but he showed that he has a good chin,' a fact that was confirmed when he went the distance with Andy Lee in 2013 and world-title contender Hassan N'Dam N'Jikam in the same year. Sutcliffe said, 'We've always called the jab "the pride", it suits Anto.'

Fitzgerald switched management and relocated to Macklin's Gym in Marbella. It wasn't just boxers who were relocating to Spain. The Costas also attracted a growing contingent of young men who were putting distance between themselves and police investigations in Ireland. A friend of the Hutch family, Fitzgerald was street smart and a popular figure. 'The atmosphere at MGM is perfect for boxing,' he told me. 'With this team around me I feel I can win titles.'

The meeting between Fitzgerald and O'Sullivan on the Macklin–Heiland card in November 2014 generated a lot of pre-fight heat. And not just because it was seen as Dublin versus Cork. The rivalry was so intense people were calling it a grudge match. Animosity had built up in Fitzgerald who explained, 'I wanted this fight when he had the middleweight title, but he wouldn't fight me.' Being coached by Seamus Macklin, Matthew's younger brother, his confidence was high. 'If I boxed Andy Lee now I'd beat him,' he said. Describing O'Sullivan as 'a one-trick pony', he promised he'd 'box the ears off him'.

Fitzgerald became a festering nest of viperish resentment leading up to the fight. The customary ritualistic wind-ups went beyond banter and bombast as social media platforms became an abusive battle ground. Scurrilous slurs and libellous allegations dangerously raised the temperature. As the personal insults fired by Fitzgerald became more inflammatory, O'Sullivan acted with restraint. The head-to-head photo-op during the final press conference in Croke Park became a mini-drama when, having belligerently shoved O'Sullivan, Fitzgerald was on the receiving end of a kiss on the cheek from Spike. Anto's rapid response was to sting O'Sullivan with a whiplash slap before officials intervened. Branding O'Sullivan as 'scared', the upstaged Fitzgerald fumed, 'I'm going to kill you.'

For the biggest grudge match in recent Irish history, the fighters were welcomed to the ring in the 3Arena by a raucous crowd. Acolytes and associates of the MGM organization filled most of the ringside seats. Members of the Byrne family, fraudster James 'Jaws' Byrne and his sons,

David and Liam, sat in the front row. Many of the crowd wore light blue MGM 'Team Fitzey' T-shirts and, as Fitzgerald approached the ring flanked by Daniel Kinahan and Seamus Macklin, noise levels rose dramatically. Fitzgerald had the more vociferous support.

In the ring, O'Sullivan barged into Fitzgerald catching him off guard. Daniel, wearing a black MGM hoodie with capital letters of the slogan 'Together Everyone Achieves More' highlighting 'TEAM', diplomatically ushered an angry Fitzgerald away from a premature confrontation. Both fighters brimmed with malevolence as Mickey Vann, the referee with the slickest footwork in the trade, kept them apart until the opening bell. Making good on his promise of war, Fitzgerald came forward with a punishment plan. His intention was to overwhelm O'Sullivan. Spike stood his ground and taunted his opponent by keeping his hands low and loose.

Favouring a similar flamboyant low-hands style, Muhammad Ali had explained, 'This way you can hit from any angle.' Having connected with a statement right uppercut after just fifty seconds, O'Sullivan put both fists behind his back, making himself an inviting target for his aggressor. Gamely, Anto pressed forward. And then it happened. Appearing casual and relaxed, his feet perfectly positioned, with the faultless timing of an orchestra conductor, O'Sullivan swung his upper-body weight behind his right arm and released an uppercut from down below his hip. The trajectory took the punch under Fitzgerald's radar. It connected with devastating ferocity, sending Anto backwards onto the canvas. The Dubliner's willpower saw him anxiously attempt to beat the count but the communication lines were down, the signals scrambled by the blast, and his legs behaved as if they belonged to a novelty act in vaudeville, wobbling and buckling like rubber stilts. The fight had lasted seventy-five seconds. 'I've fists of dynamite on both hands,' declared O'Sullivan.

Six months later, we received official confirmation of O'Sullivan's observation when scientists in Boston fixed sensors to his hands for his fight with Melvin Betancourt. O'Sullivan won by KO in the second round. When the data was analysed, it showed he'd broken the record of 1100 pounds of pressure with the damaging body shot that set Betancourt up for the knockout punch.

Sitting with O'Sullivan in an empty café beside his north Dublin training base ahead of his ill-fated IBF eliminator with David Lemieux in 2018, I discovered a detail that made a fascinating postscript to the Fitzgerald fight.

'When I was fighting Anthony Fitzgerald, I had nothing,' Spike revealed. 'There were nights when I was in camp that I didn't have the price of a dinner. I made sure my wife and kids were alright but I had nothing. I never said it to anyone. I have the financial security now to admit to it. On the day of the fight, I had 185 quid to my name. I put 100 on a bet that I'd stop him in the first round.'

O'Sullivan held back €85 because he knew he'd need to buy drinks for friends after the fight. The odds were 50-1. His wager paid off handsomely and his KO punch became one of Sky Sport's 'Knock-Outs of the Year'.

II

Like pro-tennis players, golfers and footballers, every fighter looks forward to a time when they can make big money. In reality, most are confronted with the problems of balancing the lifestyle of a professional athlete with being the family breadwinner. Every euro counts. Only a tiny percentage of fighters reach big payday status.

On the way up, things can be tight. Managers take a percentage of fees. Depending on their experience, ability or powers of persuasion, that could range from 10 per cent to 25 per cent. A coach also expects a percentage. At a certain level, a matchmaker's fee of around 5 per cent can also be built into the equation.

It's not unknown for a fighter who's signed to one promoter to take a lucrative fight arranged by another. Both promoters then demand their percentage so the fighter could come away from a punishing fight with only around 50 per cent.

Take-home money is used to pay for gym time and, when in training for a fight, a physio, a nutritionist, a sports psychologist and a cutman. The fighter also has to pay medical fees, which can often involve surgery – most often on the hand, face and shoulder – and brain scans.

Fighters understand that it's only cost-effective if they're fighting regularly. It's a complicated business. Some managers may back a fighter financially. Most don't. As we've seen, investment of time, money and know-how can be an expensive gamble. Only the anointed ones get to have their career path studiously plotted with opportunities to prove themselves in strategically positioned fights. Only the best become champions. What every fighter wants is a promoter or manager with belief, influence and business muscle. Only a few boxers have the willpower and smarts to ignore the lure of an easy path to their goal. As a general rule of thumb, a boxer can be expected to follow the money.

When Matthew Macklin's MGM operation began to gain momentum, front-of-house manager Anthony Fitzpatrick worked diligently to land meaningful fights for MGM boxers. For many boxers this was a marked improvement on the situation elsewhere earlier in their careers when most of them were being put on bills as the visiting B contestant just to make up the numbers. Now they were getting carefully gauged step-up challenges, high-profile matches, important fights that boosted their rankings. Receiving the support of other boxers in the gym, most felt they were part of a team, like when they played football as kids. While some MGM shows appeared to run at a loss, few clients asked how the company could be so generous with its terms.

III

The night John Joe Nevin made his pro debut in Boston in March 2014, super-lightweight Jamie Kavanagh beat a tough Puerto Rican fighter on the same card. It was a return to winning ways for Kavanagh who, three months earlier, had suffered his only loss in seventeen fights when he fought a vastly more experienced local contender in Quintana Roo on the Yucatán peninsula. The Dubliner, who began his pro career in 2010, had fought all his eighteen fights in America or across the border in Mexico.

During the summer of 2014 it was revealed that MGM was expanding its operations to include promotions in Ireland. Matthew's controversial business partner, Daniel Kinahan, was managing the careers of several boxers from Britain and Ireland, including Derry Mathews and Iain Butcher. Tom Stalker, Anthony Fitzgerald and Declan Geraghty were also part of an expanding crew. The company tied up a deal with iFL TV, a specialist online boxing resource that kept up a steady flow of information on MGM fighters across social media platforms, and agreed an arrangement for Matchroom to promote shows, which would air on Sky Sports. The inconvenient question of the extent of Daniel Kinahan's involvement with boxing in the light of being a person-of-interest to the police could be shrugged off when required. 'He's been convicted of nothing,' insisted two-time Olympic medallist Paddy

Barnes when he signed with the company. 'He's roaming the world free with no convictions and warrants for his arrest.'

It was against this background that, in 2015, Jamie Kavanagh joined MGM for management while remaining on the books of Golden Boy Promotions in the US. Kavanagh, whose father, Gerard, had been ruthlessly gunned down in Spain the previous year, suffered a further bereavement when his uncle and close friend, Paul (26), was murdered in a planned assassination while parking his car in Drumcondra in Dublin.

Through adversity and grief, Kavanagh clung to his dream of becoming a world champion. 'I believe that MGM and Golden Boy Promotions can bring me the best from both sides of the water,' he said. 'I know these people will do good by me. I've had enough fights to be challenging for significant tiles and that's what I'm looking for.' Despite unsubstantiated rumours that linked him to Borgia-style conspiracies and internecine score-settling in the matter of Gerard and Paul's deaths, MGM's Kinahan was also looking forward to a bright future. 'I have known Jamie and his family for a long time,' he said. 'I've followed him closely over the years, watched him train and develop here in Spain and I've seen the sacrifices he has made travelling to America while spending time away from his family and girlfriend. He is a world-class fighter and I am delighted to have him on board.'

Signed to a four-fight deal, 'the Nuisance' Kavanagh was an experienced operator in the ring. In 2008 he'd won silver at the AIBA Youth World Championships in Mexico. Training in the Wild Card Gym with Freddie Roach and coach Joel Diaz, he regularly sparred with Manny Pacquiao and Guillermo Rigondeaux. His first pro fight was on an undercard in Madison Square Garden in 2010. Jamie had a good reputation among those in the trade. A personable and obliging chap, he was prepared to step up for fights with the best in the division. 'I've shared the ring with a lot of tough Mexicans and Americans,' he told me. 'Fighters in Europe are also tough so I won't be taking them lightly. I'll need to adjust. Every fight is hard. It's about how you approach it.' With MGM, he'd have Mark Tibbs, and the old master Jimmy Tibbs, as his coaching team. When we spoke soon after he signed with MGM, there was one box he needed to tick before targeting title fights. 'I never got a chance to fight in my home town,' he said. 'A homecoming fight will be a big thing for me.'

In September 2015 few could have envisaged how the murder of gangland figure Gary Hutch would have such far-reaching effects for Irish boxing. A nephew of Gerry 'the Monk' Hutch and close associate of the Kinahan family, Hutch was shot dead while running for his life outside an apartment complex near Marbella.

Six weeks after the Hutch killing, Jamie Kavanagh had his homecoming fight in the National Stadium. On an MGM and Frank Warren bill in November, Kavanagh met Romanian journeyman Oszkar Fiko. 'This is "The Jamie Show",' he joked. 'I'm on my twenty-second fight and I'm making my home debut and I'm really looking forward to it.' It can't have been easy having his first pro fight in Dublin without his father at ringside. Fourteen months previously, dad Gerard had been shot nine times by two gunmen at an Irish bar on the Costa del Sol. Ahead of his important fight, Jamie kept his emotions in check. 'I've fought on some of the biggest cards in the world but there's no show like a home-town show,' he enthused. 'I'm still only twenty-five and I'm learning with every fight. I want to demonstrate that to Irish boxing fans.'

Part of the fascination with boxing comes from seeing how fighters cope with the test they're confronted with. Kavanagh discovered quickly that his opponent's survival gambit was to adopt spoiling tactics, which he used as cover for illegal activity. Smart fighters will attempt to blindside a referee. Though determined to cheat, Fiko wasn't smart. He received two public warnings from referee Emile Tiedt. With his friends and sometimes sparring partners Conor McGregor and Philip Sutcliffe Jr noisily supporting him at ringside, the Nuisance controlled his frustration. The loudest voice in the venue issued instructions in Spanish. Sedano Ruiz had been Kavanagh's amateur coach when he grew up in Spain. 'No one knows me like Sedano,' Jamie said later. 'He's a great man.'

Kavanagh stopped Fiko with two crippling body shots in the seventh round. Job done. 'He didn't come to fight,' said Jamie. 'It was about keeping my composure. Once I figured him out, I lined him up for the shot that finished it. I heard him wince and I knew he wouldn't be getting up from it.'

In hindsight, something peculiar occurred that evening the significance of which escaped me at the time. I was standing along the back wall watching the undercard action when, next to me, a man in a tracksuit enquired, 'Were you at the Red Cow Hotel last night?' I'd wanted to see Niall Kennedy and Gerard Whitehouse perform but had been unable to attend.

'I hear there was murder at it,' the man continued, casually.

'Really?' said I, having heard nothing of a disturbance.

'Yeah,' he added. 'You should check it out.'

Drunken rows sometimes kicked off on the fringes of events, so I thought nothing of the remark. It wasn't until much later that I learned what had occurred was infinitely more sinister than the rowdyism I'd first imagined.

This had been the second successful MGM promotion in Dublin. Things were looking up for boxers and fight fans. At the National Stadium, access to the fighters wasn't restricted, which meant us press guys could wander around and grab quotes from fighters and coaches with impunity. However, it was disconcerting that bristling young men, who were neither staff nor press, were also crowding around fighters in the changing rooms. They seemed entitled, yet appeared to have no business being there. Security was non-existent. It was still early days for the promotions team so, thinking of making life easier, and possibly safer, for the press and the fighters, I advised one of the organizers that they should consider introducing a media accreditation system.

The subject of lax security would prove germane at the public weigh-in for MGM's next event a few months later. And even more questionable in light of tabloid revelations that there had been a botched murder attempt outside the boxing show at the Red Cow on the night before Jamie Kavanagh's homecoming fight. It was reported that a masked gunman had aimed at associates of Daniel Kinahan's and pulled the trigger but the gun had jammed. Many of those attending the event rushed from the venue in a convoy of luxury cars in fear of their lives. An abandoned burnt-out vehicle, believed to have been used by the would-be assailants, was later discovered not far from the venue.

Christmas came and went and 2016 began with a good-news announcement. Kavanagh told me he was set to fight in February on MGM's 'Clash of the Clans' in Dublin. 'MGM have spoken about going for an international belt following my next fight,' he said. 'I'm happy with that plan.'

IV

Within weeks, there was even better news for Jamie Kavanagh. His fight was being upgraded. The WBO European lightweight title would be the prize when he'd meet Antonio João Bento on an exciting card that would also feature Dubliners Stephen Ormond, Philip Sutcliffe Jr and Declan Geraghty.

MGM were making good on their promise to promote an expanding roster of Irish boxers. As well as the Saturday night 'Clash of the Clans' show at the National Stadium, a second night of boxing was scheduled for the Friday evening. Stylish middleweight Luke Keeler, welterweight Tyrone McKenna, Steve Collins Jr and Sean 'Big Sexy' Turner were some of the undercard attractions set for the Roadstone Club in Clondalkin. A weigh-in for both shows was planned for Friday lunchtime with fourteen Irish boxers among those fighting over the two nights.

Early on Friday afternoon I filed copy for my weekly Saturday boxing column. It was a piece on how Stephen Ormond's demolition style had attracted the attention of fight fans in the US where Murphy's Boxing was set to announce details of an interim title shot for the Dubliner. 'This is the fight that Stephen needs,' said Paschal Collins. 'This is his year.'

An air of incipient violence, a dark foreshadowing of the brutality to come, envelops every boxing weigh-in. Stripped to their trunks, fighters preen and glower and threaten. An obligatory face-to-face stare-off between contestants enflames the passions of spectators and provides photo opportunities for fans and press alike. Combatants avail of the opportunity to impose themselves in the hope of gaining a psychological advantage ahead of the physical ordeal. Occasionally, these micro-dramas can overheat, resulting in scuffles and histrionic exchanges. These ritualistic encounters often afford a fascinating insight into a boxer's demeanour and confidence levels.

On Friday I estimated that, by the time I'd grabbed a sandwich and got across town, I'd miss most of the weigh-in action at the Regency Hotel. Knowing I'd catch up with the boxers and their trainers later, I poured a cup of coffee and put my feet up instead. Then the phone rang.

It was a news editor. There was an unsettling note of urgency in his voice.

'Where are you?' he asked.

'At home, in the kitchen. Why?'

'Are you not at the weigh-in?'

'No need. I'll be seeing the boxers later.'

'Probably not. There's been a shooting there.'

'How serious?'

'Details are sketchy. There was more than one gunman. At least three people wounded and one reported fatality.'

'When?'

'Just now. Reports are still coming through to the newsroom. I rang you immediately thinking you'd have a first-hand account.'

In an instant, a fissure had cracked wide open, plunging the future of Irish boxing into an all-consuming abyss. In an elaborate operation, on an unprecedented scale, a hit squad had targeted a sporting event in the manner of a well-planned terrorist attack, unleashing a tsunami of chaos.

In the hours that followed, details emerged of how an organized hit team that included at least five armed men, one dressed as a woman, had stampeded spectators at the weigh-in. The man in drag and another gunman had been part of a reconnaissance duo tasked with pinpointing the location of individual targets. They'd entered the hotel through a service door. When shots were fired, panic broke out among the 200 people in the function room. Those who rushed to escape through the hotel foyer were met by three men disguised as members of a police SWAT team and armed with deadly assault rifles. David Byrne, a close associate of Daniel Kinahan, and others had run into a trap. Byrne was hit twice at close range and fell to the floor. As his blood pooled around him, a hitman stood over him and shot him in the face. Describing the extreme violence, an eyewitness said, 'There was smoke coming out of his body.' Two other Kinahan associates received gunshot wounds.

Footage taken on a spectator's mobile phone went viral. It showed Gary Sweeney stepping off the scales. This was a big day for the cruiserweight who was to make his pro debut the following night. A brother of Michael 'the Storm' Sweeney, he had missed out on a chance of Olympic qualification some months previously when he picked up a nasty gash in a fight in the York Hall. When we'd spoken days earlier, he was excited about his future. 'It'll be a big night for me,' he said. 'There are titles to be won and MGM are the team to help me realize my ambitions.' Instead of enjoying his first weigh-in as a pro, Sweeney could be seen running for cover in distinctive blue Superman underpants as shots rang out and, off-camera, a terrified child's voice pleaded, 'Daddy, help me.'

I'd arranged to have breakfast the following morning with Rinze van der Meer, an eminent Dutch boxing historian who was in Dublin for the fights. A Clint Eastwood lookalike, he was on the platform taking notes when the first shots were fired. I arrived with a collection of newspapers, which carried dramatic front-page photographs of the hit squad entering the hotel. Still in shock, the visitor relived the horror of the event.

'I didn't move,' he lamented. 'When I heard the first shot, I just thought somebody had knocked over a table. I didn't duck or run. I rationalized the sound. Gunfire was too improbable.' Confused by his own response, and processing the possibility that he could have been killed by a stray bullet, the Dutchman shook his head. 'I should have known instantly,' he said in disbelief. 'I was in the military when the Soviet Union invaded Czechoslovakia in 1968.' I enquired how the police had treated him afterwards. He hadn't spoken to the police. 'I didn't see any police at the event,' he said. 'I remained there for some time after the shooting but nobody approached me.'

That there had been no obvious Garda presence or even covert surveillance at the weigh-in seemed inconceivable in light of the attempted murder of high-ranking Kinahan affiliates at the Red Cow Hotel just three months earlier. Given the absence of police at the Regency, the masked gunmen had time to stalk the corridors of the hotel searching function rooms for intended targets before abandoning their monstrous mission.

Despite ambitious planning, involving arms sourced from an illegal paramilitary organization, elaborate disguises and a fleet of getaway cars that avoided CCTV cameras in the vicinity, the audacious operation had been a failure. While Daniel Kinahan, the gunmen's prime target, escaped unscathed, press photographers captured the arrival and departure of the hit team in a series of memorable images. As the assassins sped away they left behind a scene of desolation and trauma. The vendetta proved cancerous. Within days, in a reflex born of predation, a new wave of slaughter had begun.

The public learned that this murderous initiative was just the latest development in a feud that had been brewing between two of the biggest criminal factions in the country since the murder of Gary Hutch in Spain five months earlier. The Kinahan cartel and the Hutch family, both with interests in boxing, were officially at war. Many more, including innocent bystanders, were to die as the bloodletting continued in a series of shocking and deplorable murders.

American philosopher and abolitionist Waldo Emerson once said, 'This time, like all times, is a very good one, if we but know what to do with it.' And, yes, this had been an optimistic time for Irish boxing. Irish fighters were appearing in title fights – European, inter-continental, world – and many had realizable visions of creating historic nights and big pay days. This time had been theirs to grasp, theirs to shape. Instead, we watched as the conveyor belt of emerging talent was violently derailed, flinging potential boxing stars into a doldrums of inactivity, vanishing media profiles and sporting obscurity. For fear of reprisals and further bloodshed, professional boxing events became too dangerous to stage. An emerging generation of talent was deprived of the opportunities needed to progress at a crucial stage in their career. With MTK being viewed as a pariah state, legacies were tainted or devalued. Most of those associated with the company were accused in the court of public opinion of taking dirty money. Blood money.

There's no denying that a shadow has always hung over boxing. Yet, the sound of the bell at ringside has consistently, and optimistically, signalled the telling of a new story. A complex, ritualized reimagining of a physical and psychological battle. Each time the bell, the voice of authority, sounds, a new bout, a new round, a fresh contest begins. And we are compelled to watch how the drama unfolds.

Down the centuries, the bell had its place in sacred rite. It called people to prayer, assisted in driving out evil spirits and helped purify the atmosphere. Across societies and religions, the sound of a bell, harmonizing with infinity, has evoked eternity.

Tragically, it was a muffled, mourning bell that tolled when the shadow that boxing's critics complain of strode through the room that February afternoon in Dublin. Signalling disintegration, this was darkness weighing-in. Darkness uninvited and flexing its muscle. A darkness that smothers, stains and consumes: its own eclipse; its own apocalypse.

The pall of gloom that descended on the nation that afternoon would remain in place for years. In the aftermath of the fatal events, the death toll spiralled out of control as revenge took centre stage. While the human cost is immeasurable, the damage done to professional boxing in Ireland was catastrophic and unprecedented. Once again, a golden age in Ireland had ended in a maelstrom of treachery, strife and grief.

Acknowledgments

A few who've no idea how much they helped with this book include Gerry Callan, Colm MacGinty, Paul Kimmage, Andy Cummins, Tadhg Coughlan, Bill Barich and John Wischhusen. Reassuringly, Paddy Goodwin, Mel Christle and Tom Conlon have always been on hand when required. All deserve my grateful thanks. Sadly, those no longer around to receive a 'thank you' in person include Paul Drury, George Kimball, Jim McNeill, Paddy Murray, Ulick O'Connor and Annette Tallon.

While on the beat, I've been blessed to have colleagues of wit, some wisdom and the occasional reassuring WTF? In alphabetical order we've got Kevin Byrne, Cormac Campbell, Gavan Casey, Michael Foley, Ciaran Gallagher, Mark Gallagher, David Kelly, Karl McGinty, David Mohan, Pat Myler, Tom Myler, Eamonn O'Hara, Bernard O'Neill, Joe O'Neill, Jonny Stapleton, Johnny Watterson and Steve Wellings. In truth, I wouldn't be sharing these stories had I not met Michael Brophy, Declan Cahill, Michael Denieffe, Paul Hyland, Dr Tim McDonnell, Ian Mallon, Scott Murray and Gerry O'Regan at crucial stages in my career.

I'm also indebted to Prof. Shannon McRae (New York) and Lora Lee Templeton (California). And thanks to Spomenka Lazic and the crew at Brew 204, as well as Ernesto's, for the refreshments.

Editor Seán Farrell performed miracles in helping structure my jumble of anecdotes. I've been lucky to have him on my side. My deepest thanks to Djinn von Noorden, Niamh Dunphy, Ruth Hallinan and all the Lilliput staff. With an unbeaten record in the ring, Antony Farrell was encouraging from the get-go. His coach at Trinity was the great Fred Tiedt, so the circle of gratitude is unbroken.